LIFE SENTENCE

Mark Hodkinson

The Parrs Wood Press
MANCHESTER

First Published 2001

THE PARRS WOOD PRESS
St Wilfrid's Enterprise Centre
Royce Road, Manchester, M15 5BJ
www.parrswoodpress.com

© Mark Hodkinson 2001

The right of Mark Hodkinson to be recognised as the author of this work has been asserted

ISBN: 1 903158 23 0

Printed by:
MFP Design and Print
Longford Trading Estate
Thomas Street
Stretford
Manchester M32 0JT

For Dad

Also by the author:

Life at the Top, *a brief taste of the big-time for Barnsley Football Club*
(Queen Anne Press, 1998)

Blue Moon, *Down Among the Dead Men with Manchester City*
(Mainstream, 1999)

'There are fine hills to be roamed over in Rochdale and fine lakes
for sailing, and many moorland roads where one can lose
one's fellow man.'
Official Guide to the County Borough of Rochdale
(Pyramid Press, 1960).

'They call Rochdale the town with the clean face
and the dirty neck.'
Big Cyril, the Autobiography of Cyril Smith
(WH Allen, 1977).

'While still a boy, I was lucky in being allowed to frequent a little
society of working-men naturalists in Rochdale. They were men of
rare quality; one of them, a cotton-spinner by trade, had added
several mosses to the British flora.'
Daniel Hall – Pioneer in Scientific Agriculture by HE Dale
(Wyman and Sons, 1956).

'I was born in England, in Rochdale, Lancashire, not far from
Manchester. But I couldn't help that, you know.'
The Stage Reminiscences of Mrs Gilbert edited by Charlotte Martin
(Charles Scribner's Sons, 1901).

'Rochdale has a very large Pakistani population. In 1966 they took
the largest hall, a thousand of them, to give a thank-you dinner to
the townsfolk who had made them so welcome and been so helpful during their 10 years in Lancashire.
Portrait of Lancashire by Jessica Lofthouse
(Robert Hale, 1967).

'Rochdale, then, is first and foremost an industrial town where
loom and lathe and press, mixer, retort and guillotine sing the song
of industry. It lies on the eastern borders of the great Lancashire
industrial area sometimes known as *Cottonopolis*, for want of a bet-

5

ter word, with Bury and Bolton near neighbours to the west, Oldham to the south, and Manchester to the south-west. In such a situation it might be said that you can't tell one town from t'other, but, generally speaking, it is the town centre that distinguishes one town from another, and there's no mistaking Rochdale.'
Official Guide to the County Borough of Rochdale
(Pyramid Press, 1960)

'"I come from Rochdale," were magic words which opened the portals of her home to them.'
Our Gracie by Joan Moules
(Robert Hale, 1983).

'As the daughter of a British doctor stationed in India's most discursive hospices, Miss Candace Marston was not typical of the gently bred ladies to be found in British High Society. Yet Lord Rochdale pronounced her exactly right for his urgent requirements. To inherit his fortune, they would marry instantly and divorce in one year, with no one the wiser and she a rich and free woman. There was much Candace dreamed of doing with wealth and freedom and she accepted with terms. Last to know was Lord Rochdale, that her terms would not only shock Society, but most probably land him in Bedlam!'
The Surprising Lady Rochdale by Annette Summers
(Harlequin Regency Romance, 1992)

'I had trials – being a loose word – with Man United, Halifax, Huddersfield and one of the Sheffield's, I forget which. Rochdale was the most serious. I trained with them for a couple of weeks but then I was offered a full-time job in a bank which I thought would be better than being on a YTS.'
Mark Owen (ex-Take That), *Q* magazine, July 2001.

'John Ellis, a Rochdale barber, was an official executioner for 23 years. During that period he hanged some of Britain's most celebrated criminals, including Dr Crippin.'
Diary of a Hangman by John Ellis
(Forum Press, 1990).

'Forget those traditional images of Rochdale, the mill town. Spotland is a leafy suburb, with the open moors clearly visible on the horizon.'
Football Fan's Guide (CollinsWillow, 2000).

'Lady, I am not going to Rochdale. I have been to Rochdale. I would rather have my entrails chewed by starving rats than go to Rochdale. I rest my case.'
Joe Warren, an American jazz pianist about to embark on a British tour, played by Elliott Gould in the TV film, *Doggin' Around* (1994) written by Alan Plater.

'These posters will be up for a week, then they'll be wrapping chips in Rochdale.'
Terry Woods, played by Billy Hartman, in Yorkshire Television's *Emmerdale*, when asked by his lady friend, Carol Wareing (Helen Pearson), about her appearing in fashion advertisements, Thursday, 5 July 2001

'Rochdale is indeed becoming a gutter town, full of ignorant, foul-mouthed, mentality-robbed louts.'
Mrs C.T. Brierley, letter to the *Rochdale Observer*, Saturday, 7 July, 2001

ROCHDALE AFC
Sandy Lane
Rochdale, OL11 5DS

Founded: Rochdale Town formed in 1900 and went out of existence in 1907. The present club was established in its place and joined the Manchester League, graduating to the Lancashire Combination in 1908. Rochdale AFC joined the third division (north) of the Football League in August 1921.

Colours: Blue and white.

Nickname: The Dale.

First Football League Game: 27 August 1921 v Accrington Stanley (h). Won, 6-3 with goals by Reg Owens (three), Harry Dennison (two) and Gene Carney (penalty).

Record Attendance: 24,231 v Notts County, FA Cup second round, 10 December 1949.

Record Receipts: £46,000, v Burnley, 5 May 1992.

Highest League Position: Ninth in the third division, 1969-70.

Record League Victory: 8-1, v Chesterfield, third division (north), 18 December 1926.

Record FA Cup Victory: 8-2, v Crook Town, FA Cup first round, 26 November 1927.

Record Defeat: 0-8, v Wrexham, third division (north), 19 December 1929; 0-8, v Leyton Orient, fourth division, 20 October 1987; 1-9, v Tranmere Rovers, third division (north), 25 December 1931.

Most Goals in a Game: Tommy Tippett, six, v Hartlepools United, third division (north), 21 April 1930.

Highest League Scorer in a Season: Albert Whitehurst, 44, third division (north), 1926-27.

Most League Goals in Total: Reg Jenkins, 119, 1964-73.

Most League Appearances: Graham Smith, 317, 1966-74.

Club Records: Promotion, 1968-69 from the fourth division to the third (lasted five seasons); League Cup finalists, 1961-62, lost 4-0 on aggregate, v Norwich City.

Alternatively...

Finished bottom of Football League: Six times – 1921-22, 1931-32, 1933-34, 1958-59, 1977-78, 1979-80.

Total Seasons spent in Football League's Lowest Division: 74.

English Club with Least Wins in a Season: Rochdale, two, third division, 1973-74.

Lowest Post-war Football League Attendance: Rochdale v Cambridge United, 588, 5 February 1973.

English Club Conceding Most Goals in a Season: Rochdale, 135, 1931-32, third division (north).

Lowest Percentage of Wins of Clubs with Consecutive Membership of Football League: Rochdale, 32.9 per cent.

FA Cup Exits to Non-League Teams: Seven in an 11-year period, 1972 to 1983 - Bangor City (1-2, 1972), Grantham (3-5, 1973), Northwich Victoria (1-2, 1976), Scarborough (2-4, 1977), Droylsden (0-1, 1978), Altrincham (1-2, 1982), Telford United (1-4, 1983).

Whole Seasons Without Recording an Away Victory: 1931-32, 1958-59, 1977-78, 1982-83.

Number of re-election applications: 10.

Home Attendances Below 1,000: Thirty-one times - v York City, February 1934, 800; v Shrewsbury Town, January 1974, 957; v Cambridge United, February 1974, 588; v Charlton Athletic, March 1974, 850; v Port Vale, March 1974, 982; v Aldershot, April 1984, 885; v Brentford, March 1976, 894; v Reading, April 1976, 913; v Hartlepool United, April 1977, 858; v Torquay United, April 1977, 852; v Brentford, May 1977, 977; v Bournemouth, November 1978, 962; v Southend United, December 1977, 902; v Grimsby Town, March 1978, 787; v Southport, April 1978, 966; v Hartlepool United, April 1978, 972; v Scunthorpe United, April 1978, 857; v Reading, April 1978, 734; v Torquay United, April 1978, 742; v Aldershot, May 1978, 923; v Aldershot, August 1978, 976; v Torquay United, April 1980, 958; v Scunthorpe United, April 1980, 993; v Hartlepool United, September 1982, 987; v Aldershot, December 1982, 888; v Colchester United, April 1984, 809; v Aldershot, April 1984, 853; v Torquay United, May 1984, 943; v Aldershot, October 1984, 960; v Hartlepool United, April 1985, 910; v Southend United, April 1986, 936.

Contents

Introduction

Sing your Life

The question is straightforward enough: "Why do you support Rochdale?" Watch their eyes - have they widened? Watch their lips - is there a ripple of a smile? You'll see that they are actually asking why anyone would support a football club that is famously unsuccessful and, in all probability, likely to - more or less - stay that way. 'It's like a drug,' I might say, or, 'It gets in your blood.' I'm neither being glib or evasive; it really is the best I can do.

Before the start of the 2000-2001 football season, I was invited to London to discuss a potential commission from *The Times*. I had written for the paper on a freelance basis for five years. Keith Blackmore, the head of sport, asked whether I'd like to spend the forthcoming season writing about Rochdale, from the viewpoint of a lifelong supporter. I was to bring into play the relationship with my dad (a fellow season ticket holder) and place it in the wider context of the town, the people, and the club's position in football's firmament.

I was reticent at first. My dad is a very private person. I was uncomfortable about exposing our relationship and the football side of it was about as personal as it got. We talked at football; it was probably our main forum of communication. My family was not bohemian and freethinking and an obliging source of literary anecdote. It was buttoned-up and kept itself to itself, thank you very much. Keith, with his usual mordant wit, pointed out that although I had a sporadic presence in the paper's sports pages, I was still not of significant eminence that the public cared excessively about my family life. He wanted a general sweep across the enigma of passionate, hometown club support. This was my call, and some; a song I had been waiting to sing all my life, the one I knew best.

I had undertaken similar projects during the football seasons of 1997-98 and 1998-99. The first of these was spent as a quasi writer-in-residence at Oakwell, the home of Barnsley. I produced a series of weekly dispatches during their memorable season in the FA Carling Premiership. The next season, I flitted to Maine Road, Manchester, and fastened myself to Manchester City while it was at the lowest period in its history, scrapping its way out of the second division. My brief at both these stations was to infiltrate the club and its supporters, which meant many of the articles were interview-led and, consequently, fairly standard journalism, though I tried to relate matters from the perspective of the supporter.

We decided to call the new series of articles Life Sentence. Other titles were considered, but rejected for various reasons. Among them were A Love Supreme, Talk About the Passion, Forever Blue, Marathon Man, Love Beyond Reason, Saturday Afternoon and Sunday Mourning, Yours Faithfully and Northern Songs. I'm glad we settled on Life Sentence because it has been just that, and the title suggests an appreciation of the irony and humour that has often been essential.

From the outset, it was a more challenging proposition than the earlier projects. I couldn't fall back on profiles of the club's chairman, manager and star players. It was a shot from the hip, a series of gut reactions, hunches, hopes and agonies that typified a football supporter's lot, moulded into – hopefully – lively and readable copy. While I had quickly gained affection for Barnsley and had an historical fondness for City (my family is from Manchester and pro-City), Rochdale is unequivocally *my* club.

Along the way, amid all these words and facts and opinions, I hope to have answered the question as to why they are my club. I can't summarise it neatly in a few short lines without it sounding trite and over-sentimental. My hope is that supporters of all small-time clubs with big-time obsessions will find solace and empathy here. I'd like to think, and I know it's a conceited ideal, that when a fan of a lower division team (in fact, make that anyone who doesn't support Manchester United, Arsenal, Liverpool, Leeds United or Chelsea) is asked why they support their own supposedly underachieving, going-nowhere team, they will reach for this book, and say, 'It's all in there'.

Quite rightly, during the course of the season, my credentials as a Rochdale supporter were queried. I was, after all, putting myself up as a spokesman for the faith. I have supported Rochdale since I was 10-years-old, when my family first moved to the town. I have never wavered in this support, but there were two periods when I missed a number of games – while I was away at college studying journalism and when I was asked by *The Times* to report on matches.

For a writer, getting the call from *The Times* is like a footballer joining a Premiership club, an opportunity not to be missed. My two years as a member of its match-reporting team, however, created a peculiar dilemma. I felt as if I was at a professional peak and fulfilling a childhood dream, but, as I filed reports from Anfield or Old Trafford, my heart ached to be at Spotland. I'd drive away from these famous grounds and immediately ring my dad for an update on Rochdale. When we lost, it was a relief – I hadn't missed anything, but when we won I was downhearted. Clearly, it had all left me very confused.

The period coincided with the managerial reign of Graham Barrow, which, as any Rochdale supporter will confirm, was not the most exciting in the club's history. The match report, broadcast live from my parents' living-room, was usually focused on a 0-0 draw or a 1-0 defeat, with much lamentation that Alex Russell, our most creative player, had again been left on the bench. I'd learn that we'd spent most of the match 'just booting it up the field and chasing after it like school kids'. Rather kindly, my Rochdale correspondent usually added, 'You've not missed much'.

Occasionally, while I was nibbling on triangular sandwiches – or steaming hot pots in tureens at Leeds, bless them - and generally waited upon in the sumptuous press quarters of a Premiership club, the half-time score from Spotland would flash on to the television: Rochdale 0, Hartlepool United 2. At this point, my yearning to be at Spotland seemed absurd and vain. I stomped back to the press box:

I'm a top-notch football reporter, with no time for those losers.

We did sometimes win and even my dad would concede that we had played well. He was sensitive of my feelings and could downplay a 3-0 victory ('We just got lucky. Three times.'). I remember a drive back from Middlesbrough in January, the motorway awash with cars and rain, darkness on all sides. Rochdale had drawn 1-1, Middlesbrough had won 2-1. I phoned home and dad answered. I could hear mum talking in the background and the telly was blaring away. I thought: 'What am I doing here?' I pined for the routine I'd known for more than 20 years. Like most people who are young and full of themselves, I hardly saw my parents and going to the match, and tea afterwards at their house, served as a fortnightly summit meeting, a ritual that ensured we all met up and gave each other updates from our lives. I'd gained a by-line, but lost a football club and a family.

I was unable to reconcile this dilemma between the personal and the professional and my bizarre purgatory continued until, as so often happens, the decision was made for me. I became a dad myself, and finally saw the light, and it was shining, quite beautifully, on Spotland. I resorted to the classic justification: I wanted to spend time with my child. I actually *did* want to spend more time with my baby son, but not between 3pm and 5pm on Saturdays - parents need a break, it's good for the kids, too!

Covering matches for *The Times* was actually hard work; not the game itself, but the rigmarole of getting there, parking up, waiting around afterwards for quotes from managers and players, and getting home after the match. I spent many Saturdays reporting on Newcastle, Sunderland or Middlesbrough, so I left home at 9am and didn't return until about 9pm. In comparison, going to Spotland was refreshingly straightforward. The 'spending more time with my family' line obviously suited my needs, but it wasn't completely spurious.

Incidentally, I did ponder many times on the attraction of supporting Premiership clubs. The football was manifestly of a much higher standard, but a great deal was demanded of the supporter. I realised how effortless it was to support Rochdale. I couldn't countenance the hassle of leaving home three hours before kick-off to avoid the traffic and guarantee a parking spot. I'd often walk past supporters at 1pm, sitting in their cars listening to the radio, smiling contentedly because they had managed to get within a mile and a half of St James' Park or Anfield. Afterwards, while I was still at the ground trying to wield a quote from a breathless player clutching his kit-bag in a corridor, these fans were back in their cars again, bumper to bumper, navigating streets choked with traffic.

I felt the stereotypical carping about the FA Premiership was valid. The atmosphere *was* sterile and the etiquette of support over-mannered. I recall being at Ewood Park and watching a supporter close to the press box growing increasingly frustrated by Blackburn's torpid defending. Eventually, unable to contain himself any longer, he rose from his seat and yelled: "Rovers, this defending won't do, it just won't do." At Spotland, a bloke in the same state of agitation would have proffered a coarser address: "They're useless, Parkin, get shut of the fuckin' lot of 'em." It's obviously not big or clever to swear, but it can be hilariously funny at times and supply some much needed levity, especially when your defence is playing like it's made a brief stop-off at a football ground on an annual three-day pub crawl.

I'm also used to the scale of third division football, of being part of a crowd that seldom exceeds 3,500. At Premiership grounds I felt as if my presence didn't count (it probably doesn't at Rochdale, but I delude myself that it does). We feel more part of it at Rochdale, all in it together, and we form a genuine fellowship. We are a village. They are a city. We are the intimate gig in a small nightclub. They are stadium rock.

The sub-heading of the Life Sentence columns was 'a low level love affair' and I often took it as part of my brief to justify why anyone would support a lower division team, almost as if I was running a political campaign for a minority party. When I read the pieces back, I seem unusually defensive, almost as if I need to traduce big-time football because I see it as a threat to my own version of the sport. I think this standpoint is a product of the times. We are told constantly that as football becomes increasingly commercialised, the smaller clubs face a precarious future. When we sense that we might be excluded like this, it makes us cling tighter, and we can grow territorial and testy. I love football, at any level. It's the attendant fuss over its top strata that I find repellent.

As a child, I kept meticulous scrapbooks on Rochdale, and wrote match reports that no one read. I didn't show them to anyone because at my school you were considered suspiciously effete if you liked writing, or even did your homework. During the season, as I worked on the various pieces, there were many times when I had that rare pleasure of both the joy of the moment and of being perfectly aware of it. I wasn't 'lost' in it; I savoured it. Life didn't get much better.

Although being Rochdale's most-read fan was usually a pleasant experience, it sometimes weighed heavily. I missed the free and easy nature of football support. I was constantly looking for 'lines' or angles to develop in the column. Until this season, Rochdale had been a retreat from the detail of life, and I regretted that it was impinged. Overall, it was a small price to pay.

The articles are presented as they were originally written; pressure of space meant they were pruned here and there before appearing in the newspaper. I have taken the opportunity to undertake the occasional minor rewrite where I felt the text was clumsy or long-winded. Please excuse the repetition - I had to remind the intermittent reader of a few facts, such as how long I had supported the club and regular resumes of the club's history. After some of the columns, I have added extra thoughts; a quiet word in the ear with the benefit of hindsight.

I was given complete freedom by *The Times*. Nothing was considered out-of-bounds, or, likewise, too trifling for public consumption. I have a distinctly biased perspective, but I think it is laudable that a national newspaper gave space on a weekly basis to an idiosyncratic column with undeniable minority interest (albeit with significant, wider connotations). It was a maverick stance among a media obsessed with the iconography of sport.

I was wholly responsible for the copy that formed the columns, with sub-editors at *The Times* contributing the headlines. So, spare me acclaim for wonderfully inspired tub-thumping such *as Fans Grow Old in Fear of Spotland Chainsaw Massacre* (Saturday, 10 February 2001) or censure for the more phlegmatic efforts such as *Plymouth or Not? The Most Agonising Question I Know* (Saturday, 5 May 2001). Some of the headlines may seem unwieldy, but, in defence of my colleagues, this was because they usually had to supply enough words to fit across a large expanse of narrow space. The snappy, two or three-word aphorism was denied them.

I am extremely grateful to the many people who have contributed to this project. The original idea belonged to Keith Blackmore and David Chappell, the duo at the helm of *The Times'* sports coverage. Their professional lives are extremely hectic and pressured, but they always find time to think, listen and encourage. Richard Whitehead, also of *The Times*, kindly proof-read the book at the 11th hour with remarkable professionalism. Graham Williams did the same, even though it necessitated taking it on holiday with him: a friend indeed.

Robert Kirby of PFD took care of the contractual business with aplomb, resolving to deal with The Parrs Wood Press and its indefatigable owner Andrew Searle. Several publishers expressed an interest, but Andrew's enthusiasm and vision was irresistible. He has also visited Spotland many times and knows his way around the passion and prejudices of sporting fanaticism.

Stephen Hewitt undertook some sterling research on my behalf. George Brock, managing editor of *The Times*, magnanimously waived News International's copyright to allow the material to appear in this form. Col Cavanagh of Rochdaleafc.com and Suzanne Geldard of the *Rochdale Observer* helped me gather the fans' testimonies. George Dodds and John Anson, also of the *Rochdale Observer*, allowed me access to back-issues of the paper and provided office space at its headquarters.

The following shared conversations about either the column, Rochdale, or football in general and gave me many ideas and insights for which I am grateful: Guy Patrick, John Abrahams, Tony Kerr and Karen Kerr, Neil Storey, Mike Grime, George and Beryl Ridings,

Mike Barnett, Luke Bainbridge, John McDonough, Rob Stringer, Johnny Rogan and Steve Harrison. Steve, incidentally, is a friend who became a sports agent during the course of the season and brokered a deal to bring the club's record signing, Paul Connor, to Spotland. He has reflected on this issue in the final chapter.

Richard Lysons' pastiches of my writing, performed as soliloquies in our kitchen, kept me amused and grounded. The best began, something like: 'Fathers, sons, men, football, the mill, the birth, the work, the death...' Miles Moss provided a respected opinion and a perfectly-worded message of sympathy on a long journey back from Devon. Rob Kerford, Ursula Lumb, Joanne Mortimer, Sarah Crowther, Sara Chan and James Heward took care of other important business for me while I was preoccupied with this project. Mike Barrett designed the cover. Daniel Youngs of DY Sporting Photos kindly supplied a photograph for the back cover. Alan Plater gave permission to quote from *Doggin' Around*. Mum, dad and Paula were supportive throughout.

I was summoned to an unexpected meeting with Steve Parkin, Rochdale's manager, two months after the season ended, which I have written about at the end of the book. Otherwise my formal involvement with Rochdale FC was limited, but when I did have need to contact them, Francis Collins, Les Duckworth, Tom Nichol et al were helpful and efficient. Aside from a few gripes from director Richard Bott (usually tempered by praise), the board and management team were remarkably tolerant; there were no attempts to 'pull rank' or apply any insidious pressure. Take heart, this is a club peopled by strong characters with the ability to laugh at themselves.

Finally, I'd like to thank the supporters who contacted me through the season. I received scores of letters from all parts of the country and I have included a handful of the shorter ones. They empathised with the themes and many had their own story to tell, about their own particular club. We are not alone!

It was also uplifting to discover that my adoration of Rochdale was far from unique. After the final match of the season, I issued an appeal for supporters to contact me with their stories. I expected a handful of responses, but was deluged, from all corners of the world. I had no idea of the depth of loyalty and affection people held for the club, or the way it was linked to generations of families. We form a real community and I'm proud that this project has been part of the process of drawing it together.

The supporters' contributions are included in the final chapter. I tried throughout the season (perhaps with a sly professional eye) to set the dials for the heart of this football club, but I am left with the feeling that the real love and do-or-die passion is better expressed in the blunt, heartfelt terms of these journalistic laymen.

One

The Bricks and the Dust

Saturday, 6 May 2000

Rochdale closed the 1999-2000 season with a 1-1 home draw against Barnet. They finished in 10th position, four points behind a promotion play-off place.

At the final whistle, Rochdale fans invaded the pitch to pay tribute to the players and management, with several breaking off to shake the hands of the Barnet supporters and wish them well in the play-offs.

Friday, 9 June 2000

The funeral was held of Rochdale fanatic, Derek Butler, of New Line, Rossendale. Among the mourners was his son, Dale, aged six, named after his dad's favourite team. "He was a very popular guy and loved his football, especially the Dale," said his pal, Scott Galding. "He was known to a lot of Dale fans because he always wore a bright yellow coat when he went to the matches."

Friday, 30 June 2000

Steve Parkin made his first signings of the summer - Paul Ware, aged 29, a midfielder from Macclesfield Town and the experienced defender, 32-year-old Simon Coleman from Southend United.

During his career, Coleman had attracted transfer fees totalling £1.5 million. Both players were signed on free transfers and given two-year contracts.

"I'm a defender first and foremost," said Coleman. "But I like to play football, get it down and pass it and just give 100%. Although I was captain at Southend, you could say that I'd had enough of them and they'd had enough of me."

Ware, formerly of Stockport County, had started as an apprentice at Stoke City where his duties had included cleaning Parkin's boots. He had spent a period outside the professional game, playing for Hednesford Town in the Conference.

Also in Rochdale...

June 2000

* Taxi-driver Mohammed Bhutta, aged 57, was stabbed in the head after collecting two men from the Carter's Rest pub, Spotland [Spotland is a district in Rochdale as well as the name of the club's ground].
* The Co-operative Retail Society announced it was to leave its head-quarters at Sandbrook Park just four years after moving into the £30 million purpose-built site.

Monday, 3 July 2000

Michael Oliver, a midfield player, left Darlington to join Rochdale on a free transfer, claiming, 'the ambition had gone' from his former club.

The 24-year-old began his career at his hometown club of Middlesbrough. He moved to Stockport County where he stayed two seasons before joining Darlington, for whom he made more than 200 appearances.

His last game for his former side was at Wembley in the third division play-off final when they lost to Peterborough United. He joined Rochdale on a three-year contract. "I like to get forward and score goals," he said.

Wednesday, 5 July 2000

Striker Kevin Townson signed on a free transfer from Everton. The 17-year-old was viewed as a long-term prospect, with a first-team debut predicted 'within the next year'.

Thursday, 6 July 2000

The players returned for pre-season training. Dave Bayliss badly twisted his ankle in the first session of the new season.

Monday, 10 July 2000

Jason Peake, the midfielder who had spent two periods at Rochdale, moved on again, this time to Plymouth Argyle. "This is a challenge I'm very excited by. I'm confident things will work out," he said.

Thursday, 13 July 2000

Local glamour girls were used again in the official club shop brochure. The poses were more discreet than the previous season. Dressed in various items of souvenir clothing, they were pictured outside Rochdale landmarks such as the Town Hall, Toad Lane, Cemetery Hotel and on moorland above the town. The sole risqué picture was of the girls strategically holding scarves while topless beneath a 'Welcome to Rochdale' road sign.

Friday, 14 July 2000

Carcraft renewed its sponsorship deal for an additional two years. The company's eight-year association with Rochdale made it the longest main club sponsor in English professional football. "This is without doubt the biggest signing we have made this summer," said Les Duckworth, marketing and sponsorship manager.

Rochdale beat Northwich Victoria 4-2 at the Drill Field in their first pre-season friendly, with goals from Michael Oliver (two), Clive Platt and Graham Lancashire. Steve Parkin made 10 substitutions and gave most of his squad a game. Simon Coleman was the only player to spend the entire 90 minutes on the pitch.

Friday, 21 July 2000

Motorama, Rochdale's Vauxhall dealership, signed a deal to sponsor the Main Stand for five years. It was now known as the Motorama Stand.

Monday, 24 July 2000

Paul Ware scored from a free kick to give Rochdale a 1-0 win against East Fife in the first match of their short tour of Scotland.

Tuesday, 25 July 2000

Dave Flitcroft discovered he was to face his brother, Garry, when Rochdale were drawn against Blackburn Rovers in the first round of the Worthington Cup. He immediately rang Garry and left a message that Rochdale would win.

Wednesday, 26 July 2000

Clive Platt scored after six minutes to give Rochdale a 1-0 win over Stenhousemuir. Steve Parkin again made numerous substitutions, with only Wayne Evans, Dave Bayliss and Gary Jones playing the whole match.

Friday, 28 July 2000

Rochdale's fifth new signing of the summer was the former Manchester United player, 26-year-old Simon Davies.

The winger had made four full appearances for Manchester United and seven as substitute. He played and scored in a 4-0 win against Galatasary in the European Champions League and had made one appearance for Wales. He featured in the FA Youth Cup-winning team of 1992 that also included David Beckham, Paul Scholes and the Neville brothers, Gary and Phil. While at Old Trafford, he had loan spells at Exeter City and Huddersfield Town before joining Luton Town for £200,000. He signed for Macclesfield Town on a free transfer in 1998 and was a regular member of their side before joining Rochdale for £2,000.

Saturday, 29 July 2000

Rochdale closed their pre-season tour of Scotland with a disappointing 4-1 defeat against Raith Rovers of the Scottish first division. Simon Coleman gave Raith the lead with an own goal, before Tony Ellis scored a fine equaliser. Marc Miller restored the lead for

Raith, with French trialist Ivan Mballa adding two more.

Monday, 31 July 2000

The club issued colour fixture cards for the forthcoming season. The cover photograph was of full back, Wayne Evans, clenching his fists in a goal celebration. Underneath, the caption read: 'This Time' - evidence of the club's promotion hopes.

Also in Rochdale...

July 2000

* Police launched a manhunt for a rapist who attacked a 30-year-old woman as she walked to work along the Rochdale Canal towpath at 5.30am.

* The Home Office asked Rochdale Council to provide homes for up to 200 asylum seekers from eastern Europe.

* An ex-councillor appeared at county court charged with making off without paying for a luxury holiday home he had rented on the French Riviera. He had left a note at the £700-per-week, antique-filled apartment reading, 'This is a shabby remnant of a bygone era'. He also complained that there was no parking space for his £70,000 Bentley. He was told to pay £1,844 compensation.

Tuesday, 1 August 2000

Lee Todd, a 28-year-old left back, joined Rochdale on a free transfer from Bradford City. Todd had made more than 200 appearances for Stockport County before joining Southampton for £850,000. He played just 11 times in the FA Premiership, returning north to join Bradford City in August 1998 for £350,000.

Before signing for Rochdale, Todd had appeared a few weeks earlier in Bradford's Intertoto Cup matches against FK Atalantas of Lithuania. He had also featured in Bradford's 3-1 win against Rochdale in a friendly held behind closed doors at Bradford University. Steve Parkin had been alerted to Todd's availability after the match, which was played over three 45-minute periods.

After signing in the afternoon, Todd played in a full-strength Rochdale side at Accrington Stanley of the UniBond Premier League.

Goalkeeper Neil Edwards suffered a groin strain and was replaced after 20 minutes. Keith Hill and Tony Ellis were 'sent off' by the referee; he ordered the Rochdale bench to substitute them after they were involved in separate incidents.

Paul Ware scored in the last minute to secure an ignominious 1-1 draw. Michael Holt, the former Rochdale striker, was included in the Accrington team.

Wednesday, 2 August 2000

Blackburn Rovers announced that admission to the Worthington Cup first round second-leg tie at Ewood Park would be free to their season ticket holders – significantly reducing Rochdale's proceeds from the match.

Friday, 4 August 2000

Simon Davies scored a second half goal to give Rochdale a 1-0 win in a friendly against Burnley at Spotland.

The Sandy Lane End was closed a few hours before kick-off when Rochdale Council refused to issue a safety certificate. Officials claimed the cable on the public-address system was not fireproof.

Monday, 7 August 2000

Steve Parkin completed his summer signings with the capture of 19-year-old winger Phil Hadland from Reading. York City thought they had secured Hadland's signature – and announced it on their official website – but Parkin moved quickly after Hadland impressed in a week-long trial, during which he appeared as a substitute in the friendly against Burnley.

Tuesday, 8 August 2000

Rochdale Supporters' Club announced an appeal to raise funds for a device to help ground staff fork the pitch and improve drainage. The initial plan was to tow it on the club's tractor, but the vehicle was inadequate. The appeal was broadened to also include the purchase of a new tractor at a total cost of £13,150.

Wednesday, 9 August 2000

Steve Parkin signed a new three-year deal with Rochdale, to last until the end of the 2002-03 season. "I was delighted with the offer and delighted to sign. I've enjoyed my time here so far. I hope it can continue and we can have some success," he said.

Thursday, 10 August 2000

The club had sold more than 600 season tickets. "It's a great boost for me and the players that the fans are backing us like this," said Parkin.

Friday, 11 August 2000

Nineteen-year-old Gary Hamilton was added to the squad after Graham Lancashire and Kevin Townson picked up injuries during the pre-season. The striker joined on a month's loan from Blackburn Rovers, where he was a regular member of their reserve team.

Steve Parkin said on the eve of the new season: "At the start of every campaign, all supporters have hopes and aspirations for their own team. All I can guarantee as manager, knowing the squad that I've assembled, is that the players will give 100 per cent the minute they pull on a blue shirt."

Bookmakers made Rochdale 25/1 to win the third division title.

Saturday, 12 August 2000
Rochdale 1 Darlington 1

Three new signings made their full Rochdale debuts – Lee Todd, Paul Ware and Simon Davies, with fellow newcomers Phil Hadland, Michael Oliver and Gary Hamilton appearing as substitutes.

Darlington scored first through Lee Nogan, but Rochdale equalised 10 minutes into the second half when Simon Davies converted a penalty after Paul Ware had been fouled by Paul

28

Heckingbottom. Darlington had six players booked.

Wednesday, 16 August 2000

Rochdale's Spring Hill Hospice was contacted by former Rochdale player-turned-poet Harry Boyle and offered free copies of his latest book, *Love Defined*. Harry, now 76-years-old, had played 175 league and cup games as a left back from 1950 to 1955.

He donated 240 copies to sell for funds. Harry had himself recovered from cancer.

MISTY-EYED AMONGST TALES OF WOE
(The Times, Saturday, 19 August 2000)

Welcome to Rochdale, the bricks and the dust. Manchester that way, Leeds the other, and this certain some place, somewhere in between. There used to be mills here, and the air was cotton-sweet. Now it's a picture of England - car parks, industrial estates, warehouse units, retail centres, some houses and some schools.

Up on a hill, looking down on the town, is Spotland, the home of Rochdale FC. The clock has already struck three on our new season when Darlington were the first visitors last Saturday. We strolled up in shirtsleeves with thin jackets over our arms, the tang of cut grass and optimism in the air. Sunlight danced across the pitch, silhouettes spilled everywhere. Spotland is a runty little word, but, at times like these, a quite beautiful place.

Rochdale are members of the third division of the Nationwide League. We have been in the bottom division since 1974 and our 26-year tenure qualifies us as England's least successful professional club, which sounds marginally better than England's worst.

My first love has been my only love, so I remember the date we met: Monday October 21 1974, Rochdale versus Northampton Town. We all went - mum, dad, my sister and me - which was strange because my family wasn't big on outings. Back then, you stayed in and watched telly. All week. Your mum and dad were in the kitchen or at a Tupperware party, filling time before *Bouquet of Barbed Wire*.

They'd brought you into the world, given you a plate of chips for tea: what more did you want? If you were good for a whole year, they might take you to see *Planet of the Apes* at the pictures or, in summer, your dad might roll up his sleeves and bowl a few leg-breaks in the park.

My mum and sister never went to Spotland again; my dad and me couldn't keep away. We sat in the Main Stand, the only seated part of the ground. It was a shabby wooden structure populated by middle-aged and old men, coughing and moaning. When Rochdale scored, they rose from their seats and patted each other on the arm, smiling like all was well with the world. The rain came down and the pitch and players disappeared in the mist.

Rochdale were mid-table in the fourth division. The previous season they had suffered a dishonourable relegation from the third division. They had won twice in 46 league matches and recorded the lowest ever post-war attendance when 588 supporters saw them play Cambridge United.

When I first visited, I was oblivious to this woeful legacy. Spotland was merely a place to go, somewhere it quickly felt good to be. It was the blues against the other lot, us and them, a tide of legs and boots and bodies surging towards the goal. The bit in between was inconsequential. There was no aesthetic, just athleticism - running past them, over them, flattening them, watching the ball bulge the net at the Sandy Lane End or trickling over the line. A goal was a goal, and a goal was a dance with a stranger, an embrace with your dad, a scream, a shout, a clenched fist, and the wonder: how did you get from there (your original standing position) to here (three yards farther across)?

It was also the smell of a just-lit pipe or cigar, or a tray of pies, peas and gravy. It was the camaraderie among the overcoats and the absolute theatre of mud, thud, grumble and glory. We could hear it, smell it, even touch it if we leaned over the perimeter fence. When someone broke a leg or ankle, the snapping sound reverberated around the ground and we winced. A slow watery clap and a few shouts of 'Hard luck, lad' accompanied the stretcher-bearers as they trudged to the dressing-room.

The geography and routine were important, being in the same place at a given time every other week. Once, I picked up a stone and scratched a cross on the terracing. Over the course of a few seasons, I did not stray more than a few inches from its centre. I was among the same people, kids I half-recognised from school, getting older, putting on weight, losing hair, bringing their own children along. And we hardly spoke, except to mention that Steve Whitehall was back after his injury, or that the club was looking at a young defender from Stalybridge Celtic.

Meanwhile, the season, like the summer, has already lost the lustre of absolute, enchanting newness. We drew 1-1 with Darlington. We always draw 1-1 with Darlington; it's merely routine. The rain has returned this week and streets are suffused by drizzle so there is no colour, sparkle or definition, like furniture covered by sheets. Pigeons huddle on grey sloping roofs. The Rochdale Canal shimmers and strips of wood and bottles float on the dark water. A mother pushes a pram while her son, a blond-haired boy of about four, lags behind, dipping his fishing net into the reeds. Hope is important.

Saturday, 19 August 2000
Brighton and Hove Albion 2 Rochdale 1

Rochdale scored after 14 minutes when Tony Ford headed home a cross from Simon Davies. Three minutes later, Brighton equalised through Bobby Zamora, their new £100,000 signing from Bristol Rovers.

Soon after the goal, Tony Ellis and Andy Crosby were involved in a scuffle and were both sent off.

Brighton had the better of the second half and Zamora scored again. Four Rochdale players – Phil Hadland, Lee Todd, Graham Lancashire and Paul Ware - were booked in a scrappy match.

Among the Rochdale contingent was a group claiming to be the Gay London branch of the Dale Supporters' Club. They wore straw hats to differentiate themselves from the heterosexuals.

Tuesday, 22 August 2000

Rochdale 1 Blackburn Rovers 1
(Worthington Cup, first round, first leg)

A thrilling cup tie watched by 4,873 fans saw Rochdale snatch a draw with a late headed goal by Tony Ellis.

Nathan Blake had earlier given Blackburn the lead, though Rochdale had matched their wealthy neighbours throughout. Dave Flitcroft teased his brother, Garry, afterwards, telling reporters: "He couldn't get near me!"

Before the match, a minute's silence was held for Blackburn's famous benefactor Jack Walker who had died a few days earlier. The club later received a letter from Robert Coar, the Blackburn chairman, praising Rochdale fans for, 'observing an immaculate one-minute silence for Jack – well done.'

Wednesday, 23 August 2000

Tony Ellis received a three-match ban for his sending off against Brighton. Steve Parkin claimed it had been a 'nothing incident', but the referee classed it as violent conduct.

WHAT POOR RELATIONS HAVE
THAT RICHES CANNOT BUY

(The Times, Saturday, 26 August 2000)

The photographer had to stand well back to fit them all in. Let's take a count: 34 players, 10 blokes in dark tracksuits, and, at the front, a tough-looking guy in a suit and industrial-issue moustache.

The official team photograph of Blackburn Rovers looks like an end-of-term roll call at a finishing school for broad-shouldered, thick-set young men. Graeme Souness – narrow eyes, piece of carpet underlay betwixt lip and nose – is the headmaster, no doubt with a well-worn slipper secreted inside his jacket pocket.

Assembling a football squad the size of a small army is one of the privileges afforded to a club with a rich benefactor. Blackburn came to Spotland this week for a Worthington Cup game and the death of Jack Walker was marked with a minute's silence.

The words 'Jack Walker' transcended a mere name long ago. They are a euphemism for the arrival of the dream-maker, the hand through the sky that points at your ramshackle ground and inept team and booms: 'It's you.' The received wisdom is that supporters of all clubs, especially those of Rochdale's stature, are perpetual watchers of the sky, waiting for the hand of Jack, or one of his kind.

Unfortunately, his 'kind' is so rare as to be virtually extinct. Walker was loved by Blackburn supporters not only for his philanthropy, but because he was perceived as one of them. He was no self-serving, well-buffed PR glad-hand but looked and acted like your grandad. He talked about the old days, wrapped up well in winter, and he was demure and reticent in interviews. He couldn't articulate quite why he treated his football club like a favourite nephew, but he didn't need to, supporters understood anyway.

Rochdale, trust me, would – if ever we were so 'lucky' – attract the more common variety of benefactor. Bust would inexorably follow boom and the cash would come at the price of rampant egotism and outrageous whimsicality. The ground would be renamed Dreamsville or Xanadu and the tea bars would start selling baguettes instead of pies.

Additionally, everyone would hate us. Rochdale is, more or less, a club without enemies. It is perceived as dogged and pragmatic, a doughty survivor. When we sign a few fancy-dans on £6,000 a week and have a couple of lads advertising shampoo on television, they'll be mocking us from the away end. Sure, we'll wave wads of cash in their direction and call the fanzine *Loadsamoney* (as Blackburn do), but it will still hurt.

It hurts because the nation's sporting psyche holds that success comes to those that deserve it, those that work together and main-tain the principles of fair play and decency. A sudden cash-driven upsurge makes us uneasy. It is like getting the job because your dad owns the company, or winning the race because you were the only grown-up among the under-13s. It is still a victory, but only half the size of the real thing.

The dream of unlimited resources is often a platitude, something we say impulsively, like the move to a desert island, or the date with Julia Roberts. We don't stop to think of the reality, and in football terms this may well be the stark fact that we actually quite like the struggle. It is through adversity that we shape our clubs and ourselves. Everyone covets success, but would it feel the same if our personal investment were minimal next to the pile put down by our wealthy patron? Surely, in those circumstances, we would feel less of a supporter, especially since we had relinquished independence as part of the deal.

At Rochdale, I look around at the three recently-built stands and a team that is proficient enough to hold Blackburn to a 1-1 draw and I instinctively feel part of it. I have, like a few hundred others, bought a season ticket every year and I am proud to be an investor. I form a partnership of anonymous but passionate individuals, and although we form a cumbersome whole, we control our own destiny.

Since the players earn similar wages to supporters and have chosen to play for the club chiefly through their love of football, there is a greater sense of community at Rochdale. We exercise the right to either praise or barrack, but this is based solely on their performances on the field. We do not have to consider the wider issue of whether a player is wearing our colours because of the cash-inducement or the ego trip, because these are not of our world. We're all in it together.

Saturday, 26 August 2000
Rochdale 3 Scunthorpe United 2

Tony Ellis gave Rochdale the lead with the 200th goal of his career but Scunthorpe responded with goals from Gareth Sheldon and Lee Hodges, who scored from the penalty spot soon after half-time.

Clive Platt equalised with a strike from the edge of the penalty area and substitute Paul Ware scored the winner with a fierce shot from a similar distance. Ware had lost his place in the starting line-up to Gary Jones who had been suspended for the first two games of the season.

The attendance was a disappointing 2,561, which included more than 500 from Scunthorpe.

Saturday, 26 August 2000

Richard Bott, a sports journalist and Rochdale director, mentioned Life Sentence in the match programme for the game against Scunthorpe: 'I was delighted that lifetime Rochdale supporter Mark Hodkinson will be writing on the deeds, good, bad or indifferent, of his club throughout the coming season.

'And he set the scene with a 600-word piece sub-titled *Misty-eyed amid tales of woe*. What disappointed me about the piece was that having painted a picture of how Spotland used to be 'shabby old wooden stand, pigeons huddled on grey sloping roofs, etc etc,' it did nothing to explain the transformation that finally convinced the *Mail's* Steven Baker* that we have moved into a new Millennium if not out of the lowest division.

'I'll give Mark the benefit of the doubt and assume the Fleet Street 'spin doctors' contrived to give the wrong impression and look forward to reading his next article.'

* Steven Baker of the *Daily Mail* had earlier written that, 'holding the snooker World Championship at The Crucible [Sheffield] was akin to the FA Cup Final being held at Spotland' – these were, according to Bott, 'scathing comments'. Bott said he had 'taken Baker to task' and this had led to a favourable follow-up article in the same paper, *Plush Dale Look for Cutting Edge*.

Saturday, 26 August 2000

Proud dad Colin Smith-Markl of Caldershaw showed off his two sons, Paul, aged 10, and David, aged 13, on the front page of the *Rochdale Observer*. They had gained top GCSE marks despite their young ages. More impressive to supporters was the fact that all three sported Rochdale shirts.

Monday, 28 August 2000

Halifax Town 1 Rochdale 2

Rochdale moved up to sixth with a win against local rivals Halifax Town in a poor match.

Clive Platt scored with a header from a Michael Oliver cross but Mark Bradshaw equalised for Halifax with a volley after 20 minutes. Gary Jones scored the winner with a shot from 30 yards that hit the post on its way into the net.

More than 1,200 Rochdale fans made the journey across the Pennines, including 50 who took part in a sponsored walk to raise money for the Tractor Fund. They left the Cemetery Hotel, Spotland, at 7.30am after being stoked up with complimentary sausage and bacon butties.

Wednesday, 30 August 2000

Graeme Atkinson suffered another serious injury while playing for the reserves in a 3-1 defeat against Halifax Town. He twisted his knee, damaging the cruciate and mediate ligaments, and was told his season was over.

It was one of his first comeback games after extensive treatment on the same knee for an injury he had picked up the previous season.

Also in Rochdale...

August 2000

* Emma Rhodes of Great Howarth was jailed for life for stabbing to death pensioner Hugh 'Taffy' Jones.

* Arsonists set fire to stables at Spod Row, Spotland, killing four horses and two foals.

* The Post Office announced it was considering a move back to its original headquarters in the Esplanade after five years based at Woolworth's in Yorkshire Street.

Two

The Family Business

Friday, 1 September 2000

Visitors to the Rochdaleafc.com website voted Neil Edwards as Rochdale's best goalkeeper of all time. He shaded the voting ahead of Keith Welch, with the pair amassing more than 75 per cent of the total votes. Trailing them were Chris Harker, Ted Burgin, Ian Gray and Mike Poole.

Topping the list of worst goalkeepers were two players who had been on loan from Premiership clubs, Matt Dickins of Blackburn Rovers (October 1994, four appearances) and Kevin Pilkington of Manchester United (February 1996, six appearances).

LOCAL HERO DESTINED TO BECOME
A FOOTNOTE IN HISTORY
(*The Times*, Saturday, 2 September 2000)

The Halifax Town player caught it full on the volley and the ball flashed past our goalkeeper into the net. "Took it well, didn't he?" said the bloke next to me. Took it well? Who cares? He plays for them, how can you even consider such thoughts of magnanimity at a time like this? We've lost the lead now, and I'm hurting and angry. Just get on with the game, get on with the bloody game.

I do not watch Rochdale to admire the opposition. If the Halifax player - I'm so peevish I refuse to even name him - had dribbled past eight players, doubled-back and volleyed it home from his own six-yard box, it would have meant precisely the same to me: nothing. I am blind to anything that does not benefit my club, no matter how aesthetically pretty or skilful.

I'm not always so mean-spirited. Football does it to me. It also makes me vindictive. If one of our players is the victim of a snide elbow in the ribs, I want retribution. I want the perpetrator to suffer - a stud raked down his ankle. Obviously, I don't want to see him *seriously* hurt, but if he has to limp from the pitch in a moderate degree of pain, I feel a sense of glee that might well qualify me as sick in some quarters. He deserved it. He started it.

My partisanship is central to my love of the sport. If people ask, I do not say that I am a 'football' fan because this would suggest ambiguity; I tell them I am a Rochdale fan. When I drive through the town, I see 'football' fans everywhere. They wear, among others, the club colours of Manchester United, Liverpool and Barcelona. I do not mind that they wish to declare their blandness and conformity, or their necessity to arrogate glamour, but I balk at the conceit some hold for supporters of their hometown club. They consider Rochdale as beneath them.

Media saturation has empowered these supporters, made them feel as if they belong to such an extent that there is no requirement for them to actually attend matches. Their version of football support is reflected back to them constantly while Rochdale, in such exalted company, are reduced to an anachronism, a quaint indulgence, something akin to the music hall before television was introduced.

This week, for example, our striker, Tony Ellis, scored the 200th goal of a 14-year career that has taken in six other lower division clubs. In terms of news value, this was probably equal to a Phil Neville thigh strain, the one expected to clear up by the weekend. Ellis, by rights, should be in Hollywood negotiating the film of his life story, for he is Errol Flynn in football boots, someone who can turn a crisis into a drama, every Saturday.

Unfortunately, since he is not of the FA Premiership, he is resigned to an end-of-pier tour at places like Hartlepool and Torquay. There, small but appreciative crowds will witness his mastery of the key elements of performance. 'Anger' is a punch of the air and his feet lifted off the ground; 'disbelief' is two hands on his head, his body frozen rigid (while play goes on all around him); 'regret' is a look of angelic majesty and an injured opponent's hair ruffled for a good three minutes; 'happiness' is a measured stroll towards his delirious fans after scoring. Milking it? Two extra pints, please.

Afterwards, should he get embroiled in the match, he might score a wonder goal or, alternatively, miss-time a tackle and his boots collide with a hapless defender. Ellis, disentangling himself, will apologise profusely and pull a handkerchief from his sleeve to mop away the tears of remorse. His compassion is without limits. He will beckon the physio on to the pitch: "No, not for him," he barks suddenly. "He can wait. I need more hair gel!"

Tony Ellis can emote for the rest of his playing days (and, boy, he will), but, at best, he will form a statistical footnote in the history of the game. In short, you had to be there: that swagger, the thick black hair and roguish air, the twinkle in his eyes, his dancing feet. You also had to care that the team he was playing for won the match, and that he scored the winning goal. Then, he'd throw himself at the fence, hug members of the madding crowd, and glare at the sullen rival supporters as he jogged back to the halfway line. You had to be there, just had to.

Saturday, 2 September 2000
Rochdale 1 Cardiff City 1

A shortage of strikers meant Rochdale started the game with just Clive Platt up front. Tony Ellis was suspended, Graham Lancashire injured and Gary Hamilton had played the previous night for the Northern Ireland Under-21s.

Cardiff scored through Paul Brayson and were the better team until Phil Hadland, a substitute for the injured Tony Ford, slotted home a loose ball from close range.

In the closing stages, Keith Hill and Clive Platt almost sneaked a win, but were foiled by Cardiff goalkeeper, Mark Walton.

Before the game, Rochdale's mascot Desmond the Dragon visited the town centre handing out free match tickets to schoolchildren.

Tuesday, 5 September 2000

Rochdale lost the unwanted record of appearing in front of the smallest-ever crowd for a League Cup match. Halifax Town's 'home' game against Tranmere Rovers attracted just 612 supporters after being switched to Bradford City's Valley Parade because of floodlight problems at the New Shay.

The previous lowest was 968, when Rochdale drew 3-3 draw at Scarborough in September 1990.

Wednesday, 6 September 2000

Blackburn Rovers 6 Rochdale 1
(Worthington Cup, first round, second leg)

The final score was an injustice to a Rochdale side that had matched Blackburn for much of the game and were cheered on by more than 1,500 supporters.

Blackburn took the lead through Damien Duff when his shot deflected off Dave Bayliss and beyond Neil Edwards. Clive Platt equalised, but seconds before half-time Blackburn were awarded a penalty by referee William Burns from which David Dunn, the captain of the England Under-21s, scored.

A second penalty was awarded and Dunn again scored before Kaba Diawara made it 4-1 when he outpaced Keith Hill. Rovers were awarded another penalty soon afterwards and Dunn completed a hat-trick of penalties, all scored within a 20-minute period.

In the dying seconds, Duff made it 6-1. "They put us to the sword when it mattered," said Steve Parkin. "That's why they are a good team. They do not take pity on anybody."

One of Rochdale's substitutes was second-year YTS player, David Walsh, a former pupil at St Cuthbert's High School, Rochdale. He replaced Michael Oliver in the second half.

After the game, Parkin revealed himself a devotee of the Graeme Souness school of management: "He seems to be very aggressive in everything he does and I would say that's true of myself," he said.

Thursday, 7 September 2000

An appeal went out for a new Desmond the Dragon after the club announced the original mascot had 'run out of puff'. Applicants had to be 'outgoing, vigorous and of around five ft 10 ins in height and of fairly slim build'.

SUPPORTERS BROUGHT TOGETHER
IN THE NAME OF ENMITY

(*The Times*, Saturday, 9 September 2000)

Ah, Burnley, that sweet passing side of the Sixties and Seventies, the cuddly sleeping giant among the mills, hills and terraced houses. Everyone has a tinge of claret and blue in their heart, a tender spot for this plucky club from Lancashire's football heartland. Everyone, that is, except Blackburn Rovers and us. We hate 'em.

The Burnley Non-Appreciation Society has just held two meetings, at Spotland and Ewood Park. Nominally, we were there to witness Worthington Cup matches, but this was a side issue compared with the love-in inspired by a common enemy. We stood up in the name of enmity, sat down, jigged about, and then both sets of supporters applauded one another. Strange, that naked, unashamed antipathy should meld camaraderie and also form a basis of mutual respect.

It would appear that when we take on support of a football club, it has to be counter-balanced by feelings of ill-will to another. Love thrives in the proximity of hate. Usually, this hostility is directed at the club that is geographically the closest, which is why Blackburn and Burnley are not best of friends. Oldham Athletic and Bury are Rochdale's neighbours, but our dislike of them is cursory compared with the lovingly-tended spleen we hold for everything Turf Moor way.

Many supporters of lower division teams have similar feelings about Burnley. Up until last season's promotion to the first division, they were viewed as the 'Manchester United' of our world. They tried hard - and we could tell they did, which probably made it worse – but their loftiness was transparent. They felt it was beneath them

41

to stop off at places such as Exeter and Darlington. It probably was, but some things are better left unsaid.

There were stories of dads apologising to their children that they had brought them to grounds such as Spotland. They were misty-eyed, the ghost of Ralph Coates and nights of European glory flickering across the memory. As the psychologists would concur, their real anger was with themselves, or, more accurately, their club, but they needed someone to look down upon.

An example of their haughtiness was a stark refusal to even accept Rochdale as rivals. We were of the same division for seven seasons, and separated by just 14 miles, but we were not worthy. They still claimed Blackburn as their mortal foes, despite being three divisions beneath them.

It is extremely difficult to find a rationale for anti-support. At times it can feel instinctive, something best not to think about, but to accept – and enjoy. One of the greatest moments of my life came in September 1991 when we beat Burnley at Turf Moor despite having two players sent off. Their supporters hollered for the dismissals and the match raged with shot after shot raining down on the Rochdale goal. Miraculously, we held out and, yes, some of us cried at the final whistle.

Who do we actually 'hate'? Is it the Burnley supporters, the players, or the club itself? I have had two run-ins with Burnley fans. I was talking peaceably with one in a pub when he announced abruptly: "Let's just face it, Rochdale are shit." Another time, I had been playing football and was still wearing my Rochdale shirt when I called at a shop. As I queued to pay, a Burnley fan at the front turned and asked: "What are you wearing that crap for?" He also wanted to punch me but the shopkeeper talked him out of it.

As a general body of support, I actually hold a great deal of admiration for their loyalty. No other club has underachieved so consistently in the past 25 years, and yet their support has remained steadfast. It can't be the players either, especially since many have moved from Burnley to Rochdale in the past few seasons.

My only gripe with the club as a wider entity probably qualifies as a 'spent' conviction now, but football fans have long memories when it suits. Famously, Burnley avoided relegation from the Football League with a win against Orient on the last day of the 1986-87 season. They had earlier lobbied to withdraw the automatic relegation rule. One of their officials was reported to have said, and this may be apocryphal: "This rule was meant to catch out the Hartlepool's and Rochdale's of the football world, not the Burnley's."

I must admit, the aggregate score of these half-truths, theories and supposition is still pretty much 0-0. It might be futile to search for justification and is akin to why people climb mountains: because they're there.

* Burnley were champions of the fourth division in 1991-92, the last ever, because it changed to the third division with the inauguration of the FA Premier League the following season. Their final piece of business in 1991-92 was to foil our play-off bid when they visited Spotland in the last game of the season and won 3-1, despite them having already secured the title. A Rochdale win would have lifted us above Barnet into the top seven.

Since then, apart from friendly matches, we have met only once in a competitive match, in December 1993, when Burnley won 4-1 at Turf Moor in the second round of the FA Cup. They have, then, inflicted intermittent but considerable damage on Rochdale over the years, but our main friction was confined to a definite eight-year timespan: 1985 (Burnley's first year in the fourth division) to 1993.

As the years have passed, perhaps our antipathy should have waned, but it is difficult to tell whether it has, or whether it has fermented. We are no longer of the same division, but Rochdale supporters come into regular contact with Burnley fans because of the towns' geographical closeness and - we have to reluctantly concede this - the sheer size of their support. It is noteworthy that Burnley's hatred of Blackburn Rovers (and 'hatred' is appropriate for a club many Burnley fans refer to as Bastard Rovers) appeared to intensify during the long period when they were in separate divisions.

For my part, my aversion has remained constant, which makes me uneasy about the final paragraph in my article. It was a sop, a half-hearted stab at phoney diplomacy. When writing for a national newspaper, there is tendency to camouflage (with irony or humour or downright chicanery) feelings that the reader might find unbecoming. This self-censorship does not come, in my case, from a policy emanating from *The Times*, but more from a fear of revealing too much of myself; the reader might not like me if I did.

I do not dislike Burnley because they 'are there' but because I am envious of them. They have a better ground, more supporters, a wealth of history and they win more often than Rochdale. These very factors have bred in their supporters a conceit for clubs like mine. This is probably true of many fans of 'bigger' clubs, especially those with a gilded past that has slipped away. Burnley happened to be the one 'big' club that we came into contact with on regular basis; others, such as Wolverhampton Wanderers and Sheffield United, spent only one season in the bottom division.

Our rivalry with Burnley was forged while they were at the lowest point in their history. Their fans were in an agitated state, like passengers who had boarded the wrong train. They wanted to be somewhere else, where they felt they belonged. They had, after all, been champions of the Football League on two occasions (1920-21 and 1959-60), runners-up on two occasions (1919-20 and 1961-62) and FA Cup winners in 1914. Consequently, we saw them at their worst.

They have become noticeably more relaxed now they have reached what they consider to be a their rightful place, two divisions higher. They regard it as ludicrous that Rochdale should claim to be their adversaries. Rochdale, to them, was a frivolous spat, and serves to remind them of a squalid, undignified recent past. We have not forgotten, however, how they behaved in adversity, which is always a telling insight. Some of them were insufferably condescending and disrespectful and this is why we cheer at half-time when news filters through that they are losing at Grimsby, Norwich or wherever.

Some of our supporters visit the Blackburn Rovers' websites and leave messages of congratulation when they beat the common enemy. They also upload films on to the internet of monkeys scratching themselves and claim it is a web-cam from Turd Moor (sic): childish, peevish, petty-minded and vindictive - the football supporter incarnate.

Saturday, 9 September 2000
Carlisle United 1 Rochdale 2

A goal in the 94th minute by Lee Todd made it four successive wins at Brunton Park for Rochdale and lifted them to fourth.

Clive Platt had given Rochdale the lead after 15 minutes when he headed home from a corner. Carlisle scored a similar goal just before half-time, when Ian Stevens was left unmarked at the far post.

Rochdale were awarded a late free kick and Todd sent the ball spinning past a stranded Luke Weaver in the Carlisle goal. "Rochdale didn't create their goals, we gave them to them," said Ian Atkins, the Carlisle manager.

Tuesday, 12 September 2000
York City 0 Rochdale 2

Clive Platt scored his fifth goal in six matches to give Rochdale the lead and Mark Monington, making his first appearance of the season, made it 2-0 before half-time.

The win moved Rochdale into the top three for the first time in almost a year and meant they had secured 16 points from the possible 18 in their past six matches. "Again, the players showed tremendous workrate, tremendous spirit and a ruthless determination to win," said Steve Parkin.

York's defender Wayne Hall praised Rochdale, telling reporters: "Rochdale are the best team we've played by a long way. They are quite big and physical but they play some great football on the deck. They mightily impressed me."

More than 300 Rochdale supporters made the trip to Bootham Crescent despite petrol shortages caused by fuel protests.

Wednesday, 13 September 2000

Several clubs were reported to be interested in signing Clive Platt. Scouts from Manchester City, Nottingham Forest, Blackburn Rovers, Bradford City, Sheffield Wednesday and Wimbledon had watched Rochdale's recent matches.

Thursday, 14 September 2000

Lifelong Rochdale fan Nigel MacDonald claimed divine intervention had helped him capture the glory of Spotland from high in the clouds.

Nigel and his friend Andrew Huszar were returning from Malaga, Spain, on an Airbus 320 when they flew over Spotland. Nigel passed his camera to Andrew in the window seat, but a bank of cloud spoiled the view. Suddenly, as the airplane banked, the clouds opened and Spotland, complete with its almost-built new stand, was visible.

Friday, 15 September 2000

Bury reserve striker, Lee Buggie, joined the club on a month's loan.

WHY ROCHDALE WILL NEVER
WIN THE FA CUP AGAIN
(*The Times*, Saturday, 16 September)

Clive Platt, our skinny kick-and-run striker, is no more. Over the summer he's put on half a stone in weight and the increase in bulk has been complemented by a greater poise, confidence and skill. The nicknames of 'Plattini' and 'Plattistuta' used to be ironic, but now we're not so sure.

Inevitably, the chaps in anoraks and company cars have started to turn up at Spotland, old lags searching for young legs. Football scouts are easy to spot. They are usually ex-pros, so they shift their weight awkwardly to avoid their bad knee. In the stands, they hold a pen clumsily like your old woodwork teacher as they scribble notes: 'Good left foot', 'hungry for it', 'fades away', 'attitude'. They'll make sense of it later.

Unlike, say, Crewe Alexandra, Rochdale does not have a reputation as a 'selling' club. In fact, we're rather like that dusty store on the out-skirts of town with flaking paint and the blinds half-drawn. You pass it every day but you're not quite sure if it's still open for business.

The last time we did any substantial trade was - wait for this - 25 years ago when we offloaded Alan Taylor to West Ham United. He became the star-turn on *Match of the Day*, scoring two goals in the quarter-final, semi-final and final of the FA Cup of 1975. Taylor looked like the scrawny, hollow-cheeked kid bullied into making up the numbers by the older lads on the park, someone hardly worth the bother of marking. In barely two or three touches, he'd bear down on goal, zip the ball past the goalkeeper and skip into the arms of his muscular team-mates.

During West Ham's Cup run, one newspaper dubbed Taylor 'The Rochdale Whippet'. He was actually born in Hinckley, near Leicester, brought up in Morecambe and spent just 18 months at Rochdale. No matter, whether by adoption or not, he became our most famous sporting son. He might have worn a West Ham shirt, but he was still playing for Rochdale. We had discovered him, nurtured him and primed him for glory and adulation.

My heart raced every time I heard the word 'Rochdale', which was frequent because the pundits reflected continually on Taylor's origins. It validated my club, gave it relevance. Taylor made my secret world real and supplied glamour by association. When he scored his two goals in the final, I had to race through the lounge door, charge into the hall and up the stairs to diffuse my joy. I had made a banner out of wallpaper and scrawled on it 'The Rochdale Whippet'. It was torn during the goal celebrations. It didn't matter, we'd just won the FA Cup.

Almost 20 years elapsed before we next provided a player to a club in the top division, when Alan Reeves was transferred to Wimbledon in 1994. Only two players currently with FA Premiership teams are formerly of Rochdale - Sunderland's Paul Butler and West Ham's Stephen Bywater.

When a player moves to a higher club there is a peculiar feeling of both loss and pride. I 'adopt' their new club and take a keen interest in their fortunes. I scan match reports to see if our ex-player is mentioned. I am lifted if he has played well, or deflated if he is singled out for criticism. I feel an unshakeable sense of responsibility. I want other supporters to think well of Rochdale, to view the club fondly and respect us for strengthening their own team.

The scouts watching Clive Platt will probably be from clubs higher in the Nationwide League. Premiership clubs concentrate their scouting abroad and at schoolboy level and have a mistrust of players drawn from the lower divisions. They doubt whether they will have sufficient technical ability and pace. They are also suspicious because of the efficacy of their youth scouting system – if a player is so good, why was he not spotted earlier?

The second and third divisions have effectively become football ghettos and to escape them young players must show remarkable ability, self-belief and doggedness. It isn't enough any more for a player to hit upon a run of 10 superlative performances; he must play at the peak of his game for two or three seasons to ensnare a club from the top division.

Rochdale and their contemporaries do business with clubs of their own division, or those directly above or beneath. This creates a pool of players of similar ability distributed among lower division teams. It is an egalitarian system because, where the band of ability is so narrow and uniform between clubs, there is a greater emphasis on the fundamentals of sport -- team blending and spirit, motivation, tactics and passion.

Saturday, 16 September 2000
Rochdale 2 Torquay United 1

Rochdale raced into a two-goal lead through Mark Monington and Tony Ellis in a first half during which Torquay did not have a shot on goal.

Torquay rallied after the break and pulled one back through Robbie Herrera. Afterwards, they peppered the Rochdale goal and were unfortunate not to claim a draw.

Simon Coleman made his debut for Rochdale among a trio of centre backs that also included Monington and Dave Bayliss. The win moved Rochdale into second place, behind Chesterfield.

Before the game there were fears that the petrol shortage might hit Torquay's travelling plans, but their coach company had made special provision.

Monday, 18 September 2000

Exiled fan Rory McNicholas bought a registration plate for his car - 'THE DALE' for just $35. In North Carolina, United States, where Rory lives, motorists were able to choose their own plate.

Tuesday, 19 September 2000

Joe Royle, manager of Manchester City, denied his interest in Clive Platt. "To be honest, I do not know much about him," he said.

Wednesday, 20 September 2000

Rochdale's £50,000 offer for Southend striker, Martin Carruthers, was turned down. Carruthers, aged 28, had been Southend's top scorer the previous season with 19 goals. He had started his career with Aston Villa, making a handful of first-team appearances.

AWAY WINS, ATTENDANCES UP, BUT IT WON'T LAST OF COURSE

(*The Times*, Saturday, 23 September 2000)

The bunting has yet to go up outside the Town Hall and Steve Parkin, our manager, is some way off being granted the freedom of Rochdale. We might be in second place in the league, but we're a pragmatic bunch and, besides, we're always second in September; it's pre-destined.

A rollicking good start has been a feature of our season for some time. We are the firework that catches alight too early, flaring white-hot before tumbling into the darkness, and down the league. Last year, we excelled ourselves and held second place until the beginning of October. A month later, we were 16th.

When we first take on the support of a football club we are oblivious to the innate peculiarities of our chosen team. We soon learn that, like having ginger hair or jug-ears, much of our torment is congenital, somehow passed down through the generations.

Rochdale's flawed gene is more acute than most. In blunt terms, we've made losing and suffering the family business. Even the brief moments of joy - a 4-0 win or a patch of good form - remain isolated, and are not built upon. It is not evidence of a rebirth, a reinvention, or a corner turned. That kind of kismet is for clubs that were once our equals at the foot of the Football League but progressed while we stayed-put, such as Bradford City, Wimbledon, Barnsley, Stockport County, Crewe Alexandra et al.

If we win, and win well, passing and dribbling and shooting and scoring, it is to mock the Gods and tamper with the natural order. It will incur an empirical, bitter wrath. The biggest win of the season will be followed by the biggest loss. History authenticates the claim. In our first Football League match we trounced Accrington Stanley 6-3. A week later, we played the same team and lost 4-0. We also finished the season at the bottom of the league. Our cards were marked.

So, why do I bother, when such fatalism would appear to render my support futile? In truth, my stance is a defence measure and a comfort zone. It gets me through. If I believe failure becomes us, it is paradoxically a force of hope since anything else is a bonus. It means I can also disown my team at will, claim it as something incorporeal, no longer of flesh and blood but a subordinate of a greater sorcery: we are the playthings of those pesky Gods and they deem that we should lose. Often.

Under close scrutiny, however, there is evidence that the ancestral legacy is not quite so daunting any more and we might not be such a hopeless case. For instance, we have always suffered from acute travel sickness. Our worst period spanned 1977 to 1984 when, in 138 League away matches, we won just 11 times. These days, we win more often away than we do at Spotland. To hell with hoodoo.

Rochdale were habitually the worst-supported club in the country until recently. Attendances have improved markedly and, last season, seven clubs had lower average gates. There are other signs of hope: a much-improved ground; children wearing replica shirts; a glossy, readable programme; and numerous websites dedicated to the club. These all have the effect of haranguing the hex, though to purge it completely we need to win promotion and put this woeful period of the club's history (26 seasons in the bottom division) in a black box secured with black ribbon and toss it into the sea, or Hollingworth Lake, which is a lot nearer.

If Rochdale did bring success to the town, there is further support to call upon, but the stay-aways remain justifiably sceptical. There are many who abandoned the cause years ago when supporting the club began to feel like an illness. The pain and humiliation became too great.

Many found themselves unable to break the habit without a partial abstention from their decision. They resolved to focus their support on a certain player whom they believed represented ambition, enterprise, and grounds for optimism. When that player left, be it Bob Mountford, or Steve Whitehall, or Alan Reeves, the supporter also left. This abrogation of freewill made their decision easier because it was forced upon them, a kind of mercy killing. The club, by virtue of selling its best player, had walked out on them.

These ex-supporters and the hundreds of nearly-supporters will have noticed the encouraging form and reminded themselves that it is nothing new. They want to see Rochdale in second place in December, perhaps into March, before they put their trust once more into a club that has treated them so badly in the past. Only then will they walk back in.

* This article, along with others, was not appreciated by Frank Bishop, chairman of the Rochdale Supporters' Club. He wrote:

'Anyone who reads The Times newspaper has no doubt read the regular articles on Dale by lifelong supporter Mark Hodkinson. I do not read that particular paper but have been downloading the articles from The Times website. I actually find some of the earlier articles quite depressing and downbeat. The author regales us with what makes a true Dale supporter and how we have suffered over the years with poor facilities, poor teams and no hope of a better future. He does not expect ex-supporters, non-supporters, those with only a passing interest in Dale, to regard this October to be any better than previous years in that we start well and collapse in October into freefall down the division into the basement. With matches against Kidderminster, Hartlepool, Chesterfield, Cheltenham, Macclesfield and Exeter following the Southend match this might have been so in the past. Sorry to tell the world at large that this is the year when it is not going to happen. As I write this to the background music from the motion picture Gladiator, the football team, directors, management and, most of all, the fans will not let this transpire. A new spirit flows throughout the whole club, whether you pay or are paid to be a part of Spotland. We are determined that Dale are not just going to peep over the wall between the second and third divisions. Rochdale are going to leap it with studded boots into a new Millennium Era! With the Rochdale Symphony Orchestra (a drum, bugle and trombone actually, but it is a start and growing in numbers and volume) providing quality backing to the vocal fans; a pitch you can run the Waterloo Cup on; stadium facilities better than most places the away fans will visit this season; and a team that has the skill and guts to take anyone on, times have changed. I would like to see Mr Hodkinson being far more positive in his Dale writings to encourage his readers to look upon Dale differently, unless he has a plan for the season to write about us as sheep in August with us progressing through the animal kingdom to be lions in May, kings of the third division jungle! I look forward to a more upbeat tone in his future writings.'

Saturday, 23 September 2000
Shrewsbury 0 Rochdale 4

Rochdale recorded their biggest win under Steve Parkin and scored four at Gay Meadow for the second consecutive season. It was Shrewsbury's worst home defeat for 12 years.

Tony Ellis put Rochdale ahead after 15 minutes but the visitors had to wait until 10 minutes into the second half before Clive Platt increased the lead. Defenders Mark Monington and Dave Bayliss completed the rout when they scored headed goals from corners. Monington was the first Rochdale centre half to score in three consecutive matches for 41 years.

Rochdale were awarded Performance of the Week by pundit Chris Kamara on Sky Sports.

Saturday, 23 September 2000

Ron Martin, the owner of Southend United, drafted a leaflet that was handed to fans as they went into the ground to see the match against Scunthorpe United. They were informed that Martin Carruthers was not for sale.

Monday, 25 September 2000

Rochdale's excellent form prompted bookmakers to cut the odds on them winning the third division title. They were now quoted at 9/1, fourth favourites behind Chesterfield, Cardiff and Brighton.

Thursday, 28 September 2000

Alan Little, the Southend United manager, was sacked two days before his side were due to play Rochdale at Spotland. Mick Gooding was put in temporary charge.

Little had spent his last days at the club issuing denials that Martin Carruthers was moving to Rochdale.

Friday, 29 September 2000

Neil Edwards gave an insight into the club's dressing-room philosophy. "When things are going wrong, there's no arguing. There's no slagging off anybody. We're in it together," he said.

WHY I'D RATHER NOT PLAY HAPPY FAMILIES ON MY AFTERNOON OUT

(*The Times*, Saturday, 30 September 2000)

Better make this clear - I love my children. My heart melts when Alec (21 months) tilts his head in a comic-serious manner and sings, 'Whatcha doin'?' Likewise, when my other son, George (nearly four), jumps up and down uncontrollably because he's found a woodlouse in the garden or the sweets in my jacket pocket.

All's well then, I love my children. So why do I feel uncomfortable about the admission I am about to make? Why do I worry that it may be a fatal flaw in my parental make-up? Is it a symptom of something else, like that I don't care enough? It wouldn't be too bad with daughters, but two sons? Come on.

At least once a week I'm told (not asked even) how nice it will be when I take them to watch Rochdale. It is viewed as a coming-of-age, a ritual equal to their Christening or first day at school. The problem is, I'm in no rush to take them. Boo, hiss, call the Social Services.

There are some that will say keeping my sons *away* from Spotland is the greater kindness. They have a point. Although I valiantly log our worth in this column every Saturday, I know the truth of supporting a club several fathoms below the water line of glamour and success. People scoff. It hurts. They haven't even heard of Rochdale. What division are they in? Have they ever won anything? When are they on telly? Never, ha!

I've been that kid in a blue and white scarf, so hurt by the taunts that I opted out of football conversations in the playground. It's lonely when the players you idolise don't make it on to football cards, when newspapers don't acknowledge that you exist. Billy Liar's secret world was Ambrosia; mine was Spotland.

I go to Rochdale with my dad, just my dad, and we like this arrangement. I pick him up, we drive to the ground, we watch the match – it's been this elementary for years. If we remember, we tell each other about our week just gone by. If we forget, we don't really notice. It's just good being together, and in a place where we do not feel ourselves compromised by children, women or etiquette.

If I took my sons along it would change the dynamic and tamper with a sacred custom. The match and our peculiar companionship would be secondary to my sons' welfare. For example, further down our row sits a dad of a similar age to me with his four-year-old son. I do not view this cameo with jealousy or longing. Oh no. It looks a bloody nightmare. If it's not crisps, it's pop or the toilet, not to mention facing the wrong way in his seat, jumping up and down. At the last game, they were shuffling along the row for the 14th time heading to the toilets, when the bloke behind piped up: "Sit down will you? I don't pay £10 to watch you two going to the lav all day." Ouch.

Rochdale, like most clubs, is very pro-children. They believe in initiatives like the Family Stand and Junior Dale. I'm not so sure. Attendances might double if children were banned altogether. Imagine the sheer bliss of a football ground without that high-pitched screaming and shrieks of 'off, off' when one of their players has the temerity to tackle one of ours. Also, no silly mascots; or half-time Morris dancers; or seats being tipped up noisily; or the back of the stand being whacked; or games of tig in the aisles; or crisp bags popped loudly; or Manchester United shirts. Imagine, a world without children – wonderful.

My sons will be introduced to Rochdale FC when I consider them to be no longer children. Age, or indeed gender, is of little significance here; I was about seven-years-old when I reached football fan adulthood. Essentially, they must understand the game and have the concentration span to last 90 minutes. They should also accept that, even if the behaviour of their dad and grandad is noticeably different than it is at home, they are the same caring and compassionate men as they always were, or tried to be at least.

When I first watched Rochdale in the 1970s, the team was well and truly abysmal and the ground was falling down around us. Older lads staged pitched battles on all sides and you watched your back, your front, and where the exits were. Back then, it was some achievement to become a child-bloke. These days it's too easy.

Saturday, 30 September 2000

Rochdale 0 Southend United 1

Rochdale had been strongly linked with Southend's striker Martin Carruthers and it seemed predestined that he would score.

It was the only goal of a scrappy game and it ended Rochdale's unbeaten home run. In trying to stop the ball crossing the line, two Rochdale defenders became entangled in the netting and the match was held up for 10 minutes while the damage was repaired.

Richard Bott asked supporters to help him spot 'Dale knockers' - anyone in the media declining to give Rochdale appropriate respect. 'Drop me a line if you spot a 'Dale knocker' and I will take them to task,' he wrote.

He revealed that his recent targets had been Alan Biggs of *Radio Five Live*, Des Kelly, sports editor of the *Daily Mirror* and Paul Hince, chief sports writer of the *Manchester Evening News*. 'When are people going to take their heads out of the sand and start giving this club some credit? Anyone else who takes a snipe at us is going to cop for a Bott's broadside,' he wrote in the match programme.

Also in Rochdale...

September 2000

* Eileen Jawczak, a 65-year-old mother of four and former school teacher, was attacked and killed 50 yards from her Deeplish home. She was found in a back alley close to the Weavers Arms, where she had spent a quiet night with friends.
* Health workers were threatened and abused at three petrol stations after being given special dispensation to fill-up their cars during the petrol shortage.

Three

Drifting Listlessly

Monday, 2 October 2000

Clive Platt was named as *Match* magazine's third division player of the month for September. Former Rochdale midfield player, Alex Russell, now at Cambridge United, won the award in the second division.

Wednesday, 4 October 2000

Rochdale reserves lost 2-1 against Scarborough whose team included the Senegalese international, Cerif Diallo, on trial at the Yorkshire club. Diallo was described as 'resembling a crab on ice' in the match report included in Rochdale's programme against Chesterfield. He scored both Scarborough goals.

A FUNNY OLD GAME?
WAIT UNTIL *YOUR* GOAL FALLS DOWN
(*The Times*, Saturday, 7 October 2000)

Please, no more talk of exploding goalposts, shredded netting or string and ladders. I've had it all week – a sardonic smile, a pointed finger: "Hey, your lot were in the news at the weekend, weren't they?"

Rochdale briefly found themselves on the national sporting agenda at 5pm last Saturday. I was at the match in question, so I'm not sure precisely how the news was imparted, but the nation was informed that the final score from our home game against Southend United was late because the goalposts had collapsed.

They reported that the 'incident' had occurred as Martin Carruthers scored Southend's goal. The presumption, therefore, was that he had smashed home one of those mythical net-busting goals, thought to be the sole preserve of Hot Shot Hamish or some meaty bloke called Reg or Albert who played for your club in the 1940s and chewed on bicycle chains as a pre-match snack.

Sadly, the truth rather spoils a good story. Dave Flitcroft, our well-fed midfielder, wobbled when he should have shimmied and the ball fell to a Southend player. He passed to Carruthers who side-stepped our goalkeeper and slotted it gently home. Two of our defenders, desperate to appear on television in *Nationwide Football League Extra*, hurtled into the net after the ball and dragged the lot on top of themselves

I know I take these things far too seriously, but, as this week has progressed, I've become increasingly sniffy about the whole thing. We win four consecutive league games, rise to second in the table, and no one notices. Alternatively, our winning run ends, and the whole country is made aware, in pretty emphatic fashion. Their goal, incidentally, was scored by a player we have been trying to sign all season. Lucky, the official club cat, has left the building. And been hit by a car.

Paranoid I may be, but the nature of all this attention concerns me. Is there a subtext that we are such a sorry bunch that our goalposts are made of balsa wood, the netting from donated hairnets? It feels as if Rochdale et al serve the media merely as a counterpoint to the big-name clubs. We exist to burnish their glamour and importance with our dullness and insignificance. We are not allowed to exist in our own right and respected for the passion engendered, albeit small in numerical terms. So, Rochdale's winning run, even securing pro-motion, is of the same news value as David Beckham buying a Rolo from the corner shop.

We have made the news several times recently and a theme has developed. Last season, our mascot, Desmond the Dragon, picked a fight with Freddie the Fox, his Halifax Town counterpart. It made the local television news. Rochdale were featured on *They Think It's All Over* for their 'thong' goal celebration. You must remember: goal scored, players yank up their shorts and hare off down the pitch.

Our most recent notice was in the tabloids over the club shop's saucy brochure showing naked girls (from the waist up) using Rochdale scarves to maintain their dignity.

It's all laugh-a-minute, knockabout stuff, but – stroke of the chin, furrowed brow - are they laughing with us, or at us? Have we been appointed jesters in the court of the football kingdom? The club usually goes along with the joke. They know the perils of taking themselves too seriously, but their compliance may well reinforce the stereotype. When did Sir Alex Ferguson or Arsene Wenger last have a belly laugh at some folly involving their beloved clubs.

In the circumstances, it might serve us well to pack in football altogether and trek around the country as a revue troupe. The star-turn would be the chap who ran on with string to fix the nets on Saturday. He looked like he had been on the Waltzers for three hours – probably yelling: "Spin me gypo," and we know the retribution that would bring – before being fired on to the pitch via a circus canon. Bewildered, he hit the grass at some rate and surprised many by actually locating the nets. Unfortunately, he had forgotten his ladder, so had to jump up and down on the goal line while, you've guessed it, the crowd laughed uproariously. Not one player came to his assistance, the meanies.

Mercifully, our groundsman, Craig Wooding, appeared with a set of ladders and calmly refastened the nets to the crossbar. His dizzy chum footed the ladder, and the far-away look in his eyes suggested he was already dreaming of Cleethorpes or Great Yarmouth where the Rochdale Hairnets All-Star Revue could really get them chuckling.

Friday, 6 October 2000
Kidderminster Harriers 0 Rochdale 0

Referee Mike North, well-known for his thick, bushy moustache, was the subject of controversy, making several bizarre decisions and, according to Rochdale supporters, showing favouritism to the home side.

After four successive away wins, more than 500 supporters made the difficult journey south of Birmingham in Friday's rush-hour and saw Rochdale slip back to fourth position.

The match was another milestone for Tony Ford. Aggborough was the 89th ground he had visited during his career, with only Blackpool's Bloomfield Road, Tottenham Hotspur's White Hart Lane and Wycombe Wanderers' Adams Park still awaiting a visit.

Six months after the game, North, aged 42, of Wimborne, Dorset, collapsed and died while he refereed a match between Southend United and Mansfield Town. The game was abandoned at half-time and replayed at the end of the season with proceeds donated to his family.

Friday, 13 October 2000

Rochdale's new stand, running down the Willbutts Lane side of the ground, was issued with a safety certificate from the Health and Safety Executive. It would open for the first time when league leaders Chesterfield visited on Tuesday, 17 October.

HOME IS WHERE THE HEART IS
WHEN SATURDAY COMES
(*The Times*, Saturday, 14 October 2000)

Rose and Peter are getting married today. I'm extremely happy for them, and I'm also extremely happy for me. The wedding itinerary is perfect: register office at 11am, then everyone down to the pub. Surely, amid the vol-au-vents and bonhomie, a man could slip by unnoticed, spirit himself away, and, if he wanted, maybe head Spotland way.

A 1pm start might have been problematic, a 3pm a disaster. Well, I'll own up, it wouldn't have been any such thing. Much as I like the happy couple, me and Rochdale go back a long way and we're playing Hartlepool at home today. We're fourth in the table, on a roll, and, come on, it's not as if the couple are family. Besides, I'll still be back in time to see Peter do his Billy Fury number on the karaoke and watch the bored, cake-and-pop fuelled kids sliding across the polished floorboards.

I've pulled off this wedding trick before. On December 7 1991 my sister-in-law married. A great day it was too: excellent buffet, good company, yards of ale and plenty of escape routes. I'm sure the date is etched on her memory, and, as the years go by, she will reflect on it often. When I think back, I can't recall the dress she wore or the speeches made, but with startling clarity I remember the pain of narrowly losing to Huddersfield Town in the FA Cup, of John Halpin scoring, and of 6,000 fans cheering the team on.

I have twice missed a Rochdale home match out of choice. The first was many years ago and the anguish was such that it was nearly 18 years later before I repeated the folly. Back in January 1975, Rochdale were due to play Darlington. It coincided with Andrew Bennett's fifth birthday party and I was a friend of his older brothers, Philip and Steven. I was new to the enigma of football support and foolishly chose the party. I paid dearly.

We were the only older children there. We played Crossfire and Striker while chaos reigned. Sausage rolls were trampled into the carpet and Andrew's mum kept saying it was, 'like a bloody zoo'. The little kids held a competition to see who could jump down the most stairs. Intermittently, we'd we'd hear the winner screaming in agony.

At about 5pm, my dad came to collect me. He had some good news, bad good news. Rochdale had won 2-0. He'd seen the score flash up under the wrestling on the television. I was inconsolable. It was a physical pain. I realised that the match had existed solely in the moment. I would *never* see those goals; the game was lost forever. To learn the scoreline like this, especially a winning one, was to receive a postcard, but miss out on a holiday.

I was left empty, aching, frustrated, and the only solace was the prospect of the next match, but that might be two weeks away. We'd probably lose then anyway and everyone would eulogise the match I'd missed. I swore to myself - blood on my forehead - that I would never again miss a game through free will. Only illness (acute), death (in the immediate family, but not my dad's because I would then go as a memorial tribute), or childbirth (my own children) would keep me away.

Only once have I erred. It was Christmas 1992 and I was undergoing a regular re-evaluation of my life. Who was this sorrowful twenty-something, so limited in his vision and outlook that his life was fastened to the fortunes of a mediocre third division football team? Shouldn't he cut loose, geographically and metaphorically, and seek enrichment elsewhere and by other means?

I visited a friend in Stratford-upon-Avon. I remember every detail; I would, this was my Lost Weekend. I read a biography of Albert Camus on the Friday night, proof indeed that my angst was ample. I spent the Saturday wandering around shops, ostensibly Christmas shopping, but really drifting listlessly through a chilly, dark day. I had never been so lonely. There came a point, probably half-time-ish, where it also started to feel rather indulgent. This forlorn version of myself was worse than the one I was trying to escape from.

Back at my friend's (timed, inevitably, to coincide with the results), the block of scores for the third division flashed up. I scanned down, excited, nervous: Rochdale 5, Lincoln City 1. I rang my dad and he confirmed the worst. It had been absolutely totally bloody wonderful; Andy Flounders had lobbed the goalkeeper from just past the halfway line. In the darkness, I had seen a light: I'm Dale, therefore I am.

Saturday, 14 October 2000
Rochdale 2 Hartlepool United 1

Tony Ford scored an opening goal in the 15th minute but Tony Lormor equalised after a Mark Monington effort had been disallowed.

With 12 minutes to play, a Gary Jones penalty secured three points after Lee Todd had been fouled by his former Stockport County team-mate, Darren Knowles. Afterwards, Knowles said: "Don't get me wrong, I had hold of Toddy but he had hold of me as well and it was just a bit of harmless shoving. Rochdale were as shocked as we were when they got the penalty."

At half-time, 13-year-old Chris Harris of Castleton, Rochdale, became the first winner of the *Rochdale Observer's* Kick for Cash competition when he slotted the ball through a circle cut into a huge plastic sheet. "It felt great," said Chris, who had embarked on a memorable winning celebration.

Chris spent some of his prize money on a replica shirt with 'Platt' and '21' on the back.

Tuesday, 17 October 2000
Rochdale 2 Chesterfield 2

Spotland's highest attendance of the season saw Rochdale draw with a late equaliser against the league leaders.

A penalty from Gary Jones gave Rochdale the lead. Mark Monington headed into his own goal and David Reeves, twin brother of former Rochdale favourite, Alan Reeves, gave Chesterfield the lead in a pulsating game.

Shortly before the end, Monington scored again, this time for Rochdale, and the 5,008 left the ground thoroughly entertained.

Chesterfield were cheered on by more than 1,000 supporters, which meant the Willbutts Lane stand was reasonably full on its opening night.

Wednesday, 18 October 2000

Gillingham's 25-year-old striker Christian Lee joined Rochdale on a month's loan. He had been out of the game for almost a year with an injury.

Thursday, 19 October 2000

Information on the Planet Football website surprised Rochdale fans. It listed the Spotland capacity as 'nil' and Clive Platt appeared to have undergone a body transplant – the photograph accompanying his details was someone else. Meanwhile; on the Carling Opta site, Keith Hill was listed as being 41-years-old.

SHABBY PAST GIVES WAY TO GROUNDS
OF OPTIMISM AT SPOTLAND

(*The Times*, Saturday, 21 October 2000)

Sentimentality and elaboration are not part of my dad's make-up. He tells it like it is, keeps his feet on the ground. So, please, no side-salad with his dinner (never 'lunch') or those fancy sauces in little packets (never 'sachets').

On Tuesday evening he twice tugged at my arm and said: "It looks great doesn't it?" We were playing Chesterfield and he was commenting on our new stand; nay, our new stadium. Now this, coming from him, is akin to speaking in tongues, a man barely in control. He wasn't on his own, it was that kind of night.

The stand, which holds 3,650 supporters, is the final phase in the redevelopment of Spotland that has seen three new stands built in the past 10 years and the other, the Sandy Lane End, refurbished. Words like 'redevelopment' and 'refurnish' are rather dry for what has gone on here, 'miraculous' is more apt.

Not so long ago Rochdale FC was in a parlous state. The place was falling down around us. The emphasis during most of the club's history has been on survival, so the peripherals, of which the ground was one, were left to the ravages of time. Spotland looked old; not the pleasant 'old' of syrup-brown photographic nostalgia, but a dank, murky, god-forsaken old.

The stands and huts, dugouts and out-houses, were like broken teeth, left to decay, barely upright. White paint had turned grey and flaked away like old skin. Damp had turned wood to the colour of cinder toffee, crumbling in your hands. At your feet, pressed up to the fences and retaining walls, were plastic cups, buckled and sharp, jammed in among crisp packets and chip trays.

The concrete flags on the terracing were uneven and cracked. The furnishings were like the final items at a remnant sale - £1,000 for the lot, make of them what you will. Rain seeped through the roofs. The old chap standing near you might suddenly shudder and brush water away from his shoulder, looking upwards.

In the far corner of the ground, between the Pearl Street End and the Main Stand, crash barriers had been forced down into soil and tufts of rough grass. Fans could watch from 'the hill' where it was sometimes dry enough to sit on the grass early in the season. More often, it was out of bounds, windswept and muddy, so we huddled in the stands and side-stepped puddles on the terraces.

Spotland was a seaside town out of season, but without the balm of a glorious past to bolster it to a kind of conciliatory glamour. There had been stabs of grandeur (a solitary promotion and an appearance in the League Cup final of 1962), but principally it had been a dogged pursuit of survival, a day-to-day, match-to-match drizzle of an existence. Meanwhile, the players out there on the pitch had little to offer beyond endeavour and fleeting glimpses of skill. The regulars whined that they could see better football on any of the local council-owned pitches.

The transformation has been profound and the 'before and after' shots on the website are remarkable, almost magical. Zing: colour where there was once monochrome. Zing: newness where there was decay. A board of directors of modest wealth - by today's standards – has achieved this quietly and efficiently, without recourse to egotism or self-aggrandisement.

The attendance on Tuesday was 5,008, by far the highest of the 11 matches played in our division on the night, and in excess of eight played in the division above. Chesterfield brought with them a fair number, but there had been no ticket scam or disingenuous enticement to bring out the fans on a cold, wet night. They came because the team is playing well and Spotland feels a good place to be.

The club appears to have been reclaimed by a town that had long disowned it. For years, they were not seen as a body of young men representing the town, but as outsiders, vainly clinging to a life that was made sordid by their courtship with defeat and failure. They were ridiculed, their imminent demise anticipated with a vengeful glee: they had dragged down the town for years, done nothing much apart from lose and whinge about a shortage of money.

All those years of hardship and misery add up to a fair slab of cynicism, so we view our new status with appropriate prudence. All the same, on Tuesday, for the first time ever, I thought it would be quite good (note the hereditary downbeat use of language here) to one day take my two sons with me to Spotland: decent team, not-bad ground.

Saturday, 21 October 2000
Cheltenham Town 0 Rochdale 2

A goal in each half by Mark Monington, celebrating his 30th birthday, gave Rochdale a deserved victory over a Cheltenham team that had won four of their past five games.

Despite a late rally by Cheltenham, Neil Edwards was rarely troubled. "The ref helped them win," complained Steve Cotterill, the Cheltenham manager. Rochdale's second consecutive 2-0 win at Cheltenham took them back into second place, two points above Brighton.

During the game, stones rained down on the Rochdale contingent and this led to Cheltenham's safety officer, Nick Ames, writing a letter of apology: 'There appears to be a gang of local youths, who do not attend the football, who revel in their anti-social behaviour and enjoy causing trouble.'

Tuesday, 24 October 2000
Rochdale 2 Macclesfield Town 2

Rochdale trailed at half-time after a poor performance at rain-soaked Spotland. Lee Glover and Ritchie Barker scored for the visitors.

Christian Lee and former Macclesfield midfielder Paul Ware scored to salvage a point.

Macclesfield were cheered on by a group of Luton Town fans who had travelled to Spotland after their team's match at Oldham Athletic was postponed because of a waterlogged pitch.

Thursday, 26 October 2000

Dave Flitcroft underwent a hernia operation that would keep him out of the team for a month.

OLD-TIMERS SHOULD BE CHAMPIONED
AS MUCH AS NEWCOMERS

(The Times, Saturday, 28 October 2000)

The chants were primed and, boy, were we going to blast them out loud and proud. After the first goal, we'd hit them with '1-0 to the Football League' followed by the obvious numerical change every time we stung them with another. We might also spice it with a few taunts of 'amateurs' or 'part-timers' if we were in the mood.

Rochdale, in recent weeks, have played the three nouveaux of the Nationwide Football League - Kidderminster Harriers, Cheltenham Town and Macclesfield Town. I am inordinately pleased to report that we avoided defeat in each game and represented the Football League - and, in our case, 93 years of professionalism - with aplomb.

As much as winning quickens the pulse and raises the spirit, there is a further pleasure particular to fans of lower division teams when we give these young pups a clout on the nose. It galls us that these upstarts are universally championed by football's chattering classes and are viewed as bastions of vitality and sassiness. Have they ever been to the Moss Rose, the home of Macclesfield? Imagine portside Gdansk. In the rain. In winter.

Wimbledon are to blame. They joined the League in 1977 and have performed exceedingly well. Unfortunately, their success has perpetrated the myth that former non-league clubs are 'good' for the Football League. Maidstone United - three seasons and a disreputable wind-up - weren't all that 'good' and Scarborough were mediocrity-by-the-sea until they returned from whence they came. Fellow new-boys Barnet and Macclesfield currently have the lowest average attendances in the League.

The lobby to make the Football League more fluid had its way in 1986-87 when automatic relegation was introduced for the bottom team. Before this, clubs finishing in the bottom four of the old fourth division applied for re-election. This was usually a formality. Your club chairman sent every other chairman a bottle of whisky at

Christmas, or a hamper if you were near the bottom for a second consecutive season, and, hey presto, you were reinstated.

Rochdale were the re-election kings, escapologists of distinction. In seven seasons, from 1977 to 1984, we finished in the re-election zone four times, twice at rock bottom. Luckily, our chairman, Freddie Ratcliffe, had a silver tongue. He also had a Rolls-Royce Silver Shadow and probably loaned it out to other chairman. Freddie couldn't reach the pedals anyway – he was just over five feet small.

Workington and Southport were not as fortunate and departed in 1977 and 1978 respectively. When I think of them, and also Newport County (1988) and Aldershot (1991), it is with great sadness and empathy. These towns will have had eager kids new to football support that had fallen in love with their club. Like me, they will have been enthralled by the players, the ground, the other supporters, the habit, the history. There will also have been old-boys who stood in the same place as their dads and grandads had done, season after season. We all knew our clubs had a legacy of struggle, but still felt a subliminal assurance of permanence.

We do not need to ask how it feels when your club leaves the League. We have seen the pictures. Fans climb over the fences and grab patches of turf to replant in their gardens; something has to live on, this mortality is unacceptable. They slump to the pitch, crying, and wrap their arms around one another. Kids sob into their dad's coat. If it feels like death, this isn't a coincidence. What do these people do for the rest of their lives? All those Saturdays stretch out before them, empty and hopeless.

Admittedly, the impact is not quite so dramatic these days and League clubs have tended to regain their status quickly. The swift return of Colchester United, Darlington, Lincoln City and Halifax Town has illustrated the marked difference between League clubs and the semi-professional game.

In such circumstance then, why not close the trap-door again? It is open primarily to placate the wishes of those that covet anything new and (allegedly) fresh. They know nothing of the weight of tradition that clubs such as Rochdale epitomise. We have survived on passion, commitment and sheer bloody-mindedness. There lies the cause for celebration, not newness for its own sake.

Obviously, I have had to ponder the possibility of a life outside the League, or even the club's extinction. This would not be a petty, inconsequential matter because we are 'only Rochdale'. It would feel the same as if it had happened to your club, whether that be Manchester United or Arsenal. There is no hierarchy of support in the love we hold for our clubs.

* I enjoyed writing this piece, which is probably self-evident. It irritates me a great deal that this issue has been consistently misrepresented. I obviously have a vested interest because I want Rochdale to maintain their professional status, but this does not alter the fact that the non-League case has been massively overstated.

We are almost at the point where it is now taken as a fact that the third division and the Nationwide Conference are interchangeable. The myth has been engineered by ambitious directors in the Conference and football reporters who fail to appreciate the heartfelt passion that lower division clubs engender among supporters.

I have read numerous pieces expounding the virtues of Football League interlopers – Macclesfield Town, Wycombe Wanderers, Barnet et al – but none that truthfully assess their effect and standing in the Football League. I was happy to oblige, and hoped to stir emotions.

On the same theme, more than a year earlier, I had been commissioned by *The Times* to cover Cheltenham Town's first game in the Football League, when, by coincidence, Rochdale were their opponents. Fortunately, Rochdale's performance and the result provided fuel for my standpoint and, again, I think my joy was apparent...

LATE ARRIVALS GIVEN TASTE OF NORTHERN GRIT
(*The Times*, Monday, 9 August 1999)

Laurie Lee would have been rhapsodic. A dusty heat had fallen over Cleeve Hill, the magnificent Cotswold swath framing Whaddon

Road. The world was half-asleep in the heat haze, everything hushed, still, sumptuous. But, to hell with poetry, here come Rochdale, cut from granite and adversity. Check out the steely glint in their eyes as they disembark from the team coach. There is a job to be done. No messing. No mercy. Nothing personal, it just happens to be their line of work: playing, winning, surviving, year after year.

Cheltenham Town have finally reached football's professional caste after spending 107 years in various leagues where the game was a mere addendum to the lives of its players, if not the town itself, which is stranded in a football hinterland.

Apart from the horses galloping and jumping around its famous racecourse, Cheltenham is a place where no one seems in much of a hurry. Especially in this heat.

Only when Steve Cotterill returned to his hometown three years ago to manage them was the club properly heading towards the Football League. "He has made all the difference. A great deal of our success is down to him," said Tom McNeil, a supporter for almost 60 years who works at the ground. "I used to visit other clubs and there'd be dust on the seats. I used to think 'I hope people don't come to Cheltenham and think it's dirty', so I started to help out at the ground many years ago."

To many, a game against Rochdale is not something to linger over: thud, whack, pass, goal, hit the road. Rochdale, though, are of that magical place, the other world of which boys and men dream. They are members of the most exclusive gentlemen's club in England, the Football League, and have been for 78 consecutive years. "I think we paid them too much respect," said Cotterill, after his side's 2-0 defeat. The awe of the professional, whatever its particular club colours, endures.

Romantics will find much that is reassuringly anachronistic about Whaddon Road. Rooftops peer over the tiny stand running the length of the ground: 'Anything going on over there?' There is a sign pointing to the *canteen* and, as the supporters milled in, the match announcer declared: "Let's be fair to our young siblings, let the children get to the front of the perimeter fence, would you?" Just before half-time, he excelled himself: "Ladies and gentlemen, there will be no migration during the interval, except for emergency or medical reasons." Meanwhile, the fee to use the club's official car park is just £1.

Inside the ground, the chaos was vaguely under control, but the owner of a season ticket for seat number L24 was turning red in the shade. The row ended at 23, and there was clear evidence of a section of seats sawn off to accommodate the four-man press box. "I thought something like this might happen," he muttered. Good-hearted fellow supporters squashed together, they muddled through.

Chris Banks, the Cheltenham captain, led out the team but, ominously, they ran briefly to the wrong end of the ground. They had to double back and bumped into Rochdale, which they did for the remainder of the afternoon. The visiting team often looked a class apart and by half-time were 2-0 to the better, with goals from Graeme Atkinson and Tony Ford, the league's most experienced player on his 969th appearance. After the break, Rochdale came over all cynical - some call it professional - by pinning Cheltenham, and the game, to the floor.

The received wisdom is that the lower ranks of the professional game are interchangeable with the upper echelons of the non-professional. There is much talk of Wimbledon, but little mention of Maidstone United. Just a few years ago Cheltenham had barely 300 season ticket-holders and, despite their recent success, they had sold just 1,500 for their historic first season in the League. On Saturday, fans were able to pay at the door, yet the attendance fell more than a thousand short of reaching the 6,500 capacity. It is palpably not a 'football town', though this is no slur on the club itself or its Tom McNeil's, to whom passion is nothing transient or fey.

"People underestimate the third division, but there are some good sides in it," said Steve Parkin, the Rochdale manager, afterwards. 'Two-nil to the Football League,' their supporters chanted. Indeed, on a day set up as a paean for the new, Rochdale sang the song of the stalwart. Hardy and dependable, they are rightly proud of their many years at the game's top table. They, too, are a club framed by a range of hills. These are not lush, rolling, or majestic. The Pennines above Spotland are craggy, strewn with rock and peat, not the kind of place where the novice would be advised to wander.

* During the game, I sat next to Bryon Butler, the journalist and broadcaster, who was to die 20 months later. It was bizarre hearing a voice I was so familiar with from the radio, asking me the names of the Rochdale players and from where he could get a cup of tea.

The after-match press conference was held in the sunshine out on the pitch. Steve Cotterill, Cheltenham's manager, commented to Butler that Rochdale had impressed him, and added: "They could be one of the teams up there with a chance of promotion." Butler shook his head, knowingly. "They won't be," he said. "You never know," said Cotterill. "They're not good enough," averred Butler.

I recalled the nights as a child when I'd listened to Butler's assured, luscious tones. He'd taken me to football grounds across the country and into Europe where you could almost smell the night air and sense the snap of the tackle. Suddenly, his repute had plummeted. He was right, though; we weren't good enough. He didn't have to be so adamant about it.

Saturday, 28 October 2000
Exeter City 0 Rochdale 1

Rochdale recorded their first victory at St James' Park for 37 years and their sixth win in eight league matches away from Spotland meant they had the best away record in the League.

Christian Lee and Gary Jones hit the woodwork before Exeter defender Jamie Campbell deliberately impeded Phil Hadland and was sent off. Lee Todd's free kick was flicked into the net by Clive Platt to win the game.

Michael Oliver made his first full appearance after recovering from injury, but Tony Ellis missed the game after hurting his knee in training.

Saturday, 28 October 2000

Rochdale were drawn against Cambridge United of the second division in the first round of the FA Cup. Many supporters were looking forward to seeing Alex Russell in his new club colours.

Tuesday, 31 October 2000

Tony Cottee was announced as player-manager of Barnet, replacing John Still who had switched to an executive role at the club. Cottee's first game in charge was against Rochdale in four days time.

Also in Rochdale...

October 2000

* A councillor called for an investigation into the case of a 13-year-old 'one man crime wave' who had committed more than 60 offences in two years. Eight months earlier, another Rochdale youth had also made the national news for repeat offending. "This one has the potential to be an even bigger villain," said a police spokesman.

* Coroner Barrie Williams recorded a verdict of death by misadventure on eight-hours-old baby, Aaliyah Ahmed. During her delivery, Aaliyah's head had come into contact with a lamp and trolley but the coroner said this had not played any part in her death.

Four

May I Never Cease to Love

WHERE PROGRAMMES ARE BEST
VIEWED BY AUDIENCE OF ONE
(*The Times*, Saturday, 4 November 2000)

Outside, I can hear surges of sound as cars pass by with their stereos turned up full. It's Friday night. Everyone seems to be going somewhere and if you trace the dabs of orange streetlights, they will lead to pubs and people.

I'm in the out-house with a grubby piece of paper that smells of cigarette smoke. I'm putting ticks at the end of some lines and scrubbing through others. I know the code well, I've been studying it since I was 10-years-old: 's.o.f' is score on front; 'cr' is creased; 'f' is fold; 'sl tr' is slight tear; and 's.o.s' is save our souls, mine in particular.

Please adjust the angle-poise light and black out the background, because I am about to go public with my condition: I collect football programmes, specifically Rochdale home matches. I keep them in Bisley drawers and they are filed in order of season so that each has its own reference card: '1984-85', 1985-86 etc.

Last week, I had one of those moments when a metaphorical camera suddenly flashes and provides you with a snapshot of yourself you neither asked for nor wanted. I didn't like what I saw, and it left me trembling and uncomfortable in my skin. All that space out there, all those people to meet, books to read, films to see, and I'm in here - a cold, draughty out-house, meticulously applying a tick to 'v Rotherham 3/9/88, 4 pager, low print, rare'.

It should have been the apogee of my life as a 'pg ak' (programme anorak), for my habit from hell had just acquired a supplier from

74

heaven. Almost anyone can track down a Rochdale v Lincoln, April 1964, but few can offer Rochdale v Huddersfield 10/1/76 (postponed and very rare, glossy cream four-page insert). My chap can get programmes from games that didn't even take place, or one-page printed sheets from impromptu pre-season friendlies against Forfar Athletic reserves. If I hadn't already received a bundle – with each programme presented in a small sealed bag – I'd consider him an imaginary benefactor.

While I checked his list, I felt a stab of delight every time I ran a squiggly line through a programme I already owned. It was a small revenge, as if I was putting a limit on how much hurt he could cause. I was indignant that he charged £5 for team-sheets for rearranged games. Since these were printed on plain A5-size paper, they could easily be photocopied and look identical to the original. It must be the thickness of paper, or the ingrained aroma of coffee, pipe-smoke, damp and several meat and potato pies that justifies the price.

Sheds, out-houses, garages, huts, summerhouses, gazebos - call them what you will – have long been bolt-holes for men to revisit their childhood. Some make matchstick cathedrals, others collect screws of varying threads or build radios; George Bernard Shaw wrote plays in his. Normally, it is a joy to splash about in the history of my football club (and myself) as I leaf through my programmes. There is a divine pleasure in the solitude, the memories, the cataloguing, the feel and sound of pages being turned; if the phrasing here seems vaguely pornographic, it is probably not coincidental.

So why, the other night, did my heart feel so bad? The timing might have been to blame. It's probably more of a Sunday afternoon job or best saved for an off-work-with-a-cold Monday morning. The melancholy ran too deep, however, to attribute merely to the time and day.

I think my problem was that I had remembered to think. Collecting football programmes is like falling in love or riding a bike; it is best done naturally, without thought or contemplation. Once you stop to think, it can seem absurd and futile and you can fall off and break your arm, or your heart. The solitude turns to loneliness, the nostalgia to mawkishness. The cataloguing and storing makes you leaden and vain. You suddenly feel like you should be somewhere else, and someone else too.

Thankfully, the mood is transient and we soon get to like ourselves again. Most of us don't travel light. We're collectors and archivists and happy that way. We need to feel anchored and surround ourselves with our past. It is evidence of a passion, whether Rochdale programmes, or, for example, a mint collection of postcards of British warships (1850-1944). These will be lovingly stored in a binder with plastic compartments. Their proud owner – male, obviously - will take them out when his wife goes shopping or down to the bingo. We all have the right to define our own version of Friday night fever.

* I was informed several months after this article appeared that it had been reprinted in *Programme Monthly*, the programme collectors' magazine. I used to buy the magazine as a teenager and was pleased to learn it still existed and that I'd finally made its esteemed pages. I didn't chase them for a fee; the honour was enough. I suppose by virtue of the fact that I was oblivious to its current standing, I must have tempered my collecting habit over the years. This makes me both happy and sad.

Saturday, 4 November 2000
Rochdale 0 Barnet 0

The referee inspected the soaking pitch three times before allowing the game to go ahead. Afterwards, Steve Parkin questioned the decision: "The conditions were awful and playing the game has probably set back the improvements that we have made on the pitch a long, long way."

The press box was more full than usual, with reporters dispatched to cover Tony Cottee's entrée into the third division. *The Sun's* Mike Ellis gave the club a back-handed compliment: 'Take it from me – a trip to Rochdale is not the lowest of the low.'

Keith Hill replaced Dave Bayliss who served a one-match ban for collecting five bookings. The game was evenly fought, with neither team showing much enterprise. It was Rochdale's third home match without a win.

Many local schoolchildren attended in support of Multi-Cultural Day, sponsored by the Let's Kick Racism Out of Football campaign. A steel band, Pandemonium, played before kick-off and children had their faces painted. Rochdale assistant manager and player, Tony Ford, said: "To be honest I can't really say that I've suffered from racial abuse. Either I've been very thick-skinned, deaf or I've been fortunate."

Thursday, 9 November 2000

Sky TV confirmed it would make a second visit to Spotland, on the weekend of 27-28 January 2001, to cover the promotion tussle against Leyton Orient. The fees would be £30,000 to Rochdale and £10,000 to Orient. Sky had last visited in February 1999 when Rochdale beat Hull City 3-0.

SIZE MATTERS FOR THE LITTLE MEN WITH BIG AMBITION
(*The Times*, Saturday, 11 November 2000)

The ordeal over, Tony Cottee looked positively chipper as he conducted a procession of post-match interviews. Blood hadn't been spilled, no one was stoned, and the only dastardly deed was that someone called him a 'cockney dwarf'. As insults go, at least it was succinct.

Cottee - 283 league and cup goals and seven England caps - has taken over as player-manager of Barnet. No one dare say it, but the chuckle-chortle subtext has been that poor Tony has had one collision too many with the beef stock that passes itself off as defenders in the modern game. In short, he's arrived at Barnet via Barking (mad) and the journey into the third division has been portrayed as something akin to a slow drift through the fetid swamps of Haiti. There be heads on sticks, Mr Tony, and it ain't no place for a fine and decent boy like you.

Before the advent of the FA Premiership, the Football League was a sporting kingdom. The bigger clubs obviously held sovereignty, but the movement of players and managers up and down the leagues created a sense of fraternity. It was also the convention that famous players relearnt the virtues of humility and providence by managing a lower division team.

Brian Clough served a managerial apprenticeship at Hartlepool, while in the late 1970s George Graham, then finishing his playing career at Crystal Palace, was reportedly interviewed for the managerial vacancy at Rochdale. The hysterical reaction to Cottee's decision is further proof that the lower divisions are now viewed as townships where it is best not to stray.

The leading clubs have become municipalities. Their sheer size and wealth is such that hundreds of new jobs have been created. The staff at some clubs has quadrupled in the past decade. Ex-players who might otherwise have looked to the lower reaches to find employment fill many of these positions. They are opting for the relative security of coaching one of the multitudes of youth teams, or joining the burgeoning PR ranks, rather than speculate in management. It means their lustre remains intact and is not abraded by association with a Barnet or a Rochdale.

It was inevitable that Cottee's first match should bring him to Rochdale. Likewise, that it should rain, the pitch cut-up and neither team manage to score a goal. Spotland, which has been alive with vibrancy and colour of late, put on its grey overcoat and sulked. The ball was punted randomly from one end of the field to the other and there were more than enough dead minutes to ponder: so this is life on the other side of the tracks.

Wisely, Cottee chose not to play, for his debut would have coincided with the return to Rochdale's team of Keith Hill. An encounter with the much-loved Hill would have further compounded the stereotype. He is, as they say, *old school*. He puts his head in where it hurts. In his case, this could just as easily be against the goal-post or the floodlight pylon as among opponents' elbows and ankles, for he is without fear of pain. His only concession to anything as effete as skill is to vary his punts between Row X and Row Z of the Main Stand. He would have rattled Cottee with his first tackle, 'to let him know he was there' and rattled him with the second, 'to let him know he was *still* there.'

On another day, the sun may have shone, the players might have trusted the pitch enough to pass the ball, and Cottee might have faced Dave Bayliss, another rugged defender, but with a touch more finesse than the man whose name appears to be an anagram of 'Kill Him'. Quite possibly, to further improve Cottee's day, the chap who thought it exorbitantly funny to yell 'cockney dwarf' might also have stayed at home and wallpapered the spare bedroom.

Rochdale have themselves tried 'celebrity' managers. The policy was a disaster. The Greenhoff brothers, Jimmy and Brian, arrived in March 1983 as manager and assistant manager respectively. Between them, they boasted almost 400 appearances for Manchester United and, in Brian's case, 18 England caps. Clearly, such glamour meant nought in Rochdale. We won just twice in 13 matches as the season closed, had to apply for re-election to the Football League and attendances fell below 1,000 on four occasions.

Nearly three years later, the club tried again, installing the former Leeds winger (and now assistant to David O'Leary), Eddie Gray. We stayed rooted at the bottom, but at least he brought in a few of his famous pals from Leeds, like Lyndon Simmonds, Dean Walling, Carl Harris and Brian Stanton. Surely you've heard of them.

* A few weeks later, I received a letter from Martin Dugdill of Lancaster. He was uncommonly robust in his appreciation of Rochdale's groundsman, Craig Wooding: '

Dear Mr Hodkinson,

I write with reference to your article in The Times. I think your opinion, that the ball was punted from one end of the pitch to the other, is a load of bollocks.

The Barnet match is one of the best 0-0 draws I have ever seen, with both teams, especially in the second half, trying to play football.

The last thing Rochdale's excellent groundsman needs is a so-called fan (do you think you are the only one?) slagging off his pitch in a national newspaper.

Of course it cut up, it had been pissing down all week. It was a bloody miracle the match was on at all, and the playing surface was a credit to the groundstaff.

In my opinion the players trusted the pitch to play a passing game. And just in case it passed you by, it was raining everywhere else as well last Saturday, not just in Rochdale. Stop wallowing.

Martin Dugdill

Saturday, 11 November 2000
Mansfield Town 1 Rochdale 0

A last-minute goal from Mansfield striker Chris Greenacre meant a disappointing return to Field Mill for Steve Parkin, their former manager. It was the first goal Rochdale had conceded away from home in 504 minutes of football, embracing six matches and two months.

Rochdale had numerous chances, including a penalty miss by Gary Jones, but slumped to only their third defeat of the season.

Monday, 13 November 2000

Jamie Hoyland, formerly a player with Manchester City, Bury, Sheffield United and Burnley, joined Rochdale's coaching staff. The 35-year-old revealed a pragmatic approach: "You have to pass the ball, get it into the net, and then stop the opposition doing it to you. It's not rocket science."

Wednesday, 15 November 2000

Christian Lee returned to Gillingham after a month's loan. He had made two full appearances for Rochdale, three as a substitute, and scored one goal.

THE SEARCH FOR REASON WHEN
ONE FAN'S FLAME BURNS OUT
(*The Times*, Saturday, 18 November 2000)

Bertrand Russell was cycling down a country lane one afternoon when, as if struck by a thunderbolt, he realised he no longer loved his wife. Until this point, he claimed to have had no inkling that love's rampant flame had dwindled to a softly glowing ember. He did the decent thing: took off his bicycle clips and announced his departure. He was to do this several times in his life, with several wives, but that's a different story.

My acquaintance, Andrew, has recently had a bit of a Bertrand-Russell-on-a-bike trauma. Andrew isn't his real name, but I don't want to cause him embarrassment, for this is a matter of the heart. He has a life to live, an appearance to maintain.

I last spoke to Andrew about two years ago. All was well. All was as it had been for about 25 years. He grumbled a little bit, but we all do; this is an inversion of love anyway, that we are so smitten we find enough space and have enough confidence to push at the boundaries and throw a glimmer of light between ourselves and our partners.

Andrew's love of Rochdale FC was more ardent than my own. I drew a circle 50 miles around Rochdale on the map and vowed I would only traverse it to attend an away match if we had won the previous two matches. Andrew doesn't drive, so was up and out while it was still dark, coughing in the cold, tramping through the streets to board a coach under the Town Hall clock at 7am. He travelled to Exeter, Plymouth, Colchester, Carlisle – distance couldn't stymie his ardour.

The sun never really came up on Rochdale for many years. In two seasons (1977-78 and 1982-83) we didn't win a single away match in the League and cup. There were many black days and black nights: Tuesday 6 March 1978, for example - a 4-0 defeat at Brentford, a 500-mile round trip and back home at 2am, the dog howling at the back door thinking you're a burglar.

Andrew didn't volunteer the shocking information. I stumbled on it by chance. I was enthusing about the current Rochdale team – third in the league and our longest spell in a top three position in any division for more than 70 years. He must be delighted. He went quiet, then announced: "I don't really bother any more." I didn't understand. I had to hear it spoken again. He obliged: "I've not been up there for more than a year now."

I was desperate for detail, but he was infuriatingly vague. He spoke in platitudes – 'It just happened'; 'I can do other things now'; 'I went up there for a long time, you know'. I kept pushing him, but it was as if I was asking for details about an ex-wife. It was personal, none of my business.

During my 26 years as a Rochdale supporter, I have often pondered on what it would be like to fall out of love. Was it a sudden realisation, a freeing of the soul from Saturday bondage, or was it a gradual realisation that it had slipped away, that two parallel themes (disappointment and loss of hope) had drifted together and pointed away from Spotland?

In truth, I have never come close to ambiguity about my feelings, but this has not purged the sense of being stalked by a fear that I might one day lose interest. Several times over the course of a season - and it need not be an instinctive reaction to a bad result - I imagine a life without Rochdale FC. I shudder; it feels like the axis of my inner world has shifted. My football club and my parents and sister have been my longest companions. The rest – grandparents, friends, places – have died, moved on, or been demolished.

Maybe I'm the type that doesn't fall out of love. In the real world, that frivolous concern the other side of football, I've never walked out on anybody; girlfriends have always left me. I'm not sure whether this makes me a paragon of loyalty and commitment or stubborn and witless. I'm probably not ideally placed to judge.

Anyway, back to Andrew. He talks of his new life in the same terms as a recovering addict. He likes the 'new sense of freedom' and of 'being able to do what he wants at the weekend'. This suggests that he jets off regularly to Paris or Rome, but I suspect he takes his wife and kids to Aldi, or, as a special treat, to the All-In-One Garden Centre in Slattocks, where they do a lovely pot of tea for £1.50. May I never cease to love.

Saturday, 18 November 2000

I received a cheery e-mail from a Burnley supporter who had probably missed the Life Sentence of 18 September.

Dear Mark,

As a Clarets fan I must say it is most refreshing to read a weekly column based on club I have visited many times supporting Burnley.
I was also lucky enough to come and watch the Dale on several occasions when my friend John Dawson was the physio - those were slightly darker days than now.

I came past Spotland the other day and the old ground is certainly looking good. Lancashire football is certainly looking up at the moment.

I hope you gain promotion with the common sense of your Board and committed playing and management staff. You certainly deserve to!

Steven Arnold.

* Proof indeed that Burnley have some fine, warm-hearted supporters. Many of them are actually unaware of the disdain felt by Rochdale fans for their club.

One evening I was given a lift by a Burnley-supporting taxi-driver. He spent the journey expounding on how pleased he was that Lancashire clubs were doing well, and how he had a 'soft spot' for Rochdale. He was pleasant, engaging company, but – being the partisan I am – his benign cheeriness soon began to grate.

I prefer to be among football supporters who are so passionate about their team that it pains them to proffer such a conciliatory tone. This is not to sanction downright hostility, which is never justified, but to celebrate the irrational, unabridged single-mindedness that football should excite.

Obviously, my neurosis of all things Burnley made me sceptical about the garrulous taxi-driver. How could anyone, even this kindly middle-aged chap, really want 'all the local teams to do well', when the league, in fact the whole structure of the sport, was based on the brutal premise that victory or defeat for one team meant success or failure for the other. If he didn't appreciate and embrace this, how could he purport to be a football fan? It didn't come any more basic.

I didn't want him to have a 'soft spot' for Rochdale. I wanted him to have a cruel ache of dislike and fear, seasoned with respect and reverence – much like I had for his club. Football supporters owed this to one another. It divided us and made us the same: we all burned in the same fire.

Saturday, 18 November 2000
Cambridge United 2 Rochdale 1
(FA Cup, first round)

Cambridge took the lead with an early goal from Jonas Axeldal but Rochdale equalised when Clive Platt scored his eighth goal of the season.

The winning goal came when an attempted clearance by Wayne Evans struck Cambridge's John Hansen on the backside and looped over Neil Edwards. Seconds before, a Platt effort was disallowed when Paul Ware was judged to have strayed offside, despite being uninvolved in the move that led to the 'goal'.

After the match, Roy McFarland, the Cambridge manager, visited the visitors' dressing-room to congratulate Rochdale on a battling performance and acknowledge that his side barely deserved the win.

Graham Lancashire returned after three months out through injury, replacing Tony Ford as substitute. The striker denied rumours that the club's treatment room was to be renamed *The Lancashire Suite* in his honour.

Saturday, 18 November 2000

Rochdale were drawn away at Doncaster Rovers of the Conference in the first round of the LDV Vans Trophy.

Monday, 20 November 2000

Brentford supporter, Ian Oxley of Hounslow, Midddlesex, wrote and confided that he had fallen out of love with his team after a 47-year affair, and also recalled a visit to Spotland:

Dear Mark,

Your column of 18 November really struck a chord. I began supporting Brentford in 1951 (at the age of 10) and was a season ticket holder as recently as 1998. However, I began to realise that I felt a vague sense of relief when they were away (and I didn't have to go) and that I was actually looking at my watch during the home matches and wishing they were over. It was obviously time to 'retire' and I haven't watched them for two years – and don't miss it.

Brentford have been marginally more successful than Rochdale over the past 50 years but we have had to watch 'inferior' clubs such as Millwall, Crystal Palace, Leyton Orient and even a 'non-league' club (Wimbledon) achieve top division status, even if only briefly. The height of our club's ambition seems to be a respectable place in the lower leagues.

I haven't developed 'other interests' – in fact I still attend non-league matches in the London area – but loyalty should be a two-way thing. If they take our money year after year they should at least try to fulfil their potential.

I end by wishing Rochdale every success in their bid for promotion. I remember spending a rain-soaked Monday evening there in 1974 when Brentford forced a goalless draw. That was a halfway stop from the Scottish Highlands back home to London. I got home at

2am, but at least we got a draw!

Best Wishes,
Ian Oxley.

Wednesday, 21 November 2000

A posting on the official website of Rochdale Hornets rugby league club opened the dialogue on an issue that was to cause a great deal of animosity and concern for the rest of the season – the state of the Spotland pitch. Rochdale FC shared Spotland with Rochdale Hornets under the guise of a 'stadium company' that also included representatives of Rochdale Council. Website contributor, Crede Signo [Rochdale's motto – 'Believe in the sign'] wrote:

'Last night I drove to Dewsbury to watch the Rugby League Emerging Nations final - a game that should have been played at Spotland. It was moved because last week the playing surface was deemed unsuitable due to waterlogging. Now, if the game had been called off on the day with the heavens open, then I might have understood, but to call it off four days before is patently ludicrous. I've seen half a dozen games between Thursday and yesterday and all of the playing surfaces were fine - wet, but perfectly playable. Oldham played in a downpour on Sunday and Boundary Park didn't cut up.

Rumour has it that those self-important idiots at Rochdale AFC deemed the pitch unsuitable, Hornets disagreed, and Rochdale Council had the casting vote.

If that's the case, then they have deprived Rochdale - the town, not the Rugby League club - of the chance to host a prestigious international sporting event.

Waterlogged pitches are salvageable, especially over four days. The job done on Murrayfield for the Challenge Cup Final makes the Stadium company's decision look even more pathetic.

Chances like this fall to the town of Rochdale very rarely and, despite the fact that Spotland is a stadium fitting of such an event, organisers will think twice next time.

As it was, the eyes of the world's Rugby League media were focused on Dewsbury last night, leaving Rochdale looking every inch the two-bit hick town that's on its sporting, cultural and economic arse. Dewsbury did a great job – I'd be proud to live there.'

* The message provoked the following response from Conspiracy Theory:

'You are right on every point, Rochdale in general needs a shot in the arm.'

* To which, Crede Signo retorted:

'Rochdale needs a shot in the head. It's a dying town that should be put out of its misery. It has more dickheads per capita than any other town I know.

Its populace shows less civic pride than any other town I know. It's parochial, inward-looking and deserves what it gets. It has only acquired a cinema in the last two years. It has no theatre - it doesn't even have a bookshop! Both the Dale and Hornets suffer at the hands of a fickle audience that would rather piss money up the wall watching Premier League and Super League teams. The town has a wonderful history, it's geographically very well positioned - and still it doesn't know what to do with itself. It's a crying shame.'

* I pilfered Crede Signo's theme for a Life Sentence column published a few weeks later.

FANS' LOVE AFFAIR ENDS
IN EPISODE OF PEAKE PRACTICE
(*The Times*, Saturday, 25 November 2000)

Friends and family of Jason Peake will have done well to avoid the postings on Rochdale's various websites this week, for he is not a popular man.

Peake has blond hair and is not particularly thin, so, inevitably, a theme has developed around which most of the derision is based. The rants are crabby and embittered – something akin to Jim Royle's [from the television programme, *The Royle Family*] response to his television being repossessed in the same week the chippy shuts down for a refit.

As few of you will know, Peake left Rochdale in the summer for another club in our division, Plymouth Argyle, who we play today. He has done this before. In 1996 he unexpectedly moved to Brighton and Hove Albion when they were in the middle of their infamous financial crisis. We did wonder about his judgement.

Two years later, he was back at Rochdale – via Bury – and great play was made of his homecoming. He was greeted warmly and his misdemeanour forgiven. It had been an aberration, a momentary lapse of reason. Rochdale was where he truly, madly, deeply belonged. He'd missed the pies and that look in our eyes. He scored our best goal of the season, at Halifax Town, and ran immediately towards the fans behind the goal: welcome home, son.

In the summer, by all accounts, the club was unaware of his whereabouts until he registered as a Plymouth Argyle player. According to Carling Opta statistics, Peake was the best passer in our division last season, so it wasn't like we'd lost someone who had been on trial from The Red Lion. He was, and still is, a very good player. He was also, more to the point, our prodigal son, and he wasn't supposed to go all prodigal on us again.

If Rochdale had not renewed Peake's contract and he had found himself another club, there would be no animosity. He would then be merely pursuing his vocation, but to choose to leave is – from a supporter's perspective – an act of treachery. Supporters instinctively wish upon these deserters the very worst. Well, not the *very* worst, but something close: loss of form, spells in the reserves, open goals missed, penalties given away, spectacular own goals – anything that makes them pine for the blue shirt they have forsaken.

The only pro-Peake homage on the websites has come from a

Plymouth fan making a plea for leniency, stating that Peake 'had served you well on two occasions'. Indeed he has, but it was a fundamental demand of all players that they should try their best in every game; maybe we should have left it there, and discarded notions of loyalty and commitment. If Peake moves on again, to Torquay United or Exeter City for example, our friend from Plymouth may not be quite so complaisant.

Obviously, departing players seek to validate their decision. Jason Peake might have thought he was played out of position at Rochdale; bullied by the manager; short-changed by the board; undervalued by his team-mates; or, quite simply, he may have been offered a huge signing-on fee by his next club.

As a supporter, it is my prerogative to remain oblivious to these factors. I am allowed a heartfelt response, whether it appears superficial or not. There is no amnesty for their insult. They have discarded a shirt, a colour and a club, on which I place inordinate value. I am affronted that, this afternoon, he will do everything within his power to defeat us and record a victory for his new club. He will – as all team sportsmen do - class this as professionalism, but this isn't about cool-headed, rational thought and application. This is love.

Peake will be booed every time he touches the ball today. Fans will be at the fence, shouting abuse, mocking and gesturing. Afterwards, in the changing-room among his new team-mates – or when he has a post-match drink with our players – they will scoff, and criticise the small-mindedness and hypocrisy of the supporters that formerly idolised them.

We should expect as much, and not fret. They are just footballers, gifted with a ball at their feet, but unable to grasp the enigma of those that come to support them. They do not see that by switching sides they have turned love to hate, and that people can be so sensitive and vehement about something as intangible as a football club. Only for the duration of the match do footballers and supporters inhabit the same world.

* Despite my claim to the contrary, it isn't really possible to divorce

feelings for a player from a manifest off-field situation. Despite our fanaticism, we each of us recognise the essentials of life – security, the need for recognition and appreciation, financial obligations etc. I was, in hindsight, cruel on Jason Peake. He served as a contrivance for my pontificating on loyalty and the complexities of sporting iconography.

Back in the real world, I learnt that his move from Rochdale was motivated by factors that superseded his allegiance or otherwise to the club. A fan who had known him during his time at Rochdale revealed that the player, unlike most of his team-mates, had not been offered an annual wage rise and his contract was for just one more season, whereas Plymouth were willing to provide a two-year deal.

Apart from the effect this would have on his finances and long-term security, it showed to Peake that his value to the club was low. In the circumstances, he could argue that, after his largely exemplary service, Rochdale had been disloyal to *him*.

Supporters can remain idealistic, but our clubs do not run on sentiment. They release players who have picked up injuries fighting for the cause and habitually break the hearts of teenagers who they have spent time developing and nurturing as footballers-to-be. We expect loyalty from players, but the club cannot afford to be heedlessly loyal to them. If they were, they would soon be in a financial crisis.

Unfortunately, included among my ramblings about Peake was a prophecy. He *did* suffer a loss of form and a lengthy spell in the reserves. In fact, his period at Plymouth was a disaster. The manager that signed him was sacked soon afterwards and he was released before the end of the season, joining Nuneaton Borough of the Conference.

He did return to Spotland, but he didn't make it to the pitch. He was among the Plymouth squad that pulled up on the club car park just as the game was postponed. One vengeful supporter remarked that the disappointment of a postponed game was tempered by the joy of seeing a disconsolate Peake trouping back on to the team coach, knowing he had made a futile 12-hour round journey.

* At least Jason had support from PCR, a visitor to a Rochdale web-site:

'I've just read that whining nitwit in The Times who insists on bor-ing the nation every Saturday with his tedious accounts of life as a Rochdale supporter. Who cares? Why is he allowed to fill so much space up, when it could be devoted to a genuinely interesting club like Plymouth Argyle?

And no sooner have I put the paper down than I discover people on an Argyle website with names like Alkydale or some such bleat-ing on about how much contempt they have for the Argyle general-ly and the boy Peake in particular.

There was only one team last season for which I had outright con-tempt - Rochdale. Your performance at Home Park was, as you well know, a complete disgrace. You cheated your way to a point. You certainly didn't win it playing football.

If you lot had any sense, you'd shut up. You've got precious little to shout about.'

Saturday, 25 November 2000

Rochdale's match against Plymouth Argyle was postponed at 1.40pm after prolonged heavy rain left the Spotland pitch waterlogged. Just minutes after the referee's decision, the rain cleared and the rest of the afternoon was sunny.

Tuesday, 28 November 2000

Dave Flitcroft returned to training after his hernia operation. Meanwhile, reserve goalkeeper Phil Priestley joined Scarborough on a month's loan.

Also in Rochdale...

November 2000

* Soldier Christian Garvey was found in a pool of blood in the town centre after being attacked while on a night out. He suffered a frac-

tured skull but was later said to be 'stable'.

* An armed robber mounted a raid at Tesco, Sudden, where he threatened staff with a double-barrelled shotgun.

* Hilda Redfearn, at four ft six ins, was officially recognised as Britain's smallest barmaid. She was the landlady of the Commercial Inn, Castleton.

* Rochdale Council revealed that it paid a woman to sit in an empty office and tell visitors the office was closed. The woman's 'job' was to staff the closed Littleborough Information Centre during afternoons and inform the public that it would re-open the next morning.

Five

The Rain Still Comes Down

DRIVEN TO DISTRACTION BY THOSE
RAINY DOG DAYS IN ROCHDALE
(*The Times*, Saturday, 2 December 2000)

The neighbours weren't at home, so a thorough 'pitch' inspection could take place without their prying eyes. I jabbed my foot into the lawn – a bit squelchy, but you could propel a ball across it, if you kicked it hard enough. I looked up - raining, but at least it was blowing across, rather than down: match on.

I went back in the house, shaking my head, face like thunder: "Nah, they won't play today. Too wet." No one had even rallied a counter-argument, when I reinforced the point: "It's rained all week. The pitch must be soaked through."

This was not duplicity for its own sake, but my opening gambit in a duel with God. I believe He looks down on football supporters and meddles with our emotions. If enough of us, for example, aver that a game will be postponed, it will be played, and vice-versa. It is nothing to do with the weather; it is about the power of thought and outfoxing the omnipotent.

The heavy rain that has fallen relentlessly on Britain this autumn has made all supporters watchers of the sky and prodders of the turf. They are not difficult to spot. If the bloke walking his dog in front of you suddenly mounts the grass verge and begins a series of three-yard sprints, looking anxiously at the turf behind him, it is a symptom of pre-match, possible-postponement tension.

Last Saturday, I announced defiantly that Rochdale's home match against Plymouth Argyle would be postponed. "You always say that,

93

and they always play," was the response. Indeed. Even as I spoke, I was anticipating thunderous sliding tackles and mud-bound, goal-mouth scrambles.

On Saturday mornings, I am the best dad in the world. I play 'cars' with Alec (23 months) for hours, or help George (four years) cut out dinosaur shapes from cereal packets. Last week, such was the joy in my heart, I took them out for lunch. Hardly a major extravagance, but a reasonable challenge when Alec is too old for a high chair, too young to sit still, but precisely the right age to hurl banana cake at passers-by.

They get an all-singing, all-dancing version of their dad on Saturday morning because I regard it - as they say in parenting books - as 'quality time.' Now, shame on me, but the quality of this time is enhanced considerably by the knowledge that it has a definite cut-off point. At 2pm, the dinosaurs go to sleep, Alec's Motor Mart closes and I wend my merry way to Spotland.

At a distinct point in time, probably while we were disgorging cake from inside the spout of a teapot, I realised my bluff had been called and God was about to record an away win. The rain was driving against the café window. I left my seat to look out over the Rochdale Canal. Hailstone and rain was bouncing off the water and forming pools on the towpath. In the car, the radio announcer stated the obvious: Rochdale versus Plymouth, match postponed.

Over at the ground, many Plymouth supporters had already arrived. A group of them was pictured in the *Rochdale Observer*, look-ing pantomime-glum in the stands. They had obviously arrived before the stewards, because one had his foot resting on the seat in front of him. In the hierarchy of transgressions upheld by our friends in amber, this is by far the most heinous: "Sure, you can bring an Howitzer in here, as long as you don't put your feet on the seats when you load it!"

The postponement had, at a stroke, changed the face of my week-end. No longer was my quality time neatly-packaged; it was to last all day, a day that seemed to stretch forever now its parameters had been discarded. I did what all dads would do in that situation. I drove around aimlessly.

We ended up on a moorland road. So this is what non-football dads did with their Saturdays in winter. The rain had stopped, but the light was fading. Updates came through on the radio from matches all over the country. I felt excluded, and an eeriness that was about to be exacerbated. We parked and crossed a stile. On the other side of the wall was the corpse of a dog, caught and twisted in a length of wire. We hurried the kids past and they didn't see it. It felt as if all roads away from Spotland and routine led to desolation.

On another day, the sunset might have painted the rough country-side golden, and the dog may have been alive, skipping playfully around the kids, but not last Saturday.

Saturday, 2 December 2000
Rochdale 1 Blackpool 0

A late Gary Jones goal lifted Rochdale to third place in an even con-test with mid-table Blackpool who were left trailing Rochdale by 11 points.

Steve Parkin had berated Jones at half-time. "In the first half, for me, he spent too much time moaning at other people and not con-centrating on his own game. I told him to get his game in order first and I got exactly the reaction I was looking for," he said.

During the pre-match warm-up, Keith Hill became ill. "Keith was violently sick," explained Parkin. "Although he wanted to play he looked ghastly so we brought in Dave Bayliss." Hill had gastric 'flu and was ordered to stay away from Spotland until he had recovered.

Saturday, 2 December 2000

Meteorologists recorded a day without any rainfall in Rochdale. It was only the third dry day in the last 70 – making it the town's wettest autumn since records began in 1766.

Tuesday, 5 December 2000

Doncaster Rovers 3 Rochdale 2 (aet)
LDV Trophy first round

Gary Jones gave Rochdale an early lead when he scored from the penalty spot. Mike Turner headed an equaliser before Dave Penney put Doncaster ahead with a penalty after Mark Monington had fouled.

Substitute Neil Campbell scored an own goal in injury time that took the match into extra time. Campbell scored again, this time for Doncaster, two minutes into extra time and his 'golden goal' gave the home side victory and prompted a pitch invasion.

Steve Parkin rested several first-team regulars and the players did not appear overly concerned by their early exit from the competition.

Thursday, 7 December 2000

Tony Ellis and Michael Oliver helped Sir Cyril Smith switch on the Christmas lights at Sandbrook Park, Rochdale, the location of several fast-food outlets and a cinema complex.

BLACKPOOL'S BULLY BOYS STIR UP DARK MEMORIES OF 1984

(*The Times*, Saturday 9 December 2000)

Families crossed the road to avoid them. The kids were dawdling, staring back at the noise and agitation. Farther down, a police van was pressed tight to the back of the stand.

Blackpool supporters were on the pavement outside the Church Inn, just yards from Spotland. They were singing to the street how they hated Preston North End, how they were the Blackpool boys. Some were drunk, struggling to keep their pint pots upright.

Supporters of a certain age have an inherent sense of when passion will erupt into fury at a football match. It is an instinct that was honed in the 1970s and 1980s, when you watched your back, checked where the exits were, and ensured you were among enough of your own to deter an attack. Otherwise, the boot boys were coming, to kick you down concrete steps, or corner you at the back of the stand, or down a side street on your way home.

These dark days were recalled in an article in the match programme for last Saturday's game. In March 1984, a similar visit by Blackpool led to 21 arrests; 23 damaged cars (two overturned); a pitch invasion; smashed windows at two pubs; road signs uprooted; scores of coins thrown on to the pitch; one broken arm; and a policeman's helmet knocked off by a house brick.

Back then, the primary aim was not strictly to harm opposing fans, but to lay claim on territory. Visiting supporters wanted to stand where the home fans normally stood, dislodge them, then jeer and mock because they had been driven off home ground. Charges and counter-charges took place throughout the game. Much of it was shadow-play and bravado, but anyone cut off from their allies could face catastrophic consequences. They would be battered to the ground and kicked until their friends or police pulled them free. While some were hurt and led away unconscious or groggy, most sprang up again immediately, the adrenaline lifting them back to their feet.

There was often a sly and silent drift of away supporters into the Rochdale 'end'. They carried with them a look, of cunning and daring, the feigned sure-footedness of men on a mission. The air grew cold, you could hear the crisp, dry shuffle of your feet against the cinders below, hear your heart beating. The game itself was spirited away. The players still harried and chased but it now felt as if they were the other side of a piece of glass, out of touch, drifting away. The score didn't matter: 3-0 win, 3-0 defeat, you might not get out of here alive.

At some matches, once or twice a season, the choreography and etiquette of hooliganism broke down. The slapstick was replaced by the sinister. The silhouette of violence was tolerable, and possibly enhanced an atmosphere of which partisanship and passion was an essential constituent, but to bring it for real was to thwart this delicate brinkmanship.

The chanting and threats from the other side of the ground rang more authentic. There was an edge in their voices, resentment. Fans were at the fence, spilling on to the pitch. In skirmishes with the police, we could see that their movements were frantic. They hadn't come for the hollow artifice of running and chasing. These weren't the types to jab their instep into you half-heartedly when you fell to the ground. They would kick with all their might, stamp down upon you. So, you kept silent, or ran anywhere you could – on to the pitch if necessary. If someone tripped and was immediately set upon, you closed your eyes and dreamed yourself away.

In recent years, hooliganism has become virtually extinct at Spotland and I feel a surge of joy when I see young children making their way excitedly to the ground with their parents or grandparents. It is the perfect cameo of childhood – being in the open air, feeling safe with people that care about you and sharing a passion for your team. I reflect on my own childhood as a supporter. I grew up fast. I saw things kids shouldn't see. I saw adults at their worst – fighting, destroying, hating, and all over something as trivial and beautiful as a game of football.

There was some fighting after the match on Saturday, but nothing to compare with the tumult of March 1984. The Blackpool websites have contained messages this week condemning the behaviour of their own fans. It is essential we police our fellow supporters and in most cases this is nothing more demanding or dangerous than yelling, 'give over' or 'grow up' - hopefully.

Saturday, 9 December 2000

The match against Plymouth Argyle was postponed again, this time at 9am. "There was mud half way up the ref's wellies and more rain was forecast," said Paul Sturrock, the Plymouth manager.

Thursday, 14 December 2000

Rochdale's bid of £150,000 for Torquay United's Tony Bedeau was turned down. The 21-year-old striker had scored 17 goals in the 1999-2000 season and had spent a week on trial at Sunderland earlier in the season. Bids had also been received from Sheffield Wednesday and Oxford United.

WHY ALL FANS SHOULD WORSHIP THEIR CLUB HEROES FROM AFAR

(*The Times*, Saturday, 16 December 2000)

Shop assistants had tinsel in their hair and stared blankly into the middle-distance - an early sign of over-exposure to banal songs about reindeers and log fires. The bloke juggling rolled-up socks near the precinct was getting less abuse than usual. All this goodwill; it must be Christmas.

As I walked through Rochdale town centre this week, among the fairy lights and sprayed-on snow, I recalled the ghost of Christmas past, or to be more precise, a whole squad of ghosts.

I remember it well – cue the woozy music and the wobbly visuals: Christmas 1992, and I'm walking up Yorkshire Street on a misty, rainy early evening with two carrier bags full of shopping. I look up and see the usual straggle of Rochdale folk – young, old, shell-suits and overcoats. Suddenly, like in a made-for-TV movie, the scene changes. Whoosh, a whole line of young, fidgety men are walking towards me, laughing and joking and putting their arms around one another. I know these faces; I've seen them somewhere before.

It takes at least two seconds – one, two – before I realise. Bloody hell, it's, it's, it can't be: Alan Reeves, Stevie Whitehall, Jon Bowden, it's Rochdale's first-team squad, and they're wearing normal clothes, and they look so damn happy. Mark Payne, our diminutive midfield-er, is so happy he's attempting to jump on to the back of our centre half, Alex Jones.

I did what any football supporter who spends half his life think-ing about his beloved club would do in that situation: I ignored them. I marched straight through the middle, wilfully indifferent. For all the interest I showed, they might have been bench-hands from a local engineering firm on their Christmas 'do' or trainee managers from the Bradford and Bingley.

Obviously, as soon as they passed, I stopped, turned around, and had – as we say around here – 'a good gawp', which is, in strictly formal terms, a prolonged awe-struck and inquisitive stare. I wish I hadn't. Mark Payne, dear me, had his jumper tucked *inside* his trousers and Alan Reeves was wearing a collar-less shirt, not seen on the British mainland since 1981. Strange, I hadn't realised they wore anything other than football kits. They disappeared into Yates's Wine Lodge and I vowed to spy on them on my way back.

They were still there, a huddle sitting at tables, and one or two talking at the bar. They looked younger than on the pitch. I wanted to go in and share the joke, but what would I say? It seemed perfectly acceptable to have an intimate abstract relationship with them, but hugely inappropriate to make it actual. I mean, what was my opening line to be? "Hello, I think you're a really good player," or: "What do you reckon, Scunthorpe at home on Boxing Day. Difficult game, eh?" I was cringing already and I'd not even entered the room.

I began to feel uneasy staring at these young men through a portal I had rubbed in the pub window to displace the rain. It was a busy late-night shopping evening, with lots of policemen around. I'd best move on, I thought. As I tramped back to the car, I was frustrated with myself for not making myself known to my Saturday heroes.

Afterwards, back home with my shopping, I remembered the only other time I had spoken to Rochdale players. I was about 14-years-old and, keen to break into journalism, I offered to write a page in the club programme. It was to be one of those columns like in *Shoot!* – a list of the players' hobbies and favourite films, pop groups and television programmes. The lady in the office told me they had just finished training and I should knock on the changing-room door.

It was the most intimidating assignment of a journalistic career that would later see me covering riots, murders and the Middleton Chrysanthemum Society's annual show. Not a single player said hello, or even looked up when I entered in my zipped-up snorkel jacket, shaking with nerves. In my unbroken, high-pitched voice it took me about three minutes to explain who I was and what I wanted. "I'll tell you what we like best," roared one of our strikers, "We like shagging, don't we lads?" The room rocked with laughter; I sucked on the fake fur around my hood.

Eventually, after scores of in-jokes and innuendoes, I was led away by our kindly goalkeeper, Graeme Crawford, who went through the questions with me sitting in the stand. This one good man had made the save of his life and taught me a lesson that would last the rest of mine: watch them, idolise them - and leave it at that.

Saturday, 16 December 2000
Lincoln City 1 Rochdale 1

A run of three consecutive away defeats ended when Tony Ellis slotted a second half equaliser past goalkeeper Chris Day. It was his first goal in 10 matches.

Despite early pressure from Rochdale, Lincoln had taken the lead through James Dudgeon. Phil Stant, Lincoln's manager, complained afterwards: "My players have been robbed today. We should have had two penalties."

The draw saw Rochdale slip out of a top three position for the first time in two months – their longest spell in the top three of any division since the 1926/27 season.

Monday, 18 December 2000

Mike Bateson, owner of Torquay United, revealed that Tony Bedeau, would not be joining Rochdale. "Although Rochdale have talked to Tony and offered him a very good contract, he's not remotely interested. He's going up there anyway [Rochdale] with his girlfriend because I don't think it will do them any harm to get out of Torquay for a day or two into the wider world," he said.

Tuesday, 19 December 2000

Financial analysts Deloitte and Touche published its annual list of England's richest football clubs. Rochdale were 83rd with a reported annual turnover of £1,014,000. Manchester United topped the table with a turnover of £111 million.

Wednesday, 20 December 2000

Poor ticket sales prompted Rochdale Supporters' Club to cancel its Christmas party.

SHARING NEST WITH HORNETS
SHOULD BE SOURCE OF PRIDE

(*The Times*, Saturday, 23 December 2000)

Everyone called him Starkey. It was only ever 'Mr Starkey' if he was in earshot or you were in trouble: "Mr Starkey, I've forgotten me kit again." He'd shake his head, suck in his cheeks, and then dig out a pair of huge washed-out grey shorts last seen on Billy Casper. You'd remember next time.

Starkey was your stereotypical PE teacher: crew cut, lean, sharp of movement, and no-running-on-the-corridor, Kershaw. If you ducked a tackle on the pitch, he'd want a quiet, firm word afterwards, but if he heard your gran had died, he'd have a quiet, soft word, with an arm around your shoulder. When the class bully, stricken by gastro-enteritis, had a 'trouser accident' during one of his lessons, Starkey's apres mop-up speech was magnificent. "I'm asking you, man-to-man, not to say a word to anyone about this," he began. And we didn't.

He had two jobs. He was head of PE at Thornham Middle School and coach of Rochdale Hornets. He had a problem differentiating, when it should have been obvious. We were pale skinny things with shins that went up to our waists and they were great hulking blokes with legs like oil drums.

The force of Starkey's personality meant that everyone, even the girls, knew a play-the-ball from a scrum-down, and a knock-on from a grubber-kick. He even awarded us sew-on patches if we gave up our lunch hour to complete passing drills with him across frost-rutted pitches.

Understandably, free tickets to Hornets' Athletic Grounds were plentiful, and, for a while, I considered myself a supporter of both Rochdale FC and Hornets, although my passion for football was always the greater. In 1988, Hornets sold the land on which their pitch was based for £2.6 million to Morrisons supermarket and moved to Spotland. Overnight, we inherited 'egg-chasing lodgers' – one of the more gracious euphemisms for our sporting brethren.

Obviously, since Spotland has always been our home, we seldom consider Hornets, or notice them particularly. There is one tricky issue that has caused us to bump into one another these past few weeks – the pitch. We have had two postponements while they - in extra-long, mud-churning studs - have raked up and down our beloved turf in two league matches.

Last Sunday, for the first time since Hornets relocated, I became reacquainted with Rugby League. I was going to see for myself how they mistreated this hallowed piece of England. The streets around the ground were empty; I began to wonder if they too had suffered the heartbreak of a late postponement. At the turnstiles, stewards out-numbered spectators. Inside, only two stands were open, and the Sandy Lane End had the numerical presence of a bus stop queue.

It took me a few minutes to adapt, but I was soon reminded of the sheer heroic brutality of the game. They collided, they clashed heads, they wiped off the blood and got on with it. The ball was often hidden among bodies, but then it zipped across the line, players swerving past opponents, or concealing it skilfully with a shimmy and then a move the other way, beyond desperate, grasping arms. The pitch played well too. Apart from lunges to the try-line, it was treated no worse than during a game of football.

The match programme, costing just £1, had the look and content of its football equivalent from 1978. This isn't a coincidence because, on this evidence, the Northern Ford Premiership has the unmistakable aura of a past that football has long left behind. Only 745 saw Hornets defeat Chorley Lynx 52-12 (the football club's average home attendance is almost 3,500), and there were few children among them. You could hear the players shouting and grunting. The slick, full-blooded action out there on the pitch warranted so much more from the stands.

Rochdale, like much of Britain, is a town sustained by takeaway pizzas, multiplex cinemas, drive-through fast-food outlets, late-night video shops and round-the-clock television. It does not have an authentic town centre bookshop, or theatre, or a venue for bands. It closes historic cinemas and turns them into theme pubs or carpet warehouses. It moves its head Post Office from a wonderful Georgian building into Woolworth's.

Paradoxically, it has two long-standing professional sporting clubs. These have survived through craggy determination and the commitment of the few. It is a shame that they should snipe at one another and bicker over blades of grass. Their real enemy is a populace that ignores them when it should, at the very least, see for itself. Civic pride, personal pride and pride in your hometown club are, after all, intertwined.

* The piece stirred memories for Mike Speak of Silverdale, Cumbria, a former colleague of Graham Starkey. He wrote:

Dear Mark,

I worked for a short time with Graham Starkey at Kirkholt before doing a PGCE at Loughborough and going into PE myself. I finished my working life in 1997 as Director of PE and Sports Science at the University of Hong Kong.

Your articles bring back many memories. Starkey was once asked the difference between Union and League (he had gone from Rochdale RUFC to Hornets). He said that if you were tackled in Union you could be back on your feet and rejoin the move, but in League you stayed down an awful long time.

I played for Spotland Methodists on Ings Lane in the Sixties and on match days the cheers or groans of the spectators at nearby Spotland told their own story. Very occasionally a goal at Spotland coincided with one of our own and the cheers of 2,000-plus made us smile.

Stan Milburn played for the Dale in those days. He was one of the Milburn legends and played in almost every position at an advanced age. His nephew was, of course, Bobby Charlton, and if we played an evening match towards the end of a season, Bobby and Stan, whose house overlooked our ground, would pop over the wall to watch for 20 minutes or so. It didn't half motivate the players!

Dale once had an inside-left called Eddie Wainwright, a former Everton player. As the teams ran out he was still smoking and the signal for the ref to start the game was when Eddie stubbed his fag out in the centre circle.

In FA Cup ties we saw Sam Bartram dribble to the half-way line, fifteen years before South American keepers began to leave their goal area, or Schmeichel and Barthez were born. There was no violence off the field, the FA Cup final was the only match on telly, and it was the done thing to support your local team. Adam wouldn't have dreamt of not going to watch Wetherfield with Ken! The pies were filled with meat and the Bovril warmed the cockles.

Until your articles appeared I thought those days had gone but thankfully for local communities they remain.

Best wishes, Mike Speak.

Saturday, 23 December 2000
Leyton Orient 1 Rochdale 1

Rochdale played with a five-man midfield, opting to use Clive Platt as a lone striker against a team with the best home record in the division.

Gary Jones gave Rochdale the lead through a first half penalty conceded by Orient defender Dean Smith for handball. Orient equalised when Wim Walschaerts scored after his side had dominated the second half.

Tuesday, 26 December 2000
Rochdale 1 Hull City 0

Gary Jones scored the only goal of the game with a shot that deflected off a Hull defender. Rochdale remained in fifth place.

Before the kick-off, fans witnessed a bizarre ceremony when

Desmond the Dragon unveiled his 'son', Diddy Desmond. The pint-sized dragon, wearing a baggy nappy, was produced from a box that Desmond had carried on to the pitch. Diddy Desmond cavorted energetically for a few minutes but, peculiarly, was not seen again at Spotland for the rest of the season.

Thursday, 28 December 2000
The Rochdale AFC Supporters' Band issued an appeal for a trumpet player. Potential applicants were informed the band was an equal opportunities employer and, 'welcomed applications from all ethnic minorities, except Yorkshiremen and Burnley-ites!'

Friday, 29 December 2000
Cardiff City were rumoured to have bid £650,000 for Clive Platt. They were simultaneously linked with several other players.

WHY ROCHDALE FANS ARE LEFT UNFULFILLED BY SUCCESS
(*The Times*, Saturday, 30 December 2000)

Every week, at the same time, she walks to the end of her drive, leans on the gate, and - in a dry, frail voice - asks the first person passing: "What score was it?" The old lady's house borders Spotland, so presumably she will hear the cheers and groans, but is left guessing on the actual score.

On Boxing Day, I was the bearer of the good news: 1-0 to Rochdale. "Very good," she said, and turned to walk back to the house. She was well wrapped up in a blue cardigan and stepped gingerly across the thin patches of ice. Through her doorway, I could see a small Christmas tree on the sideboard and an armchair drawn close to a gas fire.

The football season is already in its mid-life, yet it seems just weeks ago when the estate surrounding the ground was alive in the sunshine. Kids played in the streets – little girls skittering along the tarmac in their mum's shoes, the family dog reclining in the sunshine.

"You're not going to watch Rochdale are you?" they asked, grinning, "They're rubbish them!"

When we watch our football team, we also watch the seasons. Bonfires burn in back gardens and on distant hills in early November, plumes of smoke mingling with the mist and damp. The pitch is thick and soggy and the ball falls dead in puddles. Snow is shovelled into a thick buttress of white around the pitch in January. In the stands, cups of coffee are held tightly in cold, shaking hands.

The rain still comes down in March and April, though not so relentlessly. It passes and the sun splinters the damp into shards of Technicolor light. We might score at this surreal moment and it feels otherworldly, as if we are watching ourselves watching our team score. At the final games of the season, early in May, jackets are back across the arm, the warm air wafting through the shadows in the stands. The pitch is now dry and hard, the ball bouncing unevenly, the players hurrying to the touchline for bottles of water.

Heavy snow has fallen on Rochdale this week. It is a milestone, of sorts. Historical legacy has it that our season is over before the trees shed their leaves, so to reach mid-winter is reason enough to bedeck the windows in fairy lights and turn up the central heating a notch or two. Rochdale are currently fifth in the third division (with, please note, a game in hand) and have lost just three times in 22 League matches. Only once before have they lost fewer games in the opening half of the season – in 1923 when Durham City, Ashington, New Brighton and Bradford Park Avenue were among our rivals.

Obviously, then, this is a new experience for Rochdale fans. Usually, the club's fortunes is a subject best avoided, but all the munificence flowing our way is a little unsettling. Numerous times over the Christmas holiday, I have been told how wonderful, amazing, fantastic it must be to support a club doing so well, especially after all those years of struggle. I concur, but, in truth, much of this upsurge has happened on the blindside of most Rochdale fans.

Until Steve Parkin, our manager, arrived in the summer of 1999, we were a mid-table side with a good home record and dire away form. We have now become kings of the road and have conceded fewer goals away than any other team in the English professional game, with a better record than our pals 12 miles down the road, Manchester United.

In contrast, we have won just 13 times in 34 home League matches since his appointment and our biggest margin of victory is a measly 2-0. Gary Jones, our midfield terrier, warned in the match programme this week that a visiting team will 'cop for it' soon at Spotland. This has been predicted many times, yet the team still plays as if it is into the third day of a particularly heavy cold.

Understandably, the club's passive supporters have remained sceptical. They can, of course, follow the team on the road, though it means lengthy trips to places such as Plymouth, Brighton, Torquay and Exeter. Instead, when they hear of a stirring away performance, like the 4-0 win at Shrewsbury, they journey once more to Spotland with hope in their hearts. Their reward has been an almighty struggle to hold a desperate 1-0 lead against Hull City or a 2-1 against Torquay United.

So, yes, a wonderful, amazing, fantastic season, though it has often felt like it has happened to someone else, and seems as close to home as 1923.

Saturday, 30 December 2000

Heavy snow caused the postponement of Rochdale's home match against Brighton and Hove Albion.

Also in Rochdale...

December 2000

* The RSPCA announced it was to reopen its Rochdale branch in Redcross Street after the public had raised £30,000 towards costs.
* Brothers Francis and Thomas McDonagh were branded 'Britain's dopiest robbers' after they made a get-away in a hearse and then a Vauxhall Nova still covered in suds from a car-wash. They had made seven fruitless 'armed' robberies in three hours when they tried to pass off a piece of pipe as a handgun. They were jailed for seven

years. Thomas McDonagh was not as 'dopey' as first suspected – six months later he mounted a successful jail-break.

Six

Lost Souls, Found Souls

Monday, 1 January 2001

Rochdale's away game at Darlington was postponed because of a frozen pitch. It was rearranged to take place a week later.

Tuesday, 2 January 2001

Macclesfield Town striker Richard Barker joined Rotherham United of the second division despite Rochdale's offer of £100,000. The 25-year-old signed a four-year contract with the club based close to his hometown of Sheffield.

Thursday, 4 January 2001

I received a letter from Ron Murray of Woodhall Spa, Lincolnshire:

Dear Mark,

Firstly I would just like to say how much I enjoy and look forward to your Saturday stories on Rochdale FC every week, and you might be interested in my little story about them.

When I was a younger man (I am an OAP), I decided that I would like to visit all 92 Football League grounds if possible. I was living in Sutton Coldfield, near Birmingham, where I was born and bred. I have spent my whole life devoted to Birmingham City, so like you, I know what it's like to support a team that's won nothing.

I had been to all the first division and second division grounds when following Birmingham, but to go to third division grounds, I used to go on the supporters' coaches with Walsall FC, which is only six miles from Sutton Coldfield. It was a very cheap way of getting to grounds.

Well, during season 1973-1974 reports were appearing in the national newspapers that Rochdale were having things that bad, that they might go out of business. So I thought I must get to Spotland before they are gone. It was Easter Monday, 15 April 1974, and the sun was shining. It was a glorious morning and I had got nothing planned, so I thought, 'Right, Spotland here I come'.

The M6 runs through Sutton Coldfield, so by 10.30am, I was on my way. I had a very pleasant journey up there in my old Ford Anglia, and arrived at about 1pm.

Rochdale had been having some very poor gates and things were going bad. When I got to Spotland, I had a good walk around the ground outside. Aldershot were the visitors, and there were about 30 or 40 of their fans.

Well, down on one end of Spotland, there was a most bizarre sight. Somewhere in Rochdale there had been a demolition job on some council houses (this story was related to me by a 'local') and all the front doors of the demolished homes had been taken to Spotland and they were holding up the one end of the ground. When I approached, I wondered which door I would have to use to get in. However, I went in and stood by the players' tunnel and got talking to some guy who turned out to be Angus McLean, assistant manager, who invited me into his office for a cup of tea.

The outcome of this most pleasant day was that I sponsored the match ball for the next home fixture against Halifax Town, and you will see from the enclosed programme, I got my name on the back page. You are welcome to this old programme, Mark. I often think of that day with very fond memories. I was looked after so well. It was so friendly. It's all gone now.

Good Luck for 2001. I look forward to your stories. Good luck to Rochdale FC.

Sincerely, Ron Murray.

THE DAY TWEETIE PIE BROUGHT A
LITTLE GLAMOUR TO SPOTLAND

(*The Times*, Saturday, 6 January 2001)

The house smelled of paint for days. Mum had warned that it would, but dad takes some stopping when he gets an idea into his head. He had made me a Rochdale FC flag by spraying a piece of cloth with blue car paint. 'R.A.F.C' ran diagonally across the centre; he had used insulation tape to mask the letters.

I pinned it on my bedroom wall and it was taken down only when we went on holiday. I had to have it within touching distance at all times. Perversely, I never took it to matches. It was enough just to have something that reflected back to me my love of the club; I did-n't need to show it to anyone else.

Back then, the only official souvenirs with Rochdale's name on them were programmes and enamel badges. The club 'shop' was a small room at the back of the Main Stand. On match days, they lift-ed a hatch and, at best, there was room for three or four people to shuffle along and peer into the fluorescent cave. Sliding glass doors narrowed the space further, so they had to collect the money and pass the goods through a gap of about two feet wide.

They would stick pieces of paper against the windows with mes-sages written in marker pen: 'Book now for Aldershot away' or 'England U23s v Czechoslovakia U23s – programme in now.' It was-n't possible to linger; there was invariably someone shouting over your shoulder ("Do you know where the key is for the players' lounge?") or it was raining. There might have been other souvenirs - rosettes, or scarves with silk on one side and wool on the other, or teddies in blue and white knitted jumpers, but it was impossible to see them.

Rochdale, like most clubs, is now of the marketing age and will soon open a new, spacious club store. Young Rochdale supporters can walk to school in a Rochdale baseball cap, wearing a Rochdale bench jacket, over a Rochdale sweatshirt. They can check the time on a Rochdale watch, and take their Rochdale rulers and Rochdale pens out of a Rochdale pencil case. When I was at school in the late 1970s, I could either wave my home-made flag - amid much abuse and laughter- or scribble 'Up The Dale' on my rough book.

Only once did I have the opportunity to lay my hands on a bona fide, state-of-the-art Rochdale memento. I was mooching around the shopping centre when I caught sight of a clear plastic wallet hanging in a shop unit. I had to look closer; I didn't believe what I was seeing. It was divided into pockets and each contained a sticker featuring either Sylvester or Tweetie Pie. They wore football kits and beneath them was a pithy comment. Underneath the one of Sylvester leaning forward, cheeks puffed out, it read: "Join the Spotland Roar". The others had similar references to Rochdale: Tweetie Pie smiling, arms folded - 'Rochdale are Cool!'; Sylvester in a spin, feet a blur – 'Follow me to Spotland'. I bought one and placed it carefully in the pocket of my duffel coat. I only had enough money for one, but planned to return for more.

The club had never existed before beyond the actual, but it was suddenly flushed by this eccentric dab of glamour. How had the stickers come to exist? They had been professionally made. The colours were bright, the type clear.

When I returned a week later, a different lady was serving. The wallet was no longer on the wall. I asked her if there were any Rochdale stickers left.

"I don't know, I'm only working here today. I'm a friend of the owner."

She could see I was perturbed.

"What did they look like, love?"

"They were in this plastic thing, hanging up, just there."

She offered to look in the storeroom behind the counter. She brushed away the curtain across the doorway and re-emerged a few minutes later.

"I've had a good look, but I can't see anything. When you say 'Rochdale', what do you mean? Were they of the Town Hall or something?"

"No, the football club."

"I don't remember them," she said, and made a quizzical face, drawing down her mouth and tensing her forehead.

"They're not there. She must have sold them all."

There had been about 200 stickers; they couldn't all have sold in a week.

I kept my sticker. It was like something I had brought back from a dream. I stuck it on a notebook at college. Mark Witty, a fellow student, defaced it. Where it read: 'Join the Spotland Roar' he crossed out the word 'Roar' and replaced it with 'Whimper'. He wasn't to know.

Saturday, 6 January 2001
Darlington 1 Rochdale 2

Tony Ellis capitalised on Rochdale's early dominance by giving them a first half lead.

Darlington substitute Richard Hodgson equalised but Rochdale secured the victory 15 minutes from time when star performer Wayne Evans' shot hit a defender and the Darlington goalkeeper before reaching the net. "The lads are ribbing Evo because he's trying to claim the goal. It would have hit the corner flag without those two big deflections," said Parkin.

Evans was adamant that it was his goal. "There's no way anyone will be taking it off me," he said. "I'll write to the Football League if I have to!"

Wednesday, 10 January 2001

Several fans objected to comments made by the *Rochdale Observer's* columnist and Burnley supporter, Ian Ogden. He had mentioned Burnley on several occasions and, in one edition, wrote, 'What a joy it is to see Burnley doing well.'

One Rochdale fan countered: 'In my humble opinion, I shouldn't be reading about Burnley Football Club in my local paper.' He also pointed out that since receiving letters of complaint, Ogden had refrained from mentioning Burnley. 'Now, I have to wonder whether it is because he has taken heed of the advice, or whether it may be due to the fact that Burnley have since lost five games on the run,' he pondered.

Later in the season, Ogden was banished to the mythical *Room 101* on the Rochdaleafc.com website for 'force-feeding Claret propaganda on a weekly basis' and his 'one-eyed Claret obsession'.

Thursday, 11 January 2001

Rochdale issued a series of 24 'cigarette cards' featuring the first-team squad, along with Steve Parkin and Desmond the Dragon. Desmond's card revealed that he, 'joined the club in 1312 in a swap deal involving a root vegetable, a piece of sheepskin and a night-out-for-two with Tony Ford'.

Friday, 12 January 2001

Frank Bishop, chairman of the Rochdale Supporters' Club, revealed details of a typical encounter: "While I was sitting in Rochdale Shopping Centre waiting for my wife, I overheard a couple of our senior citizens discussing the contents of a newspaper they'd just bought at WH Smith's. One asked where Dale were in the league. The other replied, 'Bound to be at the bottom' and turned to the sports pages for the tables. 'They must be in the amateur leagues by now because they're not in the second or third,' he said.

"I couldn't resist going over and asking to look at the paper. I found the third division table and pointed out Dale's position. They expressed surprise and one said, 'I always look at the bottom half, I never thought to look at the top. Force of habit.' He spotted the Dale logo on my fleece and said, 'Sorry son!'"

SUPPORTERS STRUGGLE TO EMBRACE IDEAS ABOVE THEIR STATION
(*The Times*, Saturday, 13 January 2001)

Everyone's talking about not talking about it. No one dare tempt fate. A good set of results over Christmas and New Year has now made it impossible to avoid - Rochdale are on course for promotion.

They are joint third, with a nine-point cushion between themselves and the edge of the play-off zone.

Rochdale and promotion, or even Rochdale and success, is a misnomer. Where Rochdale is concerned, the words more familiar to the ear are 'lowly', 'struggling', 'minnows', and – let's face it – 'losers'. This is for good reason. We have, more or less, been all of these things throughout 94 years as a professional football club. To recap: all but five seasons have been spent in the bottom division and we are currently its longest-serving member with a tenure of 26 years, where our highest position has been eighth.

People are asking how it feels to support a club that is finally showing signs of life. Well, strange. Or should that be well strange? When I began supporting Rochdale, in their first season back in the bottom division, I was quickly made aware of the attendant social and cultural placing. We - the club, the fans, the town and myself - were the proletariats in the grand empire of the Football League. We were snotty-nosed, latchkey kids. Soup and chips for tea. The factory or, at best, an engineering works for afters.

Inevitably then, we're feeling lost, padding furtively among the marble pillars and five-course lunches of relative achievement. We don't even have lunches as our mid-day meal where we come from; we have dinners, from the chippy or from a tin. We feel like chancers, dallying with social convention. Any minute now, we'll be rumbled – we'll pick up the inappropriate piece of cutlery, say the wrong word, let slip that we never went to university.

These twitchy feelings of inferiority coexist with a growing campaign of defiance. If we are England's worst-performing team of the last 26 years, we must, therefore, be the country's most loyal supporters. Do we not deserve our place higher up the social order? Have we not suffered enough? Who makes these rules that we should be excluded anyway? Chips on our shoulder? With extra gravy, please.

Those willing to hypothesise on the subject of promotion have already started to fret. They are fearful that Rochdale in a higher division will be like going out in a snowstorm in your pyjamas. While we're shivering, they'll thump goal after goal in our net. This is to ignore the simple logic that if results show we are too good for this division, we are ready for the next.

Other clubs, such as Crewe Alexandra, Stockport County, Grimsby Town and Bradford City, have left this division in recent years and continued their ascent. They weren't mindful of their rightful place or intimidated by their new neighbourhood. They should be our role models, kids from the same streets who bought the factory where they once swept the floors. A working-class hero is something to be.

As we've not been here for a long time, we're not sure what a promotion team looks like. When it was a hypothetical notion, we imagined a team of virtuosos, 11 players with magic feet, but this lot – it has to be said – look much like every other lot we've had, except they seldom lose. Perhaps we have to hear others praise our team before we see it ourselves. We know them too well and are so tautly intertwined with their fortunes, that we fail to notice intermittent greatness.

There are some supporters who are resistant to any change. They like that we are one of the better teams of our division and, oh dear, promotion might bring with it more defeats. This particular lobby should not be underestimated. When our splendid new stand was opened earlier this season, one regular looked across and, noticing it was taller than the ramshackle shed it replaced, announced: "Bloody hell, I can't see the hills over there now. I used to like looking at them when we were playing crap!"

More than once, I've been asked what I will do if we are promoted. I feel a certain pressure, like they assume my fanaticism can only be truly memorialised through an act of delirious recklessness. I should implode or explode, drink the pub dry, climb on the roof, take a plane to Goa, or a rocket to the moon. In truth, I suspect it will be a quiet, reflective joy, something between me, my dad and my football club. Bliss, I think they call it.

Saturday, 13 January 2001
Rochdale 0 Halifax Town 1

Rochdale lost for the first time at home in more than three months when Steve Kerrigan scored for Halifax from a scissor kick. It was only Rochdale's fourth defeat in 24 matches.

The attendance was 4,123, which meant the crowd for three consecutive home games had exceeded 4,000 for the first time in 29 years.

The game held special interest for Steve Parkin because he had played alongside Halifax's manager, Paul Bracewell, at Stoke City.

Monday, 15 January 2001

The guide issued by Ondigital announced that Rochdale's forthcoming televised match against Leyton Orient would be played at Scotland, not Spotland.

Tuesday, 16 January 2001

Negotiations with Southend striker Martin Carruthers collapsed over his wage demands. Steve Parkin said the club was not willing to break its wage structure and said the player's demands had been 'ridiculous' - three or four times higher than Rochdale players were paid.

NEIGHBOURS FROM HELL: AN EVERYDAY STORY OF LIFE AT SPOTLAND
(*The Times*, Saturday, 20 January 2001)

New neighbours moved in on Saturday. They received the customary non-welcome. Although, at several points, our bodies were actually touching (anorak to anorak, that is), no conversation took place. We might, in an unguarded moment, have nodded, but hopefully no one will have spotted this act of unbecoming bonhomie.

Football has a strict code of etiquette. It takes many years to learn its complexities, which is why it is easy to spot the nouveaux. These rules are passed down from generation to generation, like a sticky

Uncle Joe's mint ball fastened to the inside of your coat pocket.

In broad terms, they are: greet your fellow supporters with wilful insouciance; do not speak about any other subject except the detail of the match you are watching; yell abuse randomly; change tack completely if your team scores – you are now permitted to hold your neighbour, hug them, or even dance down the aisle if the goal has moved your team into a play-off position.

The first of our new neighbours was in place some time before kick-off. He seemed a quiet, undemonstrative chap, the body language decidedly introspective. When his two pals arrived, the change in his demeanour was marked: "Bloody hell, where have you been?" he shouted. Thereafter, it was as if his volume control had been turned from zero to nine, occasionally hitting 10.

As usual, the refereeing was atrocious. We moaned, we shouted. Our new neighbour suddenly laughed out-loud: "He's had it him, bloody had it." His pals asked what he meant. "There'll be waiting for that ref after the match, just you see." Every few minutes, he reiterated this assertion. "I'm not joking, there'll be on the car park, after his blood." Another unfathomable decision later: "He's just making it worse for himself, now." When the half-time whistle blew, he was on his feet, looking towards the tunnel. "They're giving the ref hell down there. Just wait until after the game."

The theme continued well into the second half, his excitability honed by every peculiar decision. Finally, one of his friends spoke up: "I don't think they'll wait for him afterwards. They don't do things like that here, do they?" I expected a rebuttal, that the waspish one would declare that he knew better. Instead, in a meek, detached voice, he responded: "I suppose you're right." Subject closed. People are strange.

Down the years, we have got to know our usual neighbours fairly well. Fairly well by football terms that is, which means we do not know their surnames, their familial status, or where they live. In the absence of real names, we know them euphemistically: Little Dave, Pete the Joiner, Thingy's Dad, the Ukrainian, Bob from the Council, Mark from Accrington..

The Ukrainian, incidentally, might not actually be Ukrainian. He may be Polish or Hungarian. Whatever, he speaks in an Eastern European accent and never (ever) removes his headphones. He doesn't volunteer the football scores, so presumably he is not listening to the radio. I often deliberate on his chosen musical accompaniment to a Rochdale fixture. It might all make sense with a soundtrack by Albinoni or Offenbach, except, judging by the way he pushes past us belligerently on his way to his half-time ablutions, he might have the repeat button pressed down on The Baha Men's *Who Let The Dogs Out*.

A few years ago, we used to stand near two blokes called Jack and John. Unusually, we knew their proper first-names, although Chicken John or Bladder Jack would have been apt. John, at half-time, would disgorge pieces of smelly chicken from tin foil and – licking his lips and grunting - pick his way through, before depositing the bones and bits of skin at the back of the stand. Lovely. John, meanwhile, would drink about 12 pints of beer, wobble around, then begin numerous treks to and from the toilet. "Why does he pay to come in here and spend most of his time looking at a piss-stone?" someone shouted once. "Because it's more entertaining than watching this lot," came the reply.

Only once have dad and me made what might qualify as a 'friend' at Spotland. For several seasons we had a seat next to an old-boy called Norman. He was probably older than the club itself and had failing eyesight. He was not overly impressed by our stumpy, white-haired striker, Barry Wellings. "Get off Wellings, you're bloody awful today," he yelled joyously. This heartfelt counsel continued until half-time, when dad pulled on his sleeve: "Norman, Wellings isn't playing today." Norman was disgruntled, a little embarrassed. He thought for a minute. "Well, if he was, he'd be crap."

Saturday, 20 January 2001

After several nights where temperatures had fallen to minus five degrees, the match at Hull City was postponed because of a frozen pitch.

Wednesday, 24 January 2001

Marcus Hallows, the son of former Rochdale defender, Paul Hallows, arrived to spend a week on trial at Spotland. The striker had returned to England from Ireland where he had played for Sligo Rovers and St Patrick's Athletic. His father, an overlapping right back, had made 223 league and cup appearances for Rochdale between 1974 and 1979.

STEREOTYPING OF SACRED
TRIUMVERATE DOES US NO FAVOURS
(*The Times*, Saturday, 27 January 2001)

Shut up shop, close down t'mill, sing as you go – Rochdale's on telly, our mam. The lads and lasses from London are on their way in thundering trucks and posh cars; better bring in the washing.

Doorsteps have been scrubbed, shopping trolleys fished out of the canal, and we're all nicely scrubbed up for arrival of the television folk this weekend. Rochdale, by heck, are on the Sky Sports *2* on Sunday – weather permitting – when we play Leyton Orient.

It's not the first time they've eschewed the bright lights of nearby Manchester, Liverpool and Leeds to visit God's backyard. They came two years ago and saw us thump Hull City on a pitch so wet and muddy that our physio had to treat an outbreak of trench foot.

Obviously, I was at the game, but, like many supporters, I later took possession of a videotape of proceedings and excitedly jammed it into the player. How was my team – indeed, Rochdale itself – portrayed to the world? As the tape went in, I made my usual invocation: please, oh deities of the cathode, no mention of the Rochdale triumvirate, by name – Gracie Fields, Sir Cyril Smith and Lisa Stansfield.

Through hands clasped tightly to my face, I saw their distinctive outline. First, Gracie, caterwauling about her aspidistra and Sally, the pride of her alley. Next, Cyril, reclining in an armchair, volunteering, 'They're not doing anyone any harm' to the enigma of why people supported Rochdale FC. Finally, Lisa, a shot of the outside of her house, and a strained pun about her hit single, *All Around The World.*

Many people in Rochdale revere these as the sacred three, but others hold less determinate views. The doubters and iconoclasts are forced to meet after dark because it is a profanity to take the name of our Gracie, Cyril or Lisa in vain. The miscreant is duly ostracised – call yourself a Rochdalian? Be done with ye, to Oldham!

Undeniably, in their own disparate way, they have each defined Rochdale and its people as plucky, resourceful, forthright, cheeky, self-deprecating and with a chip-toothed charisma. An impressive list of attributes, but, lamentably, they also nail the town too rigidly to the past. They unwittingly generate a stereotype, a homily to homespun, long-gone folksiness. Gracie made her last film in 1946 and has been dead for more than 20 years. Likewise, Cyril Smith retired from political life almost 10 years ago and Lisa's big hit was in 1990, a veritable generation ago in pop terms.

When I tell people where I am from, they invariably mention one of the three. Often, they can't remember their names, so sing the song -'Salleee' (in a pitch high enough to set dogs howling), if they're thinking of Gracie; or a croon in that cod-American accent Lisa affects when she nears a microphone. If it's Cyril they mean, they invariably make reference to his girth. I've had a near-lifetime of this. I'd prefer them to say: 'Ah, Rochdale – isn't that where New Order played their first gig?' Or, 'Wasn't Bill Oddie from Rochdale?' I can then counter, stroking my chin earnestly, that indeed he was and the magnificent countryside surrounding the town first introduced him to the joys of ornithology.

I fully understand why telly people prefer the past. The Rochdale of today wouldn't make good television. It is, much like the rest of Britain, a hostage to shopping precincts and multiplexes. The pubs have polished floorboards and names like the Mucky Duck, the Regal Moon and the Country Rock Café. Everything is franchised, even the people who look much the same as one another as they skitter from bar to bar, dodging the rain on a Saturday night.

The physical, man-built remnants from the past have also been treated disrespectfully. The gothic Town Hall was set adrift and ambushed by a car park when the town centre was redeveloped, while the library was re-located from a magnificent rococo building to a couple of floors in the shopping precinct.

If I were selling Rochdale to the world, I'd show off the hills, so joyously bleak and robust. Of its people, I'd call on Don Estelle - Lofty from *It Ain't Half Hot Mum* - and we'd film him singing in the precinct to seven loyal pensioners, selling them tapes from a cardboard box. We'd move on, down Deeplish way, and find kids making on-it, up-for-it, hip-hop. We've all life here, see. Finally, I'd show them a piece of land picked out by a light at each corner (so it can be seen from heaven) called Spotland, as old as the hills, but forever young.

Sunday, 28 January 2001
Rochdale 3 Leyton Orient 1

Early morning fog threatened Rochdale`s live appearance in front of the television cameras. The rain also came down, but the ball boys were not perturbed; they had received free tracksuits and rain jackets from the club's kit suppliers, Uhlsport.

The weather improved and Rochdale eased comfortably to a half-time lead with goals from Tony Ellis and Gary Jones. Within minutes of the restart, Phil Hadland made it 3-0. Orient's consolation goal came during the closing minutes from Dean Smith.

Tommy Taylor, Orient's manager, said: "Our passing was poor. We were beaten by the better side."

Sunday, 28 January 2001

A web-surfer, writing in the programme for the Leyton Orient match, told of a 'Rochdale' few people recognised. It was home to, 'hippies, utopians, acid heads, exotic dancers, quotient dancers, bikers, flower children, acid heads, American draft dodgers, Portuguese draft dodgers, feminists, communards, lost souls, found souls, kids, Krishna's, irritating primal screamers, irritating ordinary screamers, slackers, slickers, grifters, grafters, acid heads, and drug dealers of every size, shape, disposition and level of intelligence and style.'

Rochdale had been an 18-floor tower block housing a police-free counter-cultural community in Toronto, Canada, during the late 1960s and early 1970s, Canada's equivalent of the United States' Haight-Ashbury. Former commune member, Paul Evitts, summarised it as, 'the biggest and most glorious mindfuck ever devised by man'.

Another insight into the town's namesake was provided by ex-student, Chris Hall: "Rochdale gave me a degree (for twenty-five bucks) in 'Omegapathosology,' a word I invented that means 'the end of the study of sadness.' Rochdale was a sovereign country within a great city, sort of a Vatican of the counter-culture. It was also an experiment in freedom. For example, there was crazy Smitty who spent her time strolling through the halls buck-naked except for a football helmet pulled over her head."

Monday, 29 January 2001

Kevin Kyle, a 19-year-old striker, joined on loan from Sunderland. The Stranraer-born player had scored 31 goals for Sunderland's reserves in 1999-2000 and had already appeared twice for Scotland Under-21s. He had previously had loan spells at Huddersfield Town and Darlington.

Also in Rochdale...

January 2001

* Alan Clarke, aged 61, was discovered living in a converted garden shed among trees and rocks above Newhey. He had lived alone for 22 years and had not read a newspaper since 1977. His television had been rigged up to a methane-powered electrical system a year earlier: " I turned on to watch *Coronation Street* – Ena Sharples isn't in it any more," he lamented.

* A male nurse, Neil Hartley, known to staff at Birch Hill Hospital as 'Mr Know-it-all', appeared at crown court charged with unlawfully handing out lethal injections. He was given a one-year prison sen-

tence, suspended for two years.

* Pensioner John Porter of Smithy Bridge turned his garden into a gallery of wheel trims by pinning up more than 60 to his fence. "Kids used to throw them over my hedge, so I started sticking them up," he said.

Seven

Meat and Gravy, Hit and Hope

Thursday, 1 February 2001

Rochdale players were approached by a man who worked at the Newport branch of Carcraft, the club's sponsors, as they booked into their hotel before the match against Cardiff City. He had seen their televised win against Leyton Orient and told them they had been a great advert for the company.

Friday, 2 February 2001

A headline in *The Guardian* read: *'From Rochdale to Rio via Rome, Hooliganism is Alive and Kicking'*. The article related to a thwarted pre-arranged meeting between hooligans from Leeds United and Manchester United in Rochdale. Several supporters and Richard Bott felt it unfairly implicated Rochdale FC.

"The headline was mischievous, misleading and damaging," said Bott. "A black mark to *The Guardian* who should know better. You can bet the Sports Editor doesn't live in Rochdale. But we are used to taking cheap shots and we don't intend it to let it spoil our season."

Friday, 2 February 2001
Cardiff City 0 Rochdale 0

A tight match was expected between the two clubs with the best home record and best away record in the division.

Steve Parkin surprised Cardiff by fielding three strikers – Kevin Kyle, Tony Ellis and Clive Platt. The division's highest attendance of the season so far, 11,912, saw Rochdale frustrate the home side and stop them recording their 10th consecutive home win. "We had a clean sheet against a good team. I always said it was going to be

126

tight," said Alan Cork, the Cardiff manager.

Although Rochdale's performance was based on solid teamwork, Dave Flitcroft and Lee Todd had an on-field row that culminated in Flitcroft grabbing Todd by the throat, forcing the referee to intervene.

When the attendance was announced, the 200 Rochdale supporters at Ninian Park gave the home fans a round of applause, paying respect to their large number.

ROCHDALE ON TELLY GIVES FRIGHTENING CLOSE-UP OF OUR HEROES
(*The Times*, Saturday, 3 February 2001)

Typical, we muttered. Rochdale are finally on telly, but no one can see us. We'd expected snow or rain, and an inevitable postponement, but not this: a dense, stubborn bank of fog squatting over Spotland. Is that our striker down there, or the girl bringing the pies?

Rochdale's match against Leyton Orient was the featured game last Sunday on Sky Sports 2. Anyone resolute enough to peer through the gloom, may have noticed that Rochdale won 3-1 and played with commendable heart.

Across Rochdale, contingency plans had already been made. Families settled down in front of the television and whenever the mist thickened and the players disappeared, they played 'Fantasy Patronise'. Basically, it works much like Fantasy Football, except points are scored when a pundit or commentator mentions a stereotype or cliché appertaining to Rochdale. Among the high-scorers were 'dark satanic mills', 'in the shadow of Manchester United', 'sitting at the foot of the Pennines' and an aside that Cyril Smith is 'Rochdale's biggest fan'. Ho ho.

Once we learnt that Ray Wilkins was among the telly sages, bonus points became available should he utter: 'Spotland really is a super little ground'. He didn't, actually, though he looked as if he might at several points.

The game kicked off at noon, which, for Nationwide League traditionalists such as us, is a major blow to routine. If we looked rather dazed and forlorn when the camera panned in our direction, it was with good reason Our heads said it was three o'clock on Saturday, while our stomachs were confused: why had pie and peas had so quickly followed a full English breakfast?

The boys from the telly, in all fairness, Brian, done good. They didn't patronise and they treated the club, the game, and the town with due respect. They also – somehow – brought a dash of glamour to a match that was muck and nettles, meat and gravy, hit and hope. The tag, 'Exclusively live from Spotland' raised a smile; it suggested unfettered pride, as if they had, at the eleventh hour, fended off a counter bid from the BBC or Disney Channel for the rights to point their cameras into the murk.

Two other games given significant plugs during Rochdale's on-air time were Valencia v Real Madrid and the Baltimore Ravens v the New York Giants in the Superbowl. After making reference to the Real Madrid match, the presenter said: '…but we're concentrating on events here at Spotland.' Those of us that remember the drip-drip, falling down Spotland of old, and a club teetering on extinction, have to swallow hard at times like these.

Spotland was seen a good way short of its best. The mist was like a dustsheet placed over the family silver, so the talk about the change from ramshackle tin-hut to state-of-the-art stadium was not lent much authenticity. Believe me, when the sun shines and the grass has regrown, it will form the muse for artists and poets, travelling from as far away as Bury and Accrington.

The atmosphere was also a little flat. Sky had chosen to dangle their 'crowd' microphone over four Orient fans who seemed unusually concerned about the sexual orientation of their own players. So, the country didn't get to hear the Spotland roar, which is, in truth, a long, monotonic moan of 'Daaaaayyyuuullll'.

Unlike supporters of Premiership clubs, we seldom get to see our heroes so close-up, and it was quite a shock. Dave Bayliss, our craggy centre back, had done something strange to his eyebrows. They were pulled at an acute angle and fastened down with huge blobs of

Vaseline. In all that fog, the Orient players were clearly in fear of bumping into Nosferatu in football boots. Tony Ellis' hair, as ever, was immaculate, with not a single strand out of place. When he headed the first goal, his barber could be heard sighing from the touchline.

A few weeks ago, Steve Parkin, our manager, shaved off his moustache and the cameras allowed fans a first look at his uncovered top lip. Unfortunately, his front teeth appear to have grown in direct proportion to this loss, so, as one wag put it, we've lost a Manuel (we've long memories in Rochdale) and gained a chipmunk!

Inevitably, the match video has been played more than a few times this week. The highlight isn't the goals, Nosferatu, or the chipmunk, but a cameo played out just before the kick-off. Midfielder, Dave Flitcroft, gives high-fives and embraces our goalkeeper, Neil Edwards, in the dressing-room. They look, at that moment, like two professionals who know they have a job to do. We see that they share a passion, a will to win, a team spirit and they are wearing Rochdale's colours.

Tuesday, 6 February 2001

The rescheduled home match against Brighton was postponed again because of a waterlogged pitch.

Wednesday, 7 February 2001

The Willbutts Lane Stand was renamed the Per-fit Windows Stand after the double glazing company became its sponsor.

FANS GROW OLD IN FEAR OF
SPOTLAND CHAINSAW MASSACRE
(*The Times*, Saturday, 10 February 2001)

The trees that peer over the top of the stand at the Sandy Lane End are still without leaves. In a few weeks, buds will appear, and as summer taps on branches, they will explode into a glorious panoply of dense green.

When a football match falls dull, our eyes naturally wander to the scenery around us. Close up, we see fellow supporters, and note whether they are happy, well, older or otherwise. The pitch and stands are largely unchanging, so we look beyond them, usually - in our case- to the trees. A mind can also stray at this point, to matters of mortality.

These trees are as old as the club. In black and white photos of young bucks posing in Rochdale shirts (arms crossed, short-back-and-sides, eager eyes), they form the background. In fact, any reel of photographs - whether showing standard 0-0 draws against Scunthorpe United or memorable 2-1 FA Cup wins against Coventry City – will, somewhere, include the quietly insistent outline of these sycamores.

One day, sniff-sniff, they will reach a certain maturity, become unstable, and topple to the ground. Or, and this is far more likely (if good deal less poetic), a bloke from the council will set about them with a chainsaw. He'll pile the cleaved branches and trunks into a wagon and make his way to the municipal tip. Whistling as he goes, and munching his butties, a lorry-load of secrets will trundle by unnoticed.

This issue of time passing by has been honed for many Rochdale supporters by the news that the son of a former player has been on trial at the club. Marcus Hallows, aged 25, is the son of Paul Hallows, now aged 50, who gave valuable service to the club in the 1970s.

If I close my eyes, I can still see Hallows dashing down the wing, pursued by an indignant full back. Hallows was nominally a full back himself, but he much preferred galloping down the wing. He left the mundane job of marking strikers to the likes of big Bill Summerscales or Dick Mulvaney, which was the name of our centre half, and not an affliction you went to your doctor with.

Hallows, as they all must, eventually moved on, and a host of similarly chunky full backs have since patrolled that little piece of Spotland, just to the right of the penalty area, pressed tight to the touchline. Hallows junior may soon move across the same pitch and this is irrefutable evidence that the world has moved on another generation. This wasn't supposed to happen – where have all those years gone?

When I first went to Spotland, in 1974, I could barely see over the perimeter fence. Even then, I was pondering life, death and the universe, to the extent that my uncle, when he visited, would ask whether 'Analysing Harry' was around. I analysed everything, see. On this theme, I noted the ages of the players in the Rochdale squad and distinctly recall thinking that the day I was older than any of them was the day when I was officially, undeniably old; not dad old, or grandad old, but certainly on my way there.

The day came. Wisely, I changed the rules. I didn't feel old, so why should I pander to this self-styled dictum? This was football, I could move the goal posts if I wanted. My formal coming-of-old-age was re-set at the point when I was older than every player signed to Rochdale FC. I am pleased to announce that, by this criterion, I am still young.

My extended youth is due entirely to the enlightened policy of Steve Parkin, our manager. He is of the opinion that only players who can remember *The Golden Shot* or *The High Chaparral* are worthy of a place in his team. He has 41-year-old Tony Ford at wing back, and 36-year-old Tony Ellis at striker; two players over whom I still have some time.

If I were made of stronger stuff, and my devotion to Rochdale placed in its proper context, I would probably find more valid evidence to suggest I had reached middle age. Like, why have I started writing letters to my local paper? And why do my knees click when I bend down? And why do I shout to my kids, 'Just do as you're told, and don't argue'?

Perhaps this is what being grown-up feels like. I've made it, but, then again, not quite. While Tony Ford drifts up and down that pitch and the trees stand proud behind the stand, I reserve the right to remain 10-years-old, or thereabouts.

Saturday, 10 February 2001

A team of volunteers tended the Spotland pitch through the night with pitch forks and hot-air blowers but were left disappointed when the match against Carlisle United was postponed at 1.45pm.

The board revealed that late postponements cost the club approximately £3,000 per match.

Tuesday, 13 February 2001

Scunthorpe United 0 Rochdale 0

An impressive defensive display brought Rochdale their second consecutive goalless draw away from home and kept them in fifth position. "My lads at the back were magnificent," said Steve Parkin.

Referee Ray Olivier needed an escort from the pitch at half-time and full-time after some erratic decisions. He booked Dave Flitcroft, Wayne Evans and Lee Todd.

Brian Laws, Scunthorpe's manager, accused Rochdale of playing an over-physical game: "They came here and tried to ruffle our feathers a little and see what reaction there was. We have some temperamental players here, but fair play to them, they used their heads a little bit."

Wednesday, 14 February 2000

The Sandy Lane End was officially named the Thwaites Beer Stand at a ceremony at Spotland attended by Classic and Regent, two shire horses belonging to the Blackburn-based brewers.

RAIN, RAIN, GO AWAY, GOOD OLD ROCHDALE WANT TO PLAY

(*The Times*, Saturday, 17 February 2001)

Non-mechanised digging implements are hard to find in Rochdale. If it's a spade you're after, best ask for it by name. The same logic obviously applied to the football club. Imagine the meeting of inauguration back in 1906: "Right lads, what are we going to be — Rochdale City?"

"Nah, sounds a bit grand."

"Athletic then?"

"But we might not be!"

"Academicals?"

"Now you're talking bloody stupid."

After much chin-stroking and twanging of braces, old Wilson T Arkwright or another of our semi-mythical founding fathers will have suddenly come over all sure of himself.

"Nay lads, where are we from?"

"Rochdale."

"Rochdale it is then, pure and simple, nowt fancy or too full-of-itself."

Many people are incredulous when I tell them we're known by this single moniker, rather like Liverpool or Arsenal. They think for a minute and, grinning, kindly volunteer one of their own: "How about Rochdale Nil?"

We also don't have a nickname, not a proper one anyway. We forgo anything vaguely poetic, like, for example, the Bluebirds or the Tigers, and we think commemorating industrial legacy is for cissies, as in the Iron, the Blades or the Gunners. Once more, pragmatism rules. We are 'the Dale', which is good because it rhymes with 'ale'. When we're winning, we sing that it's up with the former, and down (the neck) with the latter.

Over the last few weeks, passive supporters may be under the impression that we've finally acquired an addendum to the club's name. A 'P' has started to appear regularly after the word 'Rochdale'. We didn't ask for a P, please Bob, but we keep getting one all the same. 'P' stands for postponement. Five home matches have been called off already this season and after the postponement of last Saturday's game against Carlisle United, we are left with *six* games in hand on the league leaders, Chesterfield.

Spotland has never been the fabled 'bowling green' of which some clubs can boast. On match days, it has often looked like the day after the tractor convention of the night before. Back in 1978-79, the pitch was unplayable for an incredible three months and most seasons are punctuated by an unscheduled midwinter break. Historically, this hasn't been too much of a problem, and might have been a blessing; if we couldn't play, we couldn't lose! We now have a decent team that - at the level we play - is known for its passing game. Obviously, we can't pass the ball through a mudbath, and when a game is called off now, we take the more positive view that if we don't play, we can't win.

It emerged this week that the pitch has been damaged over the years through using the 'wrong kind of sand': take note, Sir Alex Ferguson. A lorry-load of the right kind (kiln-dried, apparently) has been delivered and 25 tons scattered over the surface. Bucket and spades are selling well in the club shop.

The club has worked valiantly to avoid postponements. Covers, special hot-air balloons and tractors have been hired. A group of officials and supporters even worked on the pitch through the night last Saturday. In a week in which Valentine's Day fell, surely this defines true love, or madness. The next step might be to scour the town for anyone of Red Indian heritage prepared to do a rain dance in reverse.

Paradoxically, the pitch has improved over the past few years, though the weather has worsened. Hearsay once had it that if we were due to be without a few key players for a certain match, the groundsman was sent out with a full bladder to 'tend' the pitch: match off. After all the pitch-improvement measures, he might need a few of his pals to achieve the same effect, should the rain abate.

Like most Rochdale supporters, I'm extremely sceptical on the day of a home match. I have taught myself to expect that it will be postponed and, instead, I'll be trailing around B & Q measuring curtain poles and discussing whether the handles on the kitchen cupboards would look better in that 'veined' effect or just normal white. Oh Lord, stop the rain.

Aside from the downpours and Rochdale Hornets clomping all over the same playing surface, this issue is really a ghost from the past tapping us on the shoulder. While we've radically improved the ground and the team, the pitch is a legacy from the dark days when paying wages and mere survival was more pressing than a few bags of grass seed. It's no longer so simple, and the pitch needs more than £100,000 of renovation. If we see the chairman with feathers in his hair, dancing backwards around the centre spot, we'll know why.

Saturday, 17 February 2001
Torquay United 1 Rochdale 0

Rochdale slumped to only their fifth defeat in 28 league games with a disappointing performance at Plainmoor.

A first half goal from midfielder Kevin Hill gave the home side three points in their struggle against relegation. "I'm aware that many fans stayed in Torquay for the weekend and I'm only sorry we were not able to make it a more memorable one," said Parkin.

Tuesday, 20 February 2001
Rochdale 0 York City 1

A defeat against bottom-of-the-table York left Rochdale without a goal in four games. It was only York's third away win in 16 league matches. "York came here and made it very difficult for us by putting men behind the ball," said Parkin.

Rochdale had most of the possession, but York had the better chances. Their winner came in the second half when midfielder Scott Emmers latched on to a mistake by Keith Hill. Rochdale had lost Clive Platt and Tony Ford earlier in the game with calf injuries.

Thursday, 22 February 2001

The Football League issued charges of malpractice against Chesterfield. These included the illegal payment of cash bonuses to players; issuing falsified contracts; the non-payment of transfer fees; and falsely declaring attendance figures.

DIEHARD FANS LOSE THEIR WAY
IN SMOKE FROM BIG GUNS

(*The Times*, Saturday, 24 February 2001)

The streetlight was on at the bottom of his drive, but Tony's face shone even brighter. He looked out of breath too, as if he'd spent 10 minutes running up and down the stairs. "It's 1-0, " he said as he opened the front door. He smiled broadly, and for a moment I thought he was going to do a jig.

"Good," I said, except I didn't know what he was talking about. Tony is a neighbour and I'd called on him to organise the rota for collecting our kids from school. As we walked down his hallway, he elaborated: "Bergkamp has just scored." Bergkamp, 1-0, suddenly it all made sense. In the front room, his family was crowded around the television. Arsenal were playing Lyon in the Champions' League and they were cheering them on because they were an English club.

As I stood there, between the propped-up bikes and piles of shoes, I realised that something significant had just happened in my life. I had forgotten Arsenal were playing, and, more to the point, I didn't care that I had. In itself, this might not appear a momentous over-sight, but I'm the bloke that can recall – in worryingly precise detail – line-ups, goalscorers, aggregate scores and goal times from all manner of matches played over the past 25 years. That I should forget a Champions' League match is evidence of a monumental change of outlook.

I trudged back up the street and began to muse: am I still a 'football' man? My self-image has been formed largely by my adoration of the sport. Football and me go back a long way, to grandad and dad playing three-and-your-in with me on the park, to *Hot Shot Hamish* and Jimmy Hill, to Esso football coins and curly perms. Football informs me, and through it I identify myself as passionate, enraptured by the collision of brutality and beauty. I also mull over the inventory of the game: statistics, match programmes, autographs - football crazy, football daft.

Disenchantment has taken a few years to fully settle in, but I can no longer feign that I want to keep a finger-hold on the sport I see reflected back at me through the media. Top-flight football is true to the stereotype. It is, by turns, a soap opera and a cartoon, populated by the self-serving and self-aggrandising. Viewed as a branch of showbusiness, it has indisputable qualities, but this Vaudevillian spectacle has found the passive, undiscerning audience it deserves.

Amid all the fuss, the sport itself seems a side issue, thrown down to legitimise the media narrative. Either side of the hyperbole, a football match remains much the same as ever, whatever the level it is played. The challenge – and I can no longer rise to it – is to divorce the celebrity from the eternal thrill of pass, tackle, shoot and score.

Elsewhere, down the professional ranks, I sense a quickening of the pulse, and a new intensity forming. My love of Rochdale has not waned, for instance, but burgeoned under the slow suffocation of a world where Manchester United play Valencia and Panathinaikos and Sturm Graz again and again until we're red in the face and howling at the moon. If you don't care about Manchester United et al, the greater the commotion, the greater the irritation. Perversely, it also hones the partisanship we feel for our own clubs. We feel annexed and our sovereignty impeached, so we drive the flag deeper into the ground.

The top clubs have made it easy for us to disown them. The media coverage suggests they play seven nights a week, so, if we miss a particular game, rest assured; there's another due very soon. The constant changes of personnel at Premiership clubs and the vogue for foreign players have dissipated their appeal. I had a fondness for the old Arsenal back four, but if I can no longer name the new incumbents, why should I care about the team they play for? At Rochdale, the team barely changes from the start of the season until the end. We know where we are then, and they have names we can remember, like Tony, Phil and Wayne.

Most authentic football fans are, by nature, reactionary, and this also fuels disaffection. Basically, we feel browbeaten by the football machine. The more PLC FC is offered, the more vehement the rejection. No one should fret or worry that they have forgotten a midweek fixture between Arsenal and Lyon. When people ask, tell them you didn't turn your back on football; football turned its back on you.

Saturday, 24 February 2001
Rochdale 1 Shrewsbury Town 7

Rochdale, boasting one of the most parsimonious defences in the whole of English football, suffered the worst home defeat in the club's history.

In the previous 14 home league matches, they had conceded just 14 goals while, on their travels, Shrewsbury were the division's lowest goalscorers with a meagre eight in 16 matches.

Steve Parkin had rearranged his team to accommodate three centre backs, with Simon Coleman brought in to play alongside Mark Monington and Dave Bayliss. The new defensive system failed in the second minute when teenager Luke Rodgers scored for Shrewsbury.

Graham Lancashire, making his first start of the season, headed Rochdale level with a deserved equaliser but within two minutes Shrewsbury regained the lead through an own goal, deflected into the net by Kevin Kyle, though Andrew Tretton claimed it. Straight after the interval, Matt Redmile scored from a corner before Ryan Lowe made it 4-1, 10 minutes later.

Wayne Evans was taken off on a stretcher after colliding with Rodgers and this caused further chaos in the Rochdale defence. Rodgers capitalised with goals in the 71st and 76th minutes. He celebrated by removing his shirt and was sent off. He had been booked earlier after a tussle with Dave Bayliss.

The rout was completed in the final minute when Steve Jagielka scored from the penalty spot. After the game, Neil Edwards slumped on to the pitch and did not leave the field with the other players. Several fans ran on and comforted the club captain.

It was Shrewsbury's biggest away win in the Football League and the first time they had scored seven goals in more than 26 years. The defeat was Rochdale's worst since losing 8-0 at Leyton Orient in October 1987.

Lee McLaughlan of the *Shropshire Star* wrote: 'Fans will be able to say 'I was there' for many years to come. The action was unrelenting and resembled one of those games your grandfather used to talk about.'

Steve Parkin said: "I hold my hands up and take full responsibility for changing the team around, but, to be truthful, too many players had an off day and personal mistakes cost us dearly."

Before the game, he had written in his programme notes: 'Our defensive record is still one of the best in the division, and we should take encouragement from that.' Despite the result, Rochdale had 28 shots, 17 of them on target, a ratio that would normally translate into a comfortable win.

Rochdale's previous worst home defeat had been 6-0 against three different teams - Plymouth Argyle in 1973, Wrexham in 1936 and Barrow in 1932.

Tuesday, 27 February 2001

The home match against Plymouth Argyle was postponed again because of a waterlogged pitch.

Wednesday, 28 February 2001

Dean Howell, an ex-Notts County trainee, joined Rochdale on a month's loan from Crewe Alexandra. He had been unable to secure a first-team place at Gresty Road, making just one appearance as a substitute.

Also in Rochdale...

February 2001

* Rochdale Council was awarded a £10 million grant from the Neighbourhood Renewal Fund to tackle problems relating to crime, unemployment, health and education.
* The outbreak of foot-and-mouth disease caused farms around Rochdale to be sealed off, animal sanctuaries to close and the suspension of livestock markets.

* Ted Stevens, a 61-year-old gas-fitter from Newbold, pushed his pal, Pat Farrell, to safety after a stolen car was driven at them. Mr Stevens took the full impact of the vehicle and was killed immediately.

Eight

Wheezing and Coughing

Thursday, 1 March 2001

Steve Parkin's bid of £100,000 for Stoke City striker Paul Connor was turned down.

Thursday, 1 March 2001

Steve Parkin appeared at a fans' forum held at Spotland just five days after the humiliating 7-1 defeat. The club, as a show of solidarity, assembled an impressive support cast including the chairman, directors, chief executive, groundsman, youth staff − in fact, it seemed the whole club was standing shoulder-to-shoulder in the midst of a crisis.

HOME IS WHERE THE HURT IS
THANKS TO REAL SHREWSBURY
(*The Times*, Saturday, 3 March 2001)

Seven bloody one. In case you missed it, Rochdale suffered their worst home league defeat of all-time last Saturday. Seven bloody one. Shrewsbury Town, in their all-white strip, might well have been Real Madrid such was their breathtaking grandeur. We were pasted, snotted, mauled, turned over, hammered.

Four days earlier we had also lost at home, to York City, who were, at that point, bottom of the Nationwide League. These aren't merely bad days at the office; we've just thrown a lighted cigarette into the waste paper bin and left the building. That burning smell is our season, our hopes and dreams, going up in smoke.

In 26 years as a Rochdale supporter, disappointment and embarrassment have dogged me, but I have never felt as humiliated as I did

141

last weekend. It hurt me in that place somewhere between heart and brain that only women ("I need more space"), illness or death can usually reach. It left me unable to sleep. When I did finally drift off, I was woken by itchy, gritty, black thoughts falling like caustic rain. I felt unclean, like I'd done something unspeakably bad the night before; blood on my knuckles, a bruise over my eye, something here doesn't add up - seven plus one equals torture.

Thankfully, no one uttered platitudes like 'It's only a game' as I made my way grumpily through the rest of the weekend. They kept a respectful distance. I couldn't even yield to the defence measure of laughing it off, pretending I didn't care. It cut too deep. I mean, 7-1 – at home, to a team near the bottom of the division. No one loses 7-1 at home. No one. Except Rochdale.

Many have asked what happened, as if I was at the scene of an accident. They expect me to tell them we had five players sent off, or the goalkeeper (and the substitute goalkeeper) was knocked out. If only there were such mitigating circumstances. Basically – and it really is this dull – our manager, Steve Parkin, made radical changes to a game-plan that has kept us in the promotion frame all season. He went from 4-4-2 to 5-2-3 and, boy, did it 'bugger up the job.'

He also introduced the stalwart, Simon Coleman, into the heart of a defence that had hitherto been performing perfectly well. Poor Simon. He has the pallor of mashed potato and the tearful expression of a boy left at the workhouse, waving his parents a last goodbye. As he lumbered hopelessly among the nippy Shrewsbury strikers, several Rochdale supporters pleaded with the bench to hurl a towel on to the pitch.

After the match, I turned to the club's websites for solace. I wanted to read the message boards and share the pain. At times like this, you want to be with your own, among family, flesh and blood, blue and white. After a few minutes I stabbed at the 'off' button on my computer. The postings were a roll-call of vindictive, gloating remarks made by fans of other clubs. What sadness permeates the lives of people who, on hearing that a team as inoffensive as Rochdale has lost 7-1, prompts them to gleefully stab at their keyboard and write: 'Seems like the rot has really set in – ha, ha, ha, ha, ha'?

On Tuesday, we were due to play Plymouth Argyle at home but the game was postponed suspiciously early. We have a few injuries in the squad, but the rumour around town was that the physio was giving intensive treatment to several broken hearts. Parkin said it was the worst weekend of his life in football and apologised to supporters. He rather spoiled his conciliatory tone by claiming there were some positive aspects of the performance, which is like saying the handrails on the *Titanic* shone beautifully in the moonlight as the ship went down.

By midweek, I'd recovered fully and managed to put my life and my football club into perspective. I even regretted some of the after-match melodrama. I am willing to put it down to a blip, a freak occurrence, like when we had snow in June in Rochdale. Really, I can't do much else, because no matter how badly I'm mistreated, I love the club and forgiveness is a tenet of the condition, whether I like it or not.

In the midst of pain, and the aftershock, I realised that my love was not limitless. Many times, drunk on romance, I have declared to friends that I would pay to watch the grass grow at Spotland, that a strange magic rose from the ground and it was almost irrelevant how we played and at what level. I know now, that a heart is only so big.

* At the start of the season I was determined not to use the column as a platform for my thoughts on the inner-workings of the club – team selection, assessing the manager's tactical acumen etc. The series had to ensnare readers from all quarters, and I considered this nitty-gritty to be indulgent and uninteresting to the general reader.

Manifestly, I am a fan before I am a writer, because I couldn't resist the opportunity to criticise and stray to areas I had mentally cordoned off. I didn't regret breaking my own code because I saw this bloodletting as an integral element of being a fan. Besides, 7-1!

Saturday, 3 March 2001
Southend United 3 Rochdale 0

A promising start was marred when Phil Whelan gave Southend the lead after 30 minutes. Paul Ware was ruled to have fouled Tesfaye Bramble and David Lee added another from the penalty spot.

In the second half, Lee made it 3-0 to record Rochdale's fourth consecutive defeat. The misery was compounded 10 minutes before the end when referee Paul Alcock dismissed Neil Edwards for handling outside the penalty area. Dave Flitcroft deputised.

"I feel like my world has fallen in," said Edwards. "I don't like conceding goals in training, so to concede seven in one game and get sent off in the next has hurt me pretty badly."

Rochdale had conceded 10 goals in their past two matches, a total that had previously taken 15 league matches to reach. They also slipped out of a play-off spot for the first time in six months. "We're going through one of those spells when nothing seems to be going right," said Steve Parkin. "Now is the time for everyone to dig deep."

Tuesday, 6 March 2001
Hartlepool United 1 Rochdale 1

A goal by Tony Lormor four minutes from the end denied Rochdale a win against Hartlepool, who extended their unbeaten run to 16 matches.

Graham Lancashire had given Rochdale the lead with a header in the first half after Gary Jones had earlier seen a 35-yard effort disallowed for pushing on the edge of the penalty area.

Lee Todd was sent off for two bookable offences. The second was given for dissent after he argued that a back pass to Edwards had been made with his knee, and not his foot. The referee later rescinded the card and admitted he had made a mistake. "I saw the ref immediately after the game and he admitted he had got it totally and utterly wrong," revealed Steve Parkin.

The draw ended Rochdale's losing streak of four matches. "The players showed the tenacity and the spirit of old and were bitterly disappointed not to pick up all three points," said Parkin.

Kevin Townson made a promising debut in an attack missing the injured Clive Platt and Tony Ellis.

Wednesday, 7 March 2001

Three Rochdale players were notified of forthcoming suspensions – Dave Bayliss (two matches) for 10 bookings, Lee Todd (one match) for five bookings and Neil Edwards (one match) for his sending off.

Friday, 9 March 2001

A press conference was held at 10am to announce the signing of the most expensive player in the club's history, Paul Connor, a £150,000 capture from Stoke City.

The 22-year-old striker was born in Bishop Auckland and started his career as a trainee at Middlesbrough. He joined Stoke on loan at the end of the 1998-99 season and scored two goals in three games. He was given a free transfer by Middlesbrough and joined Stoke permanently in June 1998, after also spending time on loan at Gateshead.

He scored 10 goals in 23 full appearances for Stoke, but was on the fringes of their first-team squad, appearing as a substitute on 25 occasions. He spent a three-month loan period at Cambridge United where he scored five goals in 14 matches.

Rochdale's other record transfers in modern times were: Clive Platt from Walsall, September 1999 (£100,000); Andy Flounders from Scunthorpe United, July 1991 (£80,000); Mark Gavin from Bolton Wanderers, August 1987 (£25,000); Les Lawrence from Aldershot, August 1984 (£17,500); and Alan Weir from Sunderland, June 1979 (£12,000).

ROCHDALE SEEK TO POSTPONE
RECKONING TO ELEVENTH HOUR
(*The Times*, Saturday,10 March 2001)

The phone rang. I was in the garden, basking in the sunshine, lost to reverie. It was a football magazine, asking me to predict Rochdale's final position of the 2000-2001 season. "Eleventh," I said, confidently. "I think you'll find we've already pre-booked it!"

I didn't really think we'd finish eleventh. I was dreaming of promotion. We had a reasonable squad, and, besides, anything seems plausible in July, when the world is warm and languid and hope glistens in the heat.

I settled on 11th for specific reasons. This was actually the lowest I envisaged us finishing. It served as a safety measure, because, in all likelihood, we'd finish higher and I could affect surprise and pretend to be mightily pleased with our season.

We lost just twice in our opening 17 league matches and I became slightly embarrassed by this public declaration of a faint heart. My prediction seemed wan and faithless while we camped defiantly in an automatic promotion position. The Dale we're going up, and now you'd better believe us – even the cautious, pessimistic bloke at the back with a degree in reverse psychology.

In the midst of our run, the unbelievers among Rochdale's townsfolk gathered like half-starved carrion crows: "You'll soon come unstuck," they mocked. "You always do!" They knew, like we all did, of the infamous Rochdale tradition. We are the marathon man, a mile clear of the field with the stadium and glory in sight. As we wave to the crowd, our shoelaces work themselves loose. Crash, we hit the shale. A blur of legs passes by. We crawl, wheezing and coughing, to fall in an undignified heap over the finishing line - and, ladies and gentlemen, in 11th place, Rochdale.

The metaphorical shoelaces came undone last month. We have collected three points out of a possible 21. Additionally, we have scored just two goals in those seven matches, had two players sent off, suffered a swathe of injuries and lost 7-1 against Shrewsbury Town. We are now ninth and the position two places below beckons.

With abject timing, the club has just held a fans' forum. The chairman, manager, groundsman, bar manager – in fact everyone connected with the club – was wheeled out. Steve Parkin, our manager, entered the room like a man on a mission. He is, like all football managers, a mixture of flintiness and charm; in plainspeak, a little tough nut. I fully expected our abysmal run to be deemed a 'blip' but we had other subjects to raise: the duff signings he has made this season and our poor home form, for example. The microphone was passed to a bloke in a replica Rochdale shirt: "Steve, why did you shave your 'tache off? It's just that ever since you did, we've been bobbins." This wasn't Steve in the Lion's Den, but Steve among the frisky, playful kittens.

The wrath was saved instead for the bar manager; we know our priorities in Rochdale. "How come it takes 20 minutes to get a pint before the game?" The bar manager, appropriately enough, was slumped against the bar as he spoke. He embarked on a long explanation, only to be interrupted by another thirsty fan. "You want to get one of those machines like they have at Blackburn that lets you pull six pints at once."

The 7-1 defeat, a lack of pace in the team, a goalkeeper palpably too small for the job, a shortage of ball-players – surely enough topics for discussion. Next question: "I got in the ground early last week and there was a massive queue to get a drink. You want to get more staff on." Haven't we been here before? Back to the big guy at the bar: "You're joking aren't you? There's no one in the ground until quarter to three!" He could support his assertion. "Look, we've got CCTV, and, if you like, I can go and get the video and show you who was in the bar at 1.30pm at the last home game. One old lady, that's all. One old lady, sitting on her own in the corner. Do you want to see the video?" The questioner didn't need time to think. "No, I'll leave it, thanks."

Little Dave, my next door-but-one neighbour in the stand, asked Steve Parkin the most germane question of the evening. "Steve, what can you do to pick the fans up after that 7-1 defeat?" Parkin rolled his head from side to side, pursed his lips. "All I can say is that it hurt, it really hurt. We're all in this together and we've got to pull each other through. I can tell you one thing though, that scoreline has been tattooed on to the brain of every one of my players." There was nothing more that needed adding after that. We'd heard what we wanted to hear.

* Once more, I took the opportunity to take a swipe at Steve Parkin. The 7-1 defeat and loss of form brought to prominence feelings I had held all season, even while we were winning matches. I was able, in a few short paragraphs (and rather slyly, I concede), to express my dissatisfaction. I had opened a direct dialogue with Rochdale fans that would run until the end of the season.

I'm sure the general reader had little concern about the stature of our goalkeeper or our infuriatingly dismal home form, but I could no longer remain equitable and 'above' the issue. I was, fundamentally, exercising my prerogative as a supporter to pick the team and have a moan about the manager.

Before these post-7-1 pieces, many Rochdale fans assumed I was 'in league' with the club; some even asked whether officials gave their approval before articles were published. I obviously have an enormous loyalty to the club, but I define 'the club' through its supporters, directors and administration staff; those that do not form football's itinerant community of managers, players and coaches.

I hold approriate respect for Parkin, but I have no great allegiance to him, or the playing staff and coaches. They are professional men, paid to do a job, and they will all eventually leave the club. Less than three years ago, Parkin was trying to inflict defeat upon Rochdale, as both a player and, later, manager of Mansfield Town. He will do the same again should he move on and his new club play against Rochdale.

Football is a messy business. It sets men against men, on the pitch and off it too. Professionals are locked into a world where your colleague covets your place, every spoken word is a half-truth or compromise, and the next tackle could be your last. The game is not really beautiful. At every turn, in every game, there is a decision that invokes bravery or cowardice, enterprise or fear. There is no shading or concealment, or the option of artifice and deception. A footballer has to believe in an absolute right to the ball, without fear of the damage he might cause himself or his opponent in collecting it. He plays for the team, but he also plays for himself. He has no sentiment. He can't afford time worrying about the player whose place he had taken or whose leg he had injured.

Inevitably, the men who thrive in this environment, and especially those that survive and become managers, are strong-willed, aggressive, savvy and autocratic. They seldom pass through football's crude and primitive system without acquiring despotic tendencies and several neuroses, not to mention a mercurial temperament. In short, it is a breed apart and happiest among its own kind.

As I sat among supporters at the forum and looked at the stern, implacable faces of Parkin's wall of pros and ex-pros, I sensed, once more, football's innate sense of superiority, a swagger and imperviousness that sees drabs of criticism deflected like rain from an umbrella.

Parkin had clearly built up a store of goodwill through the early-season form, so there was no agenda for a lynching. If there had been, it would still have taken a brave man to cross the divide between ourselves and the top-table where this squad of flinty, hobnailed, thick-skinned hired-hands was assembled.

Did we really want to cross it anyway, when, paradoxically, we were in awe of this shellac of professionalism – and, indeed, had a reluctant admiration of it? They were, after all, and despite the 7-1 defeat, making a much better job of running our club than previous legionnaires that had populated Spotland over the years.

We didn't have to like them, or brood when they paid lip service to the questions that revealed our anxiety. If they got the job done, that was enough

Saturday, 10 March 2001
Rochdale 0 Kidderminster Harriers 0

Kidderminster defended in depth to steal a point from lacklustre Rochdale, playing with one striker and five in midfield.

Paul Connor showed a willingness to run at defenders on his debut but found himself against a wall of red and white.

"To be fair to him, Jan [Molby, the Kidderminster manager] apologised for his tactics after the match. He told me it had been important to steady the ship and not concede a goal," said Parkin.

It was Rochdale's eighth game without a win, but results elsewhere took them back into the play-off zone.

Tuesday, 13 March 2001

Rochdale played a friendly at Castleton Gabriels to raise funds for the local side. Backroom staff Andy Thorpe, Jamie Hoyland and Keith Hicks starred in a 1-0 win. Hicks, incidentally, played alongside his son, Graham, Rochdale's young professional, in the second half.

LOST FOR WORDS IN THE PRESENCE
OF MY HERO PEN PAL
(*The Times*, Saturday, 17 March 2001)

Red-faced and puffed-out, Paul Connor sat down in search of air in the packed social club. Kids were loitering, autograph books at the ready. "Can you sign this for us, Paul?" Breathe in, breathe out: "Course I can."

Paul Connor had just made his debut for Rochdale against Kidderminster Harriers. He cost the club a record fee of £150,000 from Stoke City and his after-match civic duties included meeting the man from *The Times*. "I've not played a first-team game for some time. I'm knackered," he said, by way of explanation. He might also have mentioned the sodden pitch - the players had struggled like flies stuck in a bucket of wallpaper paste.

Connor is a striker, and the natives liked what they saw. He's quick, wholehearted and willing to turn and run for goal. He wanted the ball played to his feet, but it was launched mainly at his shoulders or a couple of yards over his head. As he stared incredulously at one 'pass' sailing by, one of the faithful yelled: "Don't worry Paul, you'll soon get used to it!"

He had signed for the club just the day before and was still learning the names of his team-mates. While we spoke, I thought of what Rochdale meant to me, and what it meant to him. I had 26 years of history with this club; he had 24 hours. In that time, he had done something I would never do - worn the blue shirt that is invested with so much worth, not to mention romance and passion. I wanted to take him on to the pitch and tell him the detail of every match of every season. I'd point to the stands, show him where I'd stood as a boy, the people I'd been among – my grandad, my dad, friends from school, friends from work. I'd tell him about other players that had worn the shirt – the good, the bad, and the useless: how much time do you have, Paul?

Obviously, I didn't do this. He's a professional. We have to trust footballers, like we do doctors and dentists. They know the magnitude of their job and that we acquiesce to their greater skill. We shouldn't need to burden them with a history lesson to goad them to exertion and focus their craft.

After I left his company, I realised I had met Paul without a sprig of anxiety and I recalled a long-forgotten trauma involving another Rochdale centre forward, Bob Mountford. Bob played for us back in the mid-1970s. Among a team of toilers and bruisers, each playing and looking as pale and ghostly as the other, Mountford was flesh and blood, meat and bone. He was tall and broad-shouldered with thick curly black hair - the whitey with an afro, a superfly with attitude.

His speciality was scoring from corners. The ball was dropped regularly into the middle of the penalty area and he careered recklessly through bodies to slam his forehead on to it: goal. As he disappeared under joyous team-mates, they had to pick their way through the debris of Mountford's barely-legal challenge - the shattered shin pads, ripped shirts, whimpering defenders, St John Ambulance staff, trainers passing around smelling salts.

Inevitably, he moved on, but a sensitive 12-year-old began a correspondence with his hero. In the letter in which Mountford revealed that roast duck and orange sauce was his favourite meal, he closed with: 'I might see you at Rochdale at one of the night games (don't be afraid of introducing yourself if you see me, then we can have a chat).' Oh, God.

A few months later, I was sitting in the Main Stand when

Mountford, in tight nylon trousers and a woolly tartan jacket, climbed the stairs. The stand, as usual, was almost empty. He had the choice of hundreds of wooden seats. *Hundreds.* He sat next to me. My dad asked if I was going to tell him who I was.

"No," I said, and begged him to keep quiet.

"But you've been writing to him."

"No."

"He won't mind having a chat."

"Please, dad, please don't say anything."

I couldn't bring myself to even look in Mountford's direction. When we attacked the goal to my left, which was the side where he was sitting, I watched without moving my head so that our eyes had no possibility of meeting. I was too nervous of saying something I'd regret. I was, in real life, a quiet, mundane and tense kid, where, in a letter, I could be passably engaging. I didn't want Mountford, the most perfect human being on earth – a brave, skilful footballer, *and* with the humility and decency to write to starstruck kids – to meet the real me. At least I spoke to Paul Connor and looked him in the eye. I must be growing up.

Saturday, 17 March 2001
Chesterfield 1 Rochdale 1

Paul Connor scored his first goal for the club as Rochdale mounted a dogged display against the league leaders.

Chesterfield equalised with just a minute remaining when John Howard drilled home a low cross from Rob Edwards.

Rochdale's young goalkeeper Matthew Gilks made his debut because of Neil Edwards' one-match suspension and was praised by Steve Parkin. "Everybody at the club was delighted with his contribution," he said.

The draw meant Rochdale slipped two places, to 10th, their lowest position since the start of the season. They were also at the bottom of the division's 'current form league' with three defeats and three draws in their past six matches.

Fans were surprised to find the kiosks at Saltergate selling Balti pies and called for their inclusion on the menu at Spotland.

Friday, 23 March 2001
Rochdale 1 Cheltenham Town 1

Play-off rivals Cheltenham took an early lead with a goal by Neil Grayson after he latched on to a rebound when Neil Edwards had saved.

A defensive misunderstanding between Michael Duff and goalkeeper Steve Book allowed Paul Connor to collect the ball and score an equaliser, minutes before the final whistle. "It's a point we probably didn't deserve," admitted Steve Parkin. "There were a lot of players with chins on their chests, not doing their jobs properly."

DOCTOR'S ORDERS JUST RUBBING SALTERGATE INTO THE WOUNDS
(*The Times*, Saturday, 24 March 2001)

Four novels, two remote controls (telly and CD player), one mobile phone, three magazines, several pieces of fruit; Chesterfield 1 Rochdale 1.

I should have been there last Saturday, Chesterfield that is, but I was ill in bed, flat on my back – on doctor's orders. Two days earlier, my weekly five-a-side jaunt had finished prematurely when a shot deflected into my eye. Whoosh, everything went red.

The impact had burst blood vessels and, fearing I'd also damaged the retina, I was told to spend three days in bed. The specialist thought (and the squeamish might want to bale out here…) that blood and various syrupy bits might otherwise leak into the eye.

So, for the first time in my life – and I do appreciate how lucky I've been – I was ill, properly ill, while Rochdale were playing a match. Obviously, I had one eye on the score (my good one) and at half-time we were winning 1-0. The phone went:

"Heard the score? I told you they'd do it for you."

If only I hadn't been told to avoid sudden, abrupt movements. Otherwise, I'd have laughed heartily at this point. Rochdale have seldom done anything 'for me'. They are a club of perpetual heartaches and headaches. I've been on their metaphorical sickbed for 26 years. Appropriately, we lost the lead in the final minute. We've now gone nine matches without a win.

As I lay there, surrounded by the paraphernalia of sickness, I realised the weekend would remain forever linked with a largely inconsequential third division match. I'd remember, of course, the anxious drive to the hospital and the doctor's sigh as he peered into my eye, but the Blu-Tack fastening it to my memory would be Chesterfield 1 Rochdale 1.

Other people have songs that evoke an incident that might be happy, sad or cataclysmic. The dots that, if joined, form the outline of my life comprise a handful of Rochdale matches played down the years. They mean nothing to anyone except the bloke with a piece of lint taped across his eye.

Rochdale 2 York City 0 was the end of my first long-term relationship. She'd broken the news a few days earlier. She'd met this bloke at work and she'd never felt so happy and joyous and 'in love' before. She was sorry, but she had to be with him: goodbye. Rochdale won, but I was hurting so much I felt nothing as the ball twice hit the net. I just sat there, dazed, and dad, out of respect, hardly moved either. Someone still cared.

Rochdale 2 Crewe Alexandra 1. Grandad had recently suffered a 'breakdown' or a 'stroke', the doctors weren't quite sure. He now walked with a shuffle and stared into space. He thought it was 1958, but it was actually 1978 and we'd taken him to Spotland to give my gran some respite. We scored and fans on all sides spilled down the terraces in glee.

"We've scored," I said, gripping his arm. "We've scored."

"Have we?"

Unfortunately, it isn't possible to hold sway over which matches the sub-conscious mind attaches to certain memories. I should, for example, recall who we played when my two sons were born, but I'd need to check old programmes to find out. Maybe some incidents, life or death for instance, are of such magnitude that they cannot run parallel to football; I'm not convinced though.

Several matches have stayed with me although they do not relate to a particular episode, but more a 'feeling'. They form a portal to a vividly recalled past. Rochdale drew 1-1 at Blackpool while I was on holiday in Devon. I think of the scoreline, then I think of being 15, and walking down a dusty road, kicking at the ground in my trainers, piling the towels and wind-breaks into my uncle's camper van and setting off to the beach.

A particular match can be like the touch paper on a firework display, igniting a series of memories largely unconnected to football. We lost away at Cardiff. We were driving through the Yorkshire dales when I heard the score. The garden of the hotel where we were staying was full of apple trees heavy with fruit. Dolly Parton was on the telly. We ate in a restaurant that had old photographs of racing cars on the walls. Only by first thinking of Cardiff City 2, Rochdale 1, does any of this come back to me.

When I recall these matches, I'm also reminded of my team's propensity to rain on my parade. Many otherwise happy days have been spoiled by scorelines and goal-flashes from Darlington, Colchester et al. Suddenly, a warm day can turn chilly, a good mood sour, and caring so much about your team feels more than a bit cock-eyed.

* I did ponder whether revealing details of my eye injury qualified as self-indulgence, but, after much thought, I considered missing a game through illness or injury a circumstance that would, at some point, beset most people.

Monday, 26 March 2001

Andy Turner, a 25-year-old left-sided midfielder, joined Rochdale on a month's loan from Rotherham United. He had started his career at Tottenham Hotspur and made a handful of appearances in the Premiership, before moving to Portsmouth, Crystal Palace and, finally, Rotherham.

Tuesday, 27 March 2001

Hull City 3 Rochdale 2

Goals from Gary Brabin and Mike Edwards gave Hull a deserved half-time lead. A victory looked assured when a Rodney Rowe penalty extended the lead to 3-0.

A spirited fight-back by Rochdale was inspired by goals from Dave Bayliss and Paul Connor, who had been the sole striker until the introduction of Clive Platt in the second half.

Rochdale had played 11 matches without a win, picking up six points from a possible 33.

Wednesday, 28 March 2001

Rochdale's Welsh contingent, Neil Edwards and Wayne Evans, signed new contracts to keep them at Spotland until at least the end of the 2003-2004 season.

Thursday, 29 March 2001

Rochdale terrace hero and window cleaner, Stephen Murray, better known as 'Moggy', announced a sponsored walk, carrying his ladder to Rochdale's next four away matches, at Blackpool, Macclesfield, Barnet and Plymouth.

He was raising money for GEM, an appeal for a specialist research centre into genetic diseases, and the club's Tractor Fund.

Moggy told the *Rochdale Observer* he had seen his first game at Spotland against Hull City in 1964 and was candid about his former misdemeanours: "I've been a football hooligan in the past and the trouble seems to be getting worse again. I want to show the hooligans they can't win," he said.

ROCHDALE TALISMAN MANAGES
TO STRAIN THE BOND OF TRUST

(*The Times*, Saturday, 31 March 2001)

Heads are shaken ruefully, and we're all doing those tight-lipped smiles that transmit the message: 'Oh dear.' Down by the snack bar, or on the way back from the toilets, some are even conversing in the staccato grunts that form the international language of football supporters: "Not so good, eh?" "No. Crap." Shake of the head, sigh, eyes lifted skywards.

Rochdale, after opening the season with just three defeats in their first 23 league games, are in the midst of their annual bid to avoid promotion. In two months we have slipped from fourth to 10th and have gone 11 matches without a win, during which time we have suffered our worst-ever home defeat. We are currently five points adrift of a play-off position and home attendances have fallen by almost a third.

Despite the poor run and the fractured, aimless football, our manager, Steve Parkin, has been largely free from censure. He was fortunate to arrive at Spotland as the stadium was completely rebuilt and the directors sanctioned the largest squad and biggest transfer kitty in the club's history. Parkin, therefore, is bound up with Rochdale's reinvention. The belief among fans is that he is the talisman; if he goes, the club falls back into the dark ages.

In the match programme for the last home game, against Cheltenham Town, the club appealed for local businesses to 'sponsor a youth player'. They have promised to share a portion of any transfer fee they might later receive for these players with the sponsor. In effect, we are invited to play a more substantive role in the club's administration. During the game, another dreary 1-1 draw, there was more than enough downtime to consider the offer. They were asking us to trust them to find promising young players, school them, select them for the first-team, and sell them at a profit.

Although this, in fact, happened with our former goalkeeper, Stephen Bywater (now Shaka Hislop's understudy at West Ham United), this was largely because Stephen's dad is a member of our backroom staff. In the past five years, only one player, Dave Bayliss, has graduated from the youth team to the first-team. On this evidence, my money stays in the building society.

Trust is a fundamental issue. When we take on support of a football club, we have to learn to trust. At Rochdale, I trust the directors to spend money prudently and look after the club's long-term well-being. I trust the groundsman to take care of the pitch (you can tell by his body language that he's an obsessive). I trust my fellow supporters to care deeply and passionately.

I'm not sure, any more, whether our trust in the manager is absolute. Supporters will accede to a manager's greater grasp on the vagaries of 4-5-1 or 3-5-2 formations and shop-speak like 'working the channels' but, believe me, they know their basics. When these are not upheld, they become anxious. They know it doesn't make sense to play right-footed players on the left; or sign a red-hot six ft two in striker and not play wingers; or include, at centre half, a seasoned pro woefully short of pace and confidence. Parkin did all this this against Cheltenham.

Steve Parkin, like all football managers, has gathered around him a coterie drawn from ex-team-mates and allies from his former clubs. These reflect back to him the world of football as he sees it. The rest of us - directors, staff and supporters (perversely, the very people who will remain at the club when he moves on) - are outsiders. We are, to Parkin and Co, 'civvies' and while we are thanked for our support and 'making a hell of a row' at Southend or wherever, they'd prefer our constituency to remain there. They certainly don't want our opinion, formed in the comfort of a seat in the stand. They've played the game, boy and man, and, in contrast, we're viewed as rather effete and terminally wrong-headed.

Unfortunately, supporters form a disparate bunch. We seldom speak with one voice. In fact, the voice that is most often heard invariably belongs to the prat in Row M or Z, serving up words of wisdom like: 'Flitcroft [our well-fed midfielder], you're a fat bastard'. At this point, Parkin springs to his feet, turns to face the crowd, and glowers. Suddenly, we're all true to the stereotype engendered by football's professional ranks.

Later, on the drive home, Parkin will wonder about the almost-silent majority. He will have heard the sighs and mutters and, despite the bluster of indifference, he'll be thinking: are they still with me?

* Rochdale, like several third division clubs, has a woeful record of developing home-grown players. Although the Spotland crowd is extremely critical, it is patient and charitable with players that progress through the club's youth network – for their first few games at least!

Unfortunately, there has been only a negligible trickle of players reaching the first-team via this route over the past 30 years. In fact, the harvest has been so insignificant that any youth policy (such that it is a 'policy') might as well not have existed.

Steve Parkin appears to have no more enthusiasm for the club's self-discovered young players than any previous Rochdale manager. He has, in two seasons, failed to promote anyone from the reserve team to the first-team, unless in strictly one-off emergencies. He prefers to take players on loan from other clubs, which he did on six occasions during the 2000-2001 season, with none of them particularly impressive.

Most Rochdale supporters recognise that the club has an implicit policy of finding its players from elsewhere, so they no longer hanker to see trainees in a first-team shirt. They also realised long ago that the club had severed its links with a local amateur football community that had, for many years, provided a supply-line of talent. Few, if any, of the current first-team squad live in Rochdale, let alone have any established links with the town.

Steve Parkin would counter that the young players, quite simply, have not been good enough to promote, while the pace, strength and skill required of the modern footballer has made it impossible for amateur players to cross the bridge to professionalism. He may be right, but when the issue is examined over a longer period of time (which he isn't able to do), it is easy to discern a policy of discrimination *against* home-grown players. Many times, as we have endured signings from Darlington, Scunthorpe et àl struggling to trap a ball or complete a two-yard pass, we have shouted for various managers to 'give the kids a chance' with the addendum, 'they can't do any worse than this lot'.

In defence of the club, signing free transfer and low-fee players has undeniably maintained stability and, over the past decade or so, kept the team away from the lower reaches of the division. Only three young players of the hundreds jettisoned have forged successful careers since leaving – Geoff Thomas, John Pemberton and Chris Lucketti. This suggests few mistakes have been made in their rigorous first-team selection process, but also shows that they have attracted few youngsters of real quality because of those released (or sold cheaply), none – Thomas, Pemberton and Lucketti aside - have later joined Football League clubs.

Managers habitually 'play safe' and prefer not to gamble on an untried young player, although, with five substitutes available and few authentically *vital* matches through a season, the risk is overstated. When managers are reluctant to blood youngsters, it is the board's duty to compel them, or at least reassure them that their job is safe if they want to adopt a more enterprising approach.

Supporters like to see fresh, raw talent. The heart is warmed by the sight of a 17-year-old charging around the pitch, stealing the ball from the toes of lumbering older opponents. It has the effect of rejuvenating the club, making it feel young again. When the player has been seen about the club for a year of two before – fetching balls that have been booted over the stand or wandering through the streets with a kit-bag slung over his shoulder, there is a deflected pride, like he is surrogate 'family', a favourite nephew. He is closer to supporters because, a few weeks ago, he was sitting in the stand in his tracksuit, and now he is out there on the pitch.

** I learned later that Dave Bayliss had not been a product of the club's youth system. He joined as a 17-year-old after being involved with the youth set-up at Liverpool.

Saturday, 31 March 2001

The new club shop was opened with many new lines on offer, including mouse mats, baseball hats, glassware and golf balls. Also on the way were bath towels, tea towels, duvet covers, pillow cases, valances, curtains and lamp shades.

The only item missing from the devoted fan's bedroom was Rochdale wallpaper, though the club pledged it would find a supplier.

The home match against Lincoln City was postponed at 1.45pm after another downpour. Volunteers had spent hours sweeping water from the pitch. One was asked for an update as he trudged away from Spotland. "It's like a fucking swamp," he said.

Minutes after the postponement, Rochdale was once again swathed in sunshine that lasted all afternoon.

Also in Rochdale...

March 2001

* A 93-year-old woman from Spotland bundled a bogus water authority official through her backdoor after he entered the kitchen while she was saying her rosary in another room.

* William Curwen of Kirkholt made off with a 42-seater, single-decker bus while more than three times over the legal alcohol limit. The 26-year-old ignored red traffic lights, mounted the pavement and drove through Rochdale, Heywood and Bury while still swigging from a can of cider. He was jailed for 22 months.

* Identical twins Eric and Jack Scholes, aged 63, died within three months of one another in similar circumstances. They were both members of Rochdale Town Veterans table tennis team and suffered heart attacks after playing in competitive matches.

Nine

A Piece of England That is Mine

Tuesday, April 3 2001
Rochdale 1 Brighton and Hove Albion 1

Brighton looked to have secured their first win at Spotland in 27 years but Rochdale equalised three minutes into injury time.

Richard Carpenter scored direct from a free kick in the 89th minute and sparked a pitch invasion from Brighton's bench and supporters.

Lee Todd equalised from another free kick four minutes later. Just a few hundred Rochdale fans saw the goal because many had already left the ground, believing the promotion dream was now over.

Players and officials were involved in an altercation when the match ended, with Rochdale's Michael Oliver and Micky Adams, the Brighton manager, believed to be the main culprits. "Something was said that I didn't like, but it was nothing really. Emotions were high, that was all," said Adams.

The attendance of 2,444 was Rochdale's lowest of the season.

Wednesday, April 4 2001

Photographer Tony Davis revealed details of his trip to Spotland in *When Saturday Comes*. He had called at the ground to take photographs for inclusion in a display at the national football museum in Preston.

His last assignment had been at Reading's Madejski Stadium where he had been made to sign a 'pile of legal documents' before taking pictures. 'There couldn't be a more complete contrast than at Rochdale,' he wrote. 'The groundsman made me a cup of tea, then stood and talked about the price of beer in the local working men's club and how Thatcher had fucked up the country: old values in an old setting.'

Friday, 6 April 2001

Rochdale's allocation of 1,020 tickets for the match at Bloomfield Road, Blackpool, was sold out.

YET ANOTHER TWIST OF THE KNIFE
AS LATE GOAL SEES ABANDONED HOPE RETURN
(*The Times*, Saturday, 7 April, 2001)

We are, make no mistake, getting close to the bone. The day-trippers and fair-weathers, for whom Rochdale FC registers just a frail beat, have moved on. We are down to the last 1,800; only the addicted and the afflicted remain.

The attendance for our midweek home match against Brighton and Hove Albion was 2,444, the lowest of the season. The situation is much worse than the statistics suggest, for 600 visiting supporters bolstered the figure. On the way into the ground, such was the deathly silence, an anxious Brighton fan asked me: "Is the match still on?" The message is clear: the fans have lost faith in the team, the manager and the dream of promotion, possibly that Rochdale will ever escape the bottom division.

During the game, everything that is cruel and vindictive and unfair about supporting this club was thrown like sand into our eyes. Brighton played hard and cynically. We were like kids scampering among the teachers at the end-of-term challenge match. It was obvious that our eagerness would founder, especially since their arch gamesmanship was in league with irresolute refereeing. In the 89th minute (when else?), they were awarded a free kick when their striker backed into our defender and rolled over extravagantly. The free kick became a goal.

Another defeat, 12 games without a win, let's all go home. As we tramped through the rainy streets, I could hear the Brighton fans singing their happiness. The racket ricocheted across the rooftops. I have been pressed close to the window of other people's sporting joy too often, left outside on the pavement while they dance and jig on a piece of England that is mine, not theirs. Our season was over, and they were dancing on the ashes.

Two miles from the ground, a score-flash came on the radio – Rochdale had scored in the 93rd minute. I didn't care any more; they had left me insensate. In fact, I was mildly irritated, not because I had missed the goal, but because the point it gained us had resuscitated hope and I've had a bellyful of hope.

I think I was happier when we shuffled pitifully around the bottom of the division. Our expectations were low and failure washed over us. In the past few seasons, we have been lifted higher, so, inevitably, the drop is greater. We have fallen from second to tenth this season, promotion certainties to rank outsiders, and the psychological damage is inestimable. When your life is lived vicariously, in silhouette of a football club, the sudden loss of pride, self-respect, and general wellbeing is a catastrophe.

On the drive home, still hurting, I asked myself a rhetorical question: if I lived my life again, would I still choose to support Rochdale? 'Choose' is a misnomer because I don't remember having any say in the matter, it just happened to me, like getting asthma, or needing to wear glasses (how strange, that I should automatically equate supporting the club to ill-health and imperfection). I decided, admittedly at an extremely low ebb, that, no, I would not attach myself to England's official least-successful professional football club.

At this point, my dad, or someone else with an interest in my welfare, pats me on the shoulder and mutters about it all being character-building. What character has it built, that causes me to leave the house reasonably pleased with the world, but return grumpy, frustrated and sulky? Even now, after all these years, it can take a whole day to restore my natural equilibrium after a defeat.

It's not just the losing and the disappointment, it's the peripherals, like, for example, the standard of refereeing. I don't habitually moan about referees. It's an indulgence, like telling someone the details of your last dream or your child's school report. Who, apart from you and a few others, really cares? Nevertheless, I'm going to start moaning, it is – believe me – justified. If we assume the referees in the FA Premiership are the finest (ho, ho), imagine the standard at our level. The bloke in charge of Tuesday's match was awarded 3/100 on one of Rochdale's less-hysterical websites with the comment: 'Utter shit would be a compliment.' This was only a slight overstatement.

My dad, when he reaches the point I'm at, often fibs that if he did not have a season ticket, he'd bale out on the club. He wouldn't really and neither would I. We're stuck on Rochdale FC, joined at the hip. When I try and fathom this masochism and ply my dad for an answer, he issues a peculiar, exasperated laugh and says: "I don't know, we must be bloody daft." Right now, it's a cruel madness.

Saturday, 7 April 2001
Heavy rain left Bloomfield Road waterlogged and the game was postponed at 11am. Many supporters had planned a weekend on the coast. It was the 10th postponement of Rochdale's season.

Tuesday, 10 April 2001
Chesterfield officials appeared before a panel of three Football League delegates at Hillsborough. The panel recommended that the club be docked nine points, which would still leave them comfortably in an automatic promotion spot.

Tuesday, 10 April 2001
Rochdale 6 Carlisle United 0
Rochdale finally ended their run of 12 matches without a win by thumping Carlisle 6-0, their biggest win since the promotion season of 1968-69 when they beat both Bradford City and Bradford Park Avenue by the same scoreline.

Earlier, Steve Parkin had warned: "I'm sure Carlisle will provide tough opposition. Ian's [Atkins, the Carlisle manager] teams are always well drilled defensively."

Gary Jones began the rout with an eighth-minute goal. Lee Todd extended the lead, scoring from a free kick, before two goals by Paul

Connor gave Rochdale a 4-0 half-time lead.

An error by goalkeeper Matthew Glennon presented Wayne Evans with his second goal of the season. Five minutes later, Connor secured a hat-trick with his sixth goal in six matches. "I can't ask for anything more from Paul," said Parkin. "His attitude is first class and he has been rewarded with goals of a very high standard."

The hat-trick was only the eighth scored by a Rochdale player in the past 22 years. The others were Andy Morris in 1999, Paul Moulden and Jamie Taylor in 1995, Dave Lancaster in 1994, Andy Flounders in 1992, Andy Milner in 1990 and Mickey French in 1983.

Carlisle were cheered on by more than 800 supporters, despite their position near the foot of the division.

* In the match programme Richard Bott said he was enjoying the Life Sentence series 'immensely' but commented: '…although the title 'a low level love affair' and a tendency to wallow in the clogs and caps of our past, suggests he is reluctant to embrace a new image.

'Whether the intention, originally, was to patronise or lampoon or merely to chronicle the activities of an unfashionable club, more and more people are finding us just the opposite. It won't last. Fashion never does. But let's savour it while it does and hope we can continue to make new friends for the rest of the season.'

As he had accused me several times of focusing too heavily on the club's inglorious past, and these sentiments were endorsed by Frank Bishop, the supporters club chairman, I did wonder whether I had overstated the misery of those years – for, at the most, three minutes.

I didn't respond in a formal way, although I found it difficult to resist. Rochdale FC is my specialist subject. I am understandably sensitive of any suggestion that I would seek to misrepresent it and vexed that anyone would wish to overlook or palliate the period of the club's history that I have lived through.

Bott's primary role at the club is to shape its PR and 'sell' the new-look Rochdale. He was invited on to the board, with full voting rights, specifically to plunder his contacts within the media and for the specialist knowledge he has gained during more than 40 years as a journalist. It is a time-consuming task he undertakes without any real self-gain. From his perspective, my rattling on week after week (I'm sure it seemed that way to him) about the club's past did not make easy reading. I feel, however, that I should have been spared 'Bott's Broadsides' and allowed diplomatic immunity. The readers of Life Sentence had the intelligence and good humour to understand the code.

I was told later that Bishop was a relatively new convert to the cause. I didn't feel this undermined his passion or the validity of his support, though I would question his ability to place it in an historical context.

Incidentally, I did not, at any time, mention clogs or caps. I concede that I did make one reference to pigeons huddling on grey sloping roofs, m'Lud.

SIX OF THE BEST
AND I'M SO EXCITED I CAN'T SLEEP
(*The Times*, Saturday, 14 April 2001)

The curse has been lifted, the skies have cleared and Lady Luck is back in the building, fox-trotting with Lazarus. Rochdale, after 12 matches without a win and a calamitous plummet down the table, beat Carlisle United 6-0 on Tuesday. Yes, six nil.

It's the biggest win I've seen in 26 years as a Rochdale supporter and it comes in a season when we have also recorded our worst home defeat. It's been a season of extremes and more than a touch *Twilight Zone*. First, we can't stop winning, then we can't win at all. The rain came, followed by fog and snow and 10 postponements. The nets fell down during one game, the drains under the pitch collapsed and the club mascot Desmond the Dragon became a father in an outlandish ceremony (don't ask, but it involved a large box and a baby dragon wearing a nappy). At this rate, one of our players may yet be struck down by a case of spontaneous human combustion.

While the win on Tuesday was wonderfully heart-warming, it was the nature of the victory that was most pleasing. Whisper this, but we didn't play particularly well, like we didn't play particularly badly when we lost 7-1. We just scored goals; lots of goals. Among them, for the first time I can remember, we notched a genuine, bona fide coming-to-a-video-near-you-soon *comedy* goal. Over the years, we've conceded several of these, but never recorded one ourselves.

Wayne Evans, our full back, received the ball a few yards outside their penalty area. While he's an industrious and proficient defender, he has a shot and a goal-sense akin to a Spice Girl (and not the sporty one). He responded in stereotypical fashion and you could almost hear his thoughts, 'Bugger this, I'll boot it towards the goal'. His sliced effort fell comfortably to Carlisle's goalkeeper, Matthew Glennon, at waist height. Glennon then made a bizarre movement with his hands, as if he was pulling on invisible glove puppets. Either way, he succeeded in fumbling it over the goal line. Evans, to his credit, did not celebrate.

Unusually for me, I did not feel sympathy for Carlisle. After the hurt of recent weeks, I wanted us to score more and more. I obviously regret the mismanagement of their club and their flirtation with relegation, but our cause was much the greater. The losing run has been like a cold turning to the 'flu turning to pneumonia. Besides, Carlisle have often beaten us heavily over the years and knocked us out of various cup competitions. They had it coming. Sport is cruel and selfish and we'll be someone's hapless victims soon enough.

After the game, I didn't know quite what to do. The after-match misery of the past few months has been habit forming. We're not used to all this joy. An evening match is not really conducive to a resounding knees-up. The pubs close within an hour of the match ending, and, let's be honest, a rainy Tuesday night in Rochdale, whatever the score, is no place for merriment. So, an early night it was, with all those win-induced happiness juices boiling over. At 2am, still higher than the floodlights, I was walking the landing. Shall I wake the kids up and get them to join in a few Rochdale songs? Best not, especially since the youngest asked me last week, 'Dad, is it winning or losing that's good?' There's obviously some way to go yet.

Maybe it had all been a dream. At the level Rochdale play, there is so little media attention that it can feel like a match hasn't taken place. If it had been played on Saturday, one of the *Grandstand* chaps might have raised an eyebrow when the teleprinter jabbed out: Rochdale 6 (six), Carlisle United 0. Those brackets, containing the word 'six', tell the world: someone's gone goal-happy here, and, in case you don't believe it, we're spelling it out. If yours is the team with their goals total in brackets, this forms the official opening ceremony for celebrations.

Unfortunately, Tuesday night, especially where matters involve the craggy folk of the third division, finds the world half-asleep and defiantly indifferent. A scoreline of 16-0 and an outbreak of foot-and-mouth among the substitutes might, just, have earned us a mention on the television news, directly after the piece about the singing dog from Mablethorpe.

Three days before the 6-0 win, the town's rugby league club, Rochdale Hornets, recorded their best-ever victory when they beat York Wasps 98-0 at Spotland. One of their players said after the game that 'something is happening here.' At last; it's been a hell of a wait.

* I almost had an entirely different 'angle' for this piece, but I felt the dramatic scoreline, coming after such a long run of poor results, superseded my original idea.

When I arrived in the ground for the Carlisle match and was walking up the aisle to my seat, I realised I would be sitting next to someone I'd never seen before at Spotland. Noticeably, there were spaces on all sides of him. I had no alternative but to sit with him because he was next to the seat reserved for me as a season ticket holder.

He was a dishevelled, twitchy figure, dressed in threadbare clothes. It was a fairly chilly night, but he was without a coat and the v-neck jumper he was wearing was pulled down at the front and torn. His hair was greasy and he flicked it from his eyes every few seconds. He spoke to me immediately and I saw that, although he was no older than 35, his teeth were either yellow, black, chipped or missing altogether. He looked like a refugee from a Ken Loach film shot in 1968.

His accent was cement-thick Mancunian. "It's not fucking bad here, is it?" he said. I nodded. "I've not been here before. Fucking good ground though innit, for a likkul club, like?" When we scored, he was late rising to his feet. He sat down, again a few seconds after everyone else. "He took that well then, didn't he? It was a fucking tight angle that," he said. He knew his football.

I offered him a toffee and he took it with excessive gratitude. A few seconds later a bloke a few rows down stood up and rummaged in his coat pocket. In a flash, my unkempt friend was back on his feet, shouting down: "Here, I've got a light, over here." He reached across and lit the bloke's cigarette with a disposable lighter. "I like to help, I do. Be nice to people, it gets you a long way."

A few minutes later, he sniffed the air. "I'm sure someone's lighted up. Know what I mean? There's some dope, some good weed, going down here." I scanned the motley collection of kids, dads and old blokes around us and thought it unlikely; he was pretty sure though.

When we went four goals up, he told me a little of his life story. About 12 years before, he'd fallen off a roof while working on a building site. "I did me back in, me shoulder, me leg and a fucking spike went right through me knacker-bag. I'm all right now. Everything still works, know what I mean?" He laughed, and the laugh broke into a hacking cough. He had small hands and held them close to his mouth, sucking on the back of his clenched fingers. When he recovered composure, he told me the accident had triggered epilepsy. He'd not had a fit for 'a few months now'.

I liked his company. His honesty was alarming, but also refreshing. In normal circumstances, on a train, or in a park, he was the type of person I'd take great pains to avoid. Pressed up close like this, I had no option but to talk and listen. He made me feel like a snob and I realised that football, by virtue of this peculiar meeting, had showed me for what I really was. I was hoping I might see him at another game before the end of the season, but I never did.

Saturday, 14 April 2001
Macclesfield Town 0 Rochdale 0

Rochdale were the better side in a mediocre game but could not convert possession into goals. "On another day we might have scored three or four," said Steve Parkin.

Gary Jones missed a penalty in the second half and Dave Flitcroft forced an outstanding save from Lee Martin, Rochdale's former reserve goalkeeper. "It was one of the best saves of my career," he said.

Monday, 16 April 2001
Rochdale 3 Exeter City 0

A Paul Connor goal within the first five minutes gave Rochdale the perfect start in a game they won easily.

Sustained pressure led to a Dave Bayliss goal after 20 minutes and Connor scored again 10 minutes after half-time.

Lee Todd suffered a knee injury and was told it would keep him out for the rest of the season.

Tuesday, 17 April 2001

Research by a supporter showed conclusively that Rochdale were more likely to lose against a Yorkshire side when the referee was from Yorkshire, than if he was from elsewhere.

Rochdale had lost 43 per cent of these games with a Yorkshire referee in charge, compared with 32 per cent when he was not from Yorkshire.

Friday, 20 April 2001

Rochdale announced a trading loss of £60,000 for the financial year of 2000-2001.

ROAD RAGE AND THE MAN WHO
PUT BARMY IN BLUE-AND-WHITE ARMY
(*The Times*, Saturday, 21 April 2001)

Word gets around and the travelling army (well, a battalion at least) reconstitutes at various points during the course of a season. Last Saturday, it marched into posh Cheshire, all 800 of us, chomping our way through boxes of pies and chortling at erratic water sprinklers.

We also took 1,200 to Halifax Town and more than 1,000 tickets have been sold for next week's match at Blackpool. Clearly, some games have more appeal than others, especially when the play-offs beckon.

A trip to Macclesfield is a journey 30 miles across the country and several rungs up the social ladder. Rochdale, as a town, still largely represents a bygone era, of mills and manual work; a blue-collar anachronism sunk deep into the Lancashire heartland. Macclesfield and its environs is where the business class of Manchester returns at the end of the working day for high tea on the patio, a cocked-finger on the bone-china tea cup. We like these stereotypes. It gets us through and hones our passion. It takes football deeper, into the psyche and community of the place from where we originate.

Perversely, on our travels we often meet people that we seldom see back home. Most of us have set routines for home games, so we park our car in the same place, approach Spotland from a certain direction and enter through a particular turnstile. This means we are among the same people at every match. At away games, we're forced together, ambling through unfamiliar streets to stand shoulder to shoulder as one mass of blue and white.

On Saturday, we saw Kenny for the first time in years. We heard him before we saw him, laughing when a rogue sprinkler soaked the home fans and whenever middle-aged ladies raced past carrying pie reinforcements. Kenny used to live on our street. At some point, my dad must have told him his name, but Kenny has always called him Bob, which isn't his name. He is one of those people who uses your name, or what he thinks to be your name, a lot, so when he sees my dad, he grabs him by the arm and says how good it is to see you, Bob, and how is work going, Bob?

These days, I drive to away games, but when I was a kid my presence depended on dad's work commitments, or the availability of mates' dads, dad's mates, or people who lived nearby that we half-knew; people, in fact, like Kenny. Back then, I thought of him as quite old, probably as old as 30 even. He was slightly overweight and wore a thick padded anorak. His face was the colour of a toffee apple, and still is, 23 years later.

Dad was working one Saturday, so Kenny offered to take me to see Rochdale play at Tranmere. I called at his house and he was his usual cheerful self. He jammed a scarf into the pocket of his anorak and we climbed into his new, meticulously-clean car.

We moved to join the main road. Kenny was late applying the brakes. The car jerked. He made a gasping sound. On the motorway slip road, he pulled out in front of a lorry. The lorry driver flashed his lights and drew close to our bumper. Suddenly, Kenny swore loudly into his rear view mirror, his eyes wide and mad. He turned and flicked V-signs. After a few minutes, he slowed down and gestured with his right hand that the lorry driver was a sexual virtuoso and not a team player. Wisely, our pursuer backed off.

Kenny did not speak for about 10 minutes, but snorted and emitted light, jerky coughs until, finally, he calmed down. We reached the outskirts of Tranmere. A vehicle swung in front of us and Kenny swerved. We shuddered to a stop. Two young lads were inside the other car. Kenny sprang out and pulled at their door handles. He was screaming, the words running into a long list of profanities and threats.

The lads locked themselves in. Kenny pressed his face to their windscreen, snarling. He then started looking about him as if trying to find a stone or stick. While his back was turned, they drove off. Kenny chased after them. A few yards along, he stopped and spat towards their retreating car.

Later, dad asked whether Kenny had been good company. "Well, he drives different than you, dad. And he's got a bit of a temper."

"At least you got to the match," he said. My dad has always had a keen sense of the priorities in life.

* Several readers wrote and asked whether this was a true story. It is, though the name of the protagonist and the destination of our journey have been changed. I wouldn't want to upset 'Kenny' – he probably still has 'a bit of a temper'.

Saturday, 21 April 2001
Barnet 3 Rochdale 0

Rochdale were out-played by a team that was to finish the season at the bottom of the division and suffer relegation to the Conference. Greg Heald (two) and Mark Aber scored.

"Several harsh words were spoken after the game," revealed Parkin. "And the players received some fairly scathing criticism. I feel very personally let down and upset in the way in which they rolled over and died against a struggling team. I was totally embarrassed."

Most of the teams in the top half of the table also lost, so the defeat had little impact, with Rochdale remaining 10th.

Sunday, 22 April 2001

The intrepid Moggy was questioned by a police officer while on his sponsored walk. He was spotted in the early hours carrying a ladder over his shoulder in Camberley, Surrey.

Moggy had been unable to find accommodation and was walking through the night - he even asked the officer whether they had a spare bed in one of the cells at the police station.

Monday, 23 April 2001

Steve Parkin called in his players for a meeting to discuss Saturday's defeat at Barnet. "I said my piece. A lot of it wasn't pleasant, but I felt it had to be said," he said.

Monday, 23 April 2001
Rochdale 3 Lincoln City 1

Rochdale scored after nine minutes through Clive Platt when Tony Ford's cross was headed into his path by Paul Connor. It was Platt's first league goal in 22 games, a period spanning almost six months.

Lincoln drew level 10 minutes into the second half when Lee Thorpe headed home a corner. Rochdale restored the lead four minutes later with a stunning goal by Connor. Mark Monington secured the win with a header in the 70th minute.

Tuesday, 24 April 2001

The Football League refused to endorse the decision made by its three-man panel to deduct Chesterfield nine points. "It does not significantly reflect the damage brought to the integrity of the League," said a spokesman.

The move gave rise to hopes that Chesterfield would lose more points and face demotion from a promotion position, allowing other clubs, including Rochdale, to move up a place.

Wednesday, 25 April 2001

Regular listeners to GMR's (Greater Manchester Radio) programmes *It's Kosher*, *Gaytalk* and *Asian Community News* were informed that their favourite Thursday night shows would be off-air for one week, while the station broadcast live commentary from Rochdale's crucial match at Blackpool.

Thursday, 26 April 2001
Blackpool 3 Rochdale 1

Blackpool scored after 43 minutes through Phil Clarkson who pounced on a loose ball after Neil Edwards fumbled Paul Simpson's free kick.

Two goals within 60 seconds at the start of the second half, from Brett Ormerod and John Murphy, left Rochdale with an uphill battle in a game that had been described as a 'cup final' by Steve McMahon, the Blackpool manager.

Rochdale pulled a goal back through Graham Lancashire with 10 minutes remaining but, four minutes later, Edwards was sent off after a collision with John Murphy. "We turned into a pub team once they had scored and just hit the ball long," complained Steve Parkin.

A few hours after the game, Clive Platt and Paul Connor were spotted in Rochdale's 24-hour Tesco store, buying ready-cooked curries. A supporter asked them how they were feeling after the defeat. 'They did sound rather gutted,' he reported on Rochdaleafc.com, adding: 'Let's hope they can win on Saturday, naan-nil!'

Friday, 27 April 2001

Chesterfield, in an issue separate to any Football League ruling, were served with a winding-up order demanding repayment of debts thought to be as much as £650,000. Nearly £500,000 was owed to the Inland Revenue.

THROW OUR RIVALS TO THE DOGS
AND HANG THE CONSEQUENCES
(The Times, Saturday, April 28 2001)

Season tickets used to be tatty and turning to dust in your pocket by the end of April. These days, they are wrapped in posh plastic wallets, so the only noticeable change is that they become thinner after each game. When I hold my ticket now, it is skeletal and confirms that another season, another nine months of my life, has almost slipped by.

Rochdale's season has been erratic, much the same as every other club's. We've won some, lost some, and, along the way, I've moaned and whined and cried to the sky. I think I might have even smiled once, probably when we went 6-0 up against Carlisle United. Up here in the stands, looking down, it all seems so easy: why can't they just do the obvious - like pass, dribble, shoot and score? During the course of a match, the players become us, the 'us' in our dreams (young, fit, healthy, talented), but when they founder, misplacing passes and shooting wide, it feels like our brain and our body are disconnected. Our frustration is understandable.

While the team has been wilfully inconsistent for the past few months, we have, somehow, found ourselves tapping on the shoulder of a play-off position. It is only the second time in 32 years that we have entered the final week of the season with proper blood and thunder, death or glory matches to play at the higher end of the table. Traditionally, April and May is given over to quasi-friendlies where we embark upon slapstick football with the likes of Lincoln City and give first-team debuts to a few YTS lads, or the tea lady if she asks nicely.

Among the faithful there is some trepidation about the possibility of promotion (and it is only a *possibility*, considering the one-in-four odds of the play-offs, *should* we make them). They don't think we're good enough, that we have ideas above our station. This is based on two factors: we have an undeniable historical legacy of failure and an over-familiarity with our own players. We know which are one-footed, which are slow, the ones that can't shoot. We should avert our eyes from these weaknesses and failings, and, as in life, seek out beauty and strength.

The current Rochdale team has a quality that others have lacked down the years, something that sets it apart. While Steve Parkin, our manager, makes tactical errors, plays people out of position, and has made some poor signings, he has, to his credit, given the team heart. If, during the course of a game, the ball falls between a Rochdale player and an opponent, he will - make no mistake - volunteer a forehead, a knee, a foot, or any other part of his anatomy to win the ball. We've had fancy-dans and prima donnas before and achieved nothing; this lot come out to the song *Who Let The Dogs Out* for good reason.

Unfortunately, the dogs didn't snap hard enough at the heels of play-off rivals Blackpool on Thursday when we lost 3-1. Matches at Blackpool, Brighton, Cardiff and Hull are tests of courage and self-belief. They are clubs with a history that is the antithesis of our own and form hostile ports-of-call. It is with these clubs that we must stand toe-to-toe and show that intensity and pride count for nothing.

We have plainly not done this, picking up just one point at these four grounds. All the same, we remain two points from a play-off spot, with a game in hand.

The shenanigans over at Chesterfield are being watched avidly in case they are further penalised and demoted from their promotion spot, allowing trailing clubs to shuffle up one place. A number of Rochdale fans are not keen on this scenario. We don't queue-jump at Rochdale. Straight bat, honest to God, good as gold; weaved from the highest moral fibre.

Some of us are on the change. If the team can play so fiercely (albeit with intermittent success) and deflect on to us such happiness, maybe *we* need a change of attitude too. We shouldn't, any more, confine our pride to being the friendliest club in the league or the providers of the best nosh in the lower divisions. We should adopt a manifesto of ruthlessness. So, let's send Chesterfield hurtling into the Conference pronto, and adopt the motif: by any means necessary, and to hell with pie and peas.

Saturday, 28 April 2001
Rochdale 1 Mansfield Town 0

Goalkeeper Bobby Mimms almost dashed Rochdale's play-off hopes with a string of saves.

Clive Platt headed home a cross from Paul Connor in the first half after sustained pressure on the Mansfield goal. "The all-important thing was the result. Nothing else mattered and thankfully we got it," said Steve Parkin.

Rochdale's play-off fate now rested with consecutive games against Plymouth Argyle, played over a four-day period.

Saturday, 28 April 2000

The annual auction of players' shirts was held at Spotland to raise money for club funds. The highest bids were £200 for Neil Edwards' and Paul Connor's, with Clive Platt's fetching £180.

Sunday, 29 April 2001

Rochdale players were overlooked in the PFA's team-of-the-year for the third division. Their peers chose players drawn mainly from Brighton, Chesterfield and Cardiff.

The last Rochdale player selected was Alan Reeves at the end of the 1993/94 season.

Monday, 30 April 2001

Steve Parkin was chosen as the third division Manager of the Month for April after guiding his team to four wins, two draws and two defeats. Rochdale's recovery had taken them to eighth.

Also in Rochdale...

April 2001

* Nadeem Ajmed of Heybrook was jailed for two months after he spat at a woman during a 'road rage' incident and called her a 'white bitch.'

* Mary Malone and Malcolm Vickers of California left Rochdale disappointed after visiting especially to see Don Estelle. They thought he sang daily in Rochdale's shopping precincts but were told no appearances were planned. "We will keep trying to track him down," said Mary.

Ten

In Some Strange Way

Tuesday, 1 May 2001
Rochdale 2 Plymouth Argyle 1

Rochdale moved back into a play-off spot, one point ahead of Blackpool, for the first time in two months after an end-to-end match against Plymouth.

They also set a new club record with a points tally of 70, which made it their most successful season since returning to the bottom division in 1974.

Plymouth took the lead through Michael Evans but Rochdale scored two in a five-minute second half spell. Plymouth defender Stuart Elliot headed into his own goal before Paul Connor scored a memorable volley, his 10th goal in 13 matches.

Dave Flitcroft was sent off on 77 minutes after a mistimed tackle earned him a second yellow card.

Rochdale's fifth consecutive home win meant that another victory, in Saturday's return at Plymouth's Home Park, would secure a place in the play-offs. Defeat, and a draw or victory for Blackpool at Darlington, would end any hopes of promotion.

The game provided a special memory for eight-year-old Laura Wild of Littleborough. She had waited six months for her mascot appearance after the Plymouth match had been postponed three times. "She's always been mad about the Dale," said her mum, Karen. "Her grandad first took her when she was just two-years-old."

She was presented with a cake by the club as a thank you for her patience and had her photograph taken with her favourite player, Mark Monington. She had no doubt about the highlight of her evening: "The best bit was when the Plymouth player put the ball in his own net. I was quite pleased about that!"

After the match, Chris Errington of the *Plymouth Evening Herald* asked Keith Hill, a former Argyle player, whether he could 'spare a few minutes.' "I'm sorry, I don't do interviews any more," laughed Hill, as he filed into the players' lounge, his team-mates chuckling at his impudence.

The aside was not appreciated, as the defender discovered four days later in the match programme for the game at Plymouth. 'Now if I had got the brush off from David Beckham or Michael Owen I would not have minded so much,' grumbled Errington. 'But we are talking about a third division footballer who celebrates his 32nd birthday later this month. I was surprised by Keith's attitude but I suppose it made him feel better about himself.'

Thursday, 3 May 2001

The club reduced the fare on official coaches travelling to the vital final match of the season at Plymouth. The cost was reduced from £19 to £10, with fans asked to rendezvous at Spotland at 8am.

PLYMOUTH OR NOT?
THE MOST AGONISING QUESTION I KNOW
(*The Times*, Saturday, 5 May 2001)

Coins have been tossed, bottles spun, and I've even asked my two-year-old son for guidance. "Should dad go to Plymouth?" "Yes," he blurted instinctively. That's it then, 608-mile round trip, nearly 11 hours of driving, away we go. "No," he yelled, a second later. Come on, lad, where do you get all this indecisiveness from?

Rochdale play at Plymouth Argyle today in our most important match for more than 30 years. If we win, we will make the play-offs for the first time. We might also qualify if we lose, should those wonderful, big-hearted chaps at Darlington beat Blackpool today. The other permutations are (and bear with me here): we draw, Blackpool win – we miss out; we draw, Blackpool draw – we make it; we lose, Blackpool draw – we miss out; we win, they win – we might both make it, should Leyton Orient lose.

Basically, it's one of those situations that Alan Green habitually describes as 'on a knife edge' and then adds for dramatic effect, 'It really is." If our game were on telly, they'd be swinging the cameras round to face the fans, picking out haunted faces, anxious glances at watches and transistors pressed to ears. I'm the one in the periphery of your vision, being taken away on a stretcher, twitching and pleading for more oxygen.

Hundreds of Rochdale supporters have already pledged to make the long journey to Home Park. The club has generously reduced the cost to a mere £10 return and extra coaches have been added throughout the week. One particular Rochdale fan, may, or may not, be heading to Plymouth, and is quite envious of fellow supporters who have had the conviction to book their seat.

Since Tuesday, when we beat Plymouth 2-1 in a rearranged match (yes, two matches against Plymouth in five days), my life has been in turmoil. I have passed through this world, seemingly affixed to it, but really somewhere else. All the time, tapping away at my mind with a toffee hammer has been the dilemma: Plymouth, or not Plymouth?

The emotional permutations are every bit as enigmatic and complex as the mathematical. If we miss out – by whatever course – the anguish will be unbearable. I can hear the cruel Argyle fans singing now, as their team take the lead and news filters through that Blackpool are beating Darlington: 'Staying down, staying down', followed by mock cheers for Blackpool. And that long, long journey home, in silence, with anger and bitterness and frustration chewing at every nerve-end.

"But the lads need us," I was told by one supporter. They might need you, I thought, but they don't need me: an apoplectic wreck, too nervous to raise a pathetic, bone-dry whisper of 'Come on the 'Dale.' During my truly morbid moments, I've even considered that this might all be a nefarious plot. We're taken to the other end of the country, pumped up with hope and excitement, and dropped from a great height, well 304 miles, such is the distance from Rochdale to Plymouth.

Another entreaty has been that I should go down and to hell with the result. The claim is that pleasure or pain is a condition of football support, and I should trust to fortune. At most other clubs, this might stand, but, apart from the odd winning run, Rochdale haven't really been over-generous with pleasure. In football terms, after 27 years supporting the club, Pain FC is 8-0 up on Pleasure, so I'm rightly sceptical about a sudden comeback.

So, that's it, I'm not going. I'll dig the garden. I might even assemble that exercise bike that's still in its box two months after we bought it. Football? Rochdale FC? Nothing to do with me, pal. As if. I know where my tremulous heart will be and should news filter through ("Who left that telly on, stuck on Teletext?") that we're winning, or Blackpool are losing, what will my thoughts be then?

I'll be pining, with a sickening, mixed-up feeling I've not known since I was six-years-old and I went on holiday with my best mate and his family. We got to the main road and I realised I wanted to be somewhere else - back home with my mum and dad. Today, should I stay at home and we win, I'll ache to be among the boys in blue, punching the air and hugging kids I half-remember from school who are now all big and grown up.

Bugger it, I'm going. I'll send you a postcard from Devon next week. I went on that holiday when I was six, despite the tears and whimpering. My mate's mum, Joan, kept telling me how much I'd enjoy myself. It was the best holiday of my life.

* I wrote this piece two days before the match at Plymouth and, at that point, was genuinely still unsure of whether to travel down. I actually made up my mind while I was writing and once I'd finished I was relieved because it meant I had to hold to my decision.

I suppose there was an element of professional duty to my attending, though I think *The Times* sportsdesk would have understood if I had explained my reasons for not going.

A few hours after e-mailing the article to London, I deliberated whether I was being over-optimistic in the final paragraph and should have tempered it with a hint of caution. I decided to let the copy stand.

Saturday, 5 May 2001
Plymouth Argyle 0 Rochdale 0

Rochdale started nervously but dominated the closing stages of the first half. As the second half progressed, news filtered through that Blackpool had taken a 3-1 lead at Darlington: Rochdale had to win.

In the final few minutes, Clive Platt shot narrowly wide and a goal-bound shot from Gary Jones struck a defender and flashed past the post.

At the final whistle, it was obvious the players knew the scoreline at Feethams. They assembled on the half-way line, heads in their hands, before walking a few yards towards the end containing the massed Rochdale supporters, who sang for some time after the game had finished.

"It's heartbreaking. We went into the game firmly believing we could do it. It doesn't get any harder than losing out on the last day of the season," said Steve Parkin.

Sunday, 6 May 2001

Players and supporters joined together at the club's end-of-season awards party. Gary Jones won four trophies, as the Chairman's, Manager's, Rochdaleafc.com's and Pomona's [a club sponsor] player-of the-year.

Lee Todd was the Supporters' Club player-of-the-year and also won an award for the club's goal-of-the-season – his free kick against Brighton at Spotland.

Clive Platt was 'the most improved player of the season' and Dave Flitcroft won the Players' player-of-the-season award. "That's right, pick the fat, shit one!" was his gracious acceptance speech.

Wednesday, 9 May 2001

Clive Platt was linked with a £650,000 move to Grimsby Town. The rumour was quickly scotched. "We'd only sell Clive if we were talking about stupid money for him," said Parkin.

CRYING GAME CONTINUES FOR
THE PLYMOUTH BRETHREN
(*The Times*, Saturday, 12 May 2001)

Leaning against a wall, head hung low, a lad of about 10-years-old sobbed. The Rochdale shirt he was wearing shuddered every time he drew breath. His dad put a hand on his shoulder and gestured as we filed past. The expression – imagine a smile ironed flat - told us, 'He's got a lot to learn.'

We have each of us learnt about this football club down the years and the pain that it can inflict. It has made some of us old before our time and has turned idealists into cynics. The end of our promotion dream came in a wholly appropriate way, a wholly Rochdale way. We were taken hundreds of miles from home, to Home Park, Plymouth, for the final torment. A win, no matter how slender, would have propelled us into the play-offs but chance after chance was spurned. We drew 0-0, while Blackpool won 3-1 at Darlington and took our place in the play-off zone.

Many of us felt it would end this way. We have a sixth sense, a feeling 'in our bones' that we are perpetually destined to fail, and not just conventionally, but with added, twisted cruelty. We are persecuted by bad luck. Supporters of all clubs make this claim, but we are the majesty of the suffered, as our record of 27 seasons in the bottom division testifies.

As I filed past the crying boy and towards the exit gate at Home Park, several thoughts flickered across a mind beset by stultifying melancholy. Why was I tied so tightly to this football club when the balance between victory and defeat, pleasure and pain, has always been hugely disproportionate in favour of the negative? Why, at some point in the midst of all this year-on-year misery, had I not walked-out and make my escape?

My friends don't like me talking like this. I sense it makes them uneasy. They feel I am defined by my support. As a person, I'm perceived as fiercely loyal, a champion of the underdog and an optimist, so to forsake Rochdale FC is to forsake myself. I don't like that I'm swathed in this peculiar sporting martyrdom. I'd prefer to possess these qualities without them being imbued in my football club. Football is supposed to provide an escape from real life, not more of the same.

When I saw the lad being comforted by his dad, I thought of my own two sons, aged two and four, and whether I should pass on this broken heirloom of a football club. I hitched myself to Rochdale in 1974, when the ground had the crooked, knocked-together look of a shanty town, 20 years after the gold had run out. Boot boys waged a futile, evil war on all sides and we finished bottom of the Football League every other season.

Rochdale FC is a different entity in 2001 and I must take heart from this at times like these. The club is a professional set-up with unmistakable ambition and only an unmitigated disaster (please God, no!) would cause it to slip back. My children will inherit a club that has risen to its feet from its belly - if I wrote 'knees' here, it would be to understate its accomplishment. So, if they show sufficient interest and promise not to pop inflated crisp bags near me or run up and down the aisles, I have no qualms about taking them to Spotland. I have a feeling that their experience of Rochdale FC will be much happier than mine.

My final thought, as 1,000 of us shuffled disconsolately down those steps, was an incongruous stab of happiness that I didn't make sense of until a few days later. It really was something to be among people from your hometown, all that way from familiar streets, and know that everyone of us believed in the worth of us being there.

It's some gang too. We won't win any modelling contracts – unless mullets, shaved heads, acne and fezzes (blue, aptly enough) become *de rigueur* - but these hearts are forged from solid gold. While apathy and fickleness has prospered elsewhere, they have remained steadfast and loyal and have refused to renounce hope and belief. They have also trusted in something outside their control – 11 young men in blue football shirts – and, let's face it, no one trusts anyone any more.

Evidently, our reward was abject disappointment, but this was to subjugate a greater truth. We were alive last Saturday, truly alive, no longer passive or indifferent like most of the rest of the human race, but teetering on the edge of glory or despair, up to our eyeballs in it. We lost out on a play-off spot and possible promotion, but our lives felt to be enriched in some strange way. If I were that lad's dad, I'd be proud.

* The disappointment was every bit as painful as I had expected. I don't normally sing or chant at matches, but I joined in at the end; everyone did. It was the most emotional moment of my years as a Rochdale supporter. We were singing to stop ourselves from crying.

I wanted the players to draw closer to where we were standing, but they appeared reticent, almost as if they felt they had let us down. At that moment, they were forgiven every stray pass and every miss-hit shot in every match, because we saw that they had given their all.

Towards the end of the game, players such as Mark Monington, Dave Bayliss, Clive Platt and Gary Jones, seemed in danger of getting seriously hurt as they threw themselves at the ball, heedless to their own safety. We could see how much they wanted it; they should have come to the fence and accepted out appreciation at closer quarters.

Supporters were reluctant to disperse afterwards because we knew the loneliness that awaited us. We felt wrapped up warm on that terrace, safe from our sorrow. On the way through the park in which Plymouth's ground is situated, a group of fans began singing, *Always Look on the Bright Side of Life*. Some found this a solace, but, to me, it is a song that belongs to Manchester United. I would have preferred silence, once we'd reached the path through the sycamores.

As we continued the walk towards the car park, Plymouth fans passed in the opposite direction. They were unusually quiet and I detected an unspoken empathy. One or two old-boys caught my eye and shook their heads as if they understood the emotions we were feeling.

This was in stark contrast to the Plymouth fans in the ground who had behaved peevishly. They cheered and danced ecstatically when news came through of every Blackpool goal and a group in the seats next to the Rochdale fans spent most of the match shouting, swearing and making gestures.

At half-time, Moggy trouped around the pitch on the final few steps of his sponsored walk. One of his pals, a member of the fez-wearing posse, was allowed access to the pitch with a collection bucket. A mob of Plymouth fans ran to the fence to attack him and stewards had to hold them back. As Moggy drifted past, wilfully indifferent to the hostility, an ironic chant broke out on the terraces, one that hadn't been heard for more than 20 years: 'Moggy's gonna get yer, Moggy's gonna get yer.'

This same group of Plymouth fans refused to throw back the ball after it had entered their stand. When the final whistle blew, Plymouth's goalkeeper clenched his fists and jumped into the air; it seemed odd that a 0-0 home draw should bring him such happiness.

The journey back was long and tedious. I was tired. It was probably all the driving. I also had a real sense of the 27 years as a Rochdale fan weighing me down, too. It was like being hungover, but not being able to recall having had a drink.

In the days afterwards, several fans of other clubs told me it was best that Rochdale had missed out as they did, rather than losing out in the play-offs. I didn't agree. We viewed the play-offs as a novelty, a cause of celebration in itself, with promotion as a possible bonus. We wanted a few more days in the sunshine, to all be together again, singing that we were Rochdale 'til we died.

Tuesday, 15 May 2001

Supporters were shocked to learn that two Rochdale stalwarts, Mark Monington and Keith Hill, were among six players given free transfers by Steve Parkin.

Also released were injury-prone striker Graham Lancashire (96 total appearances, 25 goals) and the 36-year-old striker Tony Ellis (68 appearances, 18 goals) who had not featured in the team, even as substitute, for the last 12 games of the season. Goalkeeper Phil Priestley (four appearances) and winger Simon Davies (16 appearances, one goal) were the other players released. Davies had not started a match since January.

The release of Monington and Hill effectively dismantled a Rochdale defence that had proved highly competent for most of the season. Keith Hill had played 200 games (seven goals) for Rochdale, and Mark Monington 110, which included 16 goals – an admirable tally for a defender.

Wednesday, 16 May 2001

Tony Ford, who had just celebrated his 42nd birthday, was told he was part of Parkin's plans for the forthcoming season. "Tony will still be involved in the capacity of having a player's contract. Whether or not he will be fit enough to play as many games, we will have to see," he said.

Saturday, 19 May 2001

Steve Parkin explained his decision to release Mark Monington and Keith Hill. "I wouldn't have a bad word said against them because I like them as people, not just as a manager. But I felt we were found wanting a bit at times in defence, especially away from home."

Monday, 21 May 2001

The club sold more than 100 season tickets for the 2001-2002 season within one week of them going on sale.

Wednesday, 23 May 2001

A group of 14 division three chairmen, led by York City's Douglas Craig, called for an extraordinary general meeting of the Football League to review the case involving Chesterfield. Craig said Chesterfield's punishment of a £25,000 fine and a deduction of nine points was 'too lenient' and a 'cheat's charter'.

They called on Chesterfield to be relegated to the Conference, a move that would cause chaos – Hartlepool, who finished fourth could demand automatic promotion, Barnet could push for reinstatement in the division, and Rochdale could seek recompense for missing out on a play-off place. "Chesterfield supporters say they are the ones being punished but they forget that supporters of 23 other clubs, not least Rochdale and Barnet, have been affected and punished, too," said Craig.

The Football League was expected to agree to the meeting which would be held in June.

Thursday, 24 May 2001

Cheltenham Town signed Keith Hill on a three-year contract. Hill said he was looking forward to the move, especially because Cheltenham were one of the few clubs that provided players with a top-notch post-match meal!

Saturday, 26 May 2001

Blackpool beat Leyton Orient 4-2 at Cardiff's Millennium Stadium to clinch promotion from the third division. Hartlepool and Hull City had earlier been knocked out in the semi-final matches.

Blackpool's promotion meant that Rochdale were the only Lancashire club remaining in the third division.

Tuesday, 29 May 2001

A group of Blackpool fans voted Rochdale top of the division for match day facilities and hospitality.

Rochdale topped two of the four separate categories, for 'best ground' and 'best fans' – the latter based on vocal support and the friendliness shown to visitors.

Rochdale were judged to have the third-best match programme in the division and the seventh-best catering facilities. Runners-up were Exeter and Cheltenham, with Chesterfield at the bottom of the fans' table.

Wednesday, 30 May 2001

Readers of *FourFourTwo* magazine voted four Rochdale players into the third division's top 50 list. They were Neil Edwards (16th), Mark Monington (24th), Gary Jones (31st) and Wayne Evans (40th). The division's top player was Bobby Zamora of Brighton with Cardiff's Robert Earnshaw the runner-up.

At the season's end, both Steve Parkin and Rochdale's chairman David Kilpatrick issued statements reflecting on the club's fortunes:

Steve Parkin:

I would like to say a big thank you all for the fans' fantastic support throughout the campaign. On the whole, I think we've had a great season. Attendances are up, the team has finished with its highest points tally ever and the players - through most of the season - have been superb. I really wish we could have finished it off with a win at Plymouth and got that last play-off place.

High points of the season? Well, for me, it must be winning the final five home games. It was vital, as they were high-pressure games. We had to win and we managed to do it. These games kept the season alive. They were very tense, very exciting and very enjoyable.

Obviously the lowest point, of not just the season but my career, was when the final whistle blew at Plymouth. I, and everyone else was bitterly disappointed, not just for the team, the staff and everyone at the club, but for so many supporters who made the trip to see us hopefully get into the play-offs. The last 10 minutes were very exciting and we did have some good chances to win the game.

If I could change one thing about the season it would be the pitch, without a doubt. If the games had been played when they should have been, there wouldn't have been as much pressure on the lads at the end of the season to win every game. I feel we would have got a few more points if we'd have played them first time round.

Even though the lads did very well at the back end of the season, the amount of games, in my mind, proved too much. To ask them to not only play, but win 13 games in five and a half weeks is far too much for a small squad.

I set a personal target every season to finish one place higher than the previous season. Obviously, if that was the case next season we would be in the play-offs, but before we can even think about it there are a few things we need to sort out. The first thing is the pitch. We need a playing surface that gives us at least a chance to get games on. The other thing is training facilities. We need suitable training grounds on which to train professionals, on a regular basis. This is one thing we have not been able to do this season and it certainly needs sorting out.

I am hoping to bring in two or three new players who will strengthen the squad. We do have a couple of names to follow-up, but we must wait until the list of available players comes out in a couple of weeks.

There is a lot of talk about us going for John Doolan from Barnet, but John has pledged his future to Barnet for five years. Obviously, with Barnet entering the Conference this may change things, but I'm sure Barnet would want a substantial fee for him, and we have used the money we had on signing Paul Connor which was the right thing to do.

The lads are still down, but hopefully after we all have a good holiday, a good pre-season and get to Scotland to play a few games we will have everyone fit and raring to go.

David Kilpatrick:

We are all desperately disappointed that we missed out on the play-offs and the chance to go up to the second division after years of waiting. Steve Parkin and his staff and players put in a tremendous effort when faced with a congested fixture list. Having to play 10 high-pressure games in 33 days, because of a backlog of fixtures, was asking too much. Yet we took our promotion effort to the very last league game, at Plymouth, and a win would have put us in the play-offs for the first time.

I want to congratulate the manager, who thoroughly deserved his award as the division three Manager of the Month for April, and his players for their efforts throughout the season and to say a particular 'thank you' to our supporters. We took nearly 1,000 to Plymouth, a round trip of 600 miles. Our fans did the team and the town proud, as they did all season.

We have made excellent progress for two seasons but we do not want to experience ever again the disappointment we all felt after the game at Plymouth. The final table shows that we were the eighth best team in the third division, regardless of whether we feel that, in other circumstances, we should have finished higher.

Basically, the reason we are not in the play-offs is because of our results against the likes of Shrewsbury, York, Barnet and Kidderminster. Look at our performances against the top teams: Chesterfield - drew both games; Leyton Orient - beat them at home, on Sky TV, and drew away; Hartlepool - won at home, drew away; Cardiff - drew home and away; Brighton - lost away (with 10 men), and drew at home. And so on. We experienced a very poor run in February and March, when we went 12 games without a victory, but most of those were drawn. We finished the season very strongly at home, winning our last five, and our new striker Paul Connor was in superb scoring form. More about him later.

We are already planning for next season. We appreciate the playing surface is a vital consideration because we cannot afford to have games postponed in such numbers in future. This was the cause of the fixture congestion and contributed to our eventual disappointment.

We drowned our sorrows at the end-of-season party on Sunday, where Gary Jones was a popular winner of the Player-of-the-Year awards, and then got down to business. You can rest assured that the only thing we will allow to grow under our feet this summer is the grass at Spotland, once we have sorted out the drainage problem.

The pitch caused us a tremendous amount of embarrassment this year and we aim to rectify it over the summer months. Personally, I don't think the pitch is quite as bad as some people believe. If you put a plug in a sink and turn on the tap, it soon fills up. Our problem is with the drainage, not the pitch itself. One problem is that we only have a small amount of time for the work to be carried out because Rochdale Hornets could well be involved in the rugby league play-offs and the Northern Ford Premiership Grand Final is scheduled to be played at Spotland at the end of July.

The atrocious weather this winter has been a contributory factor to our pitch problems and particularly what I call 'the one o'clock monsoons'. Sometimes I wonder whether God realises it is Saturday and we are at home! I remember the postponement of the home game against Plymouth. I only went across to the garage near my home and when I came out it was absolutely belting down. I thought then that we had no chance of playing and was proved right.

The Lincoln fixture was another that fell victim to monsoon-type weather conditions. Nevertheless, the rain stopped at 2pm and we felt we could get the pitch playable. Unfortunately, the referee had already decided at 1.45pm to call off the game. The Carlisle game was also called off in similar circumstances. It was postponed at 1.30pm but was playable at 3pm. Even the Carlisle manager wanted to wait and was prepared to play.

Steve Parkin has made his feelings known about the pitch, the postponements and the difficulties in finding suitable training facilities, particularly when the weather is bad. All these problems are being addressed. My relationship with the manager is extremely open and communication between us is excellent. We speak most days but he is allowed to manage the club his way and I have no influence on team selection.

Finally, the background to the arrival of our record signing, Paul Connor, who is proving to be an excellent acquisition on the evidence of his first few weeks at the football club. We had continued to watch Paul when he was playing for Cambridge United on loan and it was clear, when he returned to Stoke after three months, that Cambridge were interested in signing him on a permanent basis. However, we had been led to understand that they couldn't afford to buy him.

One problem at Stoke these days is that, under the present regime, everything has to be sanctioned by the head office in Iceland. In order to progress the deal we lodged an official bid with John Rudge [Stoke's director of football], who we knew would pass it on to

Iceland. Not surprisingly, our initial bid, which was £75,000, was refused, so we upped it to £100,000. This was also refused. We then increased our bid to £125,000 and that, subsequently, was also not accepted. A few weeks passed and I think I am right in saying we were now talking to Southend again about Martin Carruthers.

Finally, I told our manager to phone John Rudge and ask him how much Stoke wanted for Connor. And I emphasised, 'Tell Rudgey half the people in Rochdale don't even believe we are in negotiations with you. Tell him people just think it is easy for us to say we have had another bid turned down and that we are not serious. Well, we are'.

Eventually, word came back that they didn't actually want to sell him. Then we were told that £150,000 was what they were looking for, so Steve Parkin was told to put in a final offer of £150,000 - take it or leave it. Paul was pencilled-in to play in Stoke's LDV Trophy game that night. When he was pulled out, we knew we had got our man.

The fee was a new club record, easily beating the £100,000 we had paid to Walsall for Clive Platt. Earlier in the season, when we knew we had to provide cover for Tony Ellis and Platt, we did not have the finance to pay out such a substantial amount. If you spend £150,000 on a player and pay him wages commensurate with that fee, it is always going to be money the club hasn't got, despite the increased revenue from gate receipts and the excellent contribution of the Goldbond Weekly Draw. But the time comes when you have to take a risk and so far it has proved to be a risk well worth taking.

Also in Rochdale...

May 2001

* Police feared racial violence could spill over into the town after several nights of rioting in nearby Oldham. They were called to a pitched battle between rival gangs outside a pub in Belfield.
* Desert Orchid made an appearance at the Sacred Heart Church Fair in Kingsway and attracted more than 2,000 visitors.
* Scotland-born Christine MacKinnion claimed she was the victim

of a race attack when she returned from holiday to find someone had thrown a haggis through the window of her home in Spotland. "They probably thought they were being clever. I can't stand haggis," she said.

Tuesday, 5 June 2001

Kevin Townson was called into the England Under-17s squad for their forthcoming match against Italy. On the same day, former Rochdale goalkeeper Stephen Bywater made his full debut for the England Under-21s in their 3-1 defeat against Greece.

Bywater's appearance was thought to have netted Rochdale an additional £25,000 under the terms of his transfer to West Ham United.

Thursday, 7 June 2001

Parliamentary candidate Nick Harvey of the Green party received just 728 votes standing for the Rochdale constituency in the General Election. He said the biggest regret of his campaign was not revealing his love of Rochdale FC: "I've been a fan since I was a child. Perhaps if I said I was a supporter I could have won a few more votes from the fans."

Sunday, 10 June 2001

The extraordinary general meeting called to discuss the possible demotion of Chesterfield to the Conference was cancelled when League chairmen met at their annual conference.

The League's chief executive David Burns said there was little support for the motion to further penalise Chesterfield, with only seven clubs from the third division still upholding a complaint. "I am pleased that we can now draw a line under this affair," he said.

Eleven

Home is Where the Heart is

I put out an appeal for fans to write to me with their stories and memories of Rochdale and to reflect on why they supported the club. They were asked to limit their submissions to 500 words, but many had difficulty containing their fervour. The response was astounding, both in number and in the quality of the writing. They are published here, with only minor editing. A box of tissues may be required as you read these eulogies to hope, optimism, loyalty, tradition and kinship.

Jeff Greenwood, Rochdale: I am 27 and my life changed in 1985 when I went to watch my first football match, between Rochdale and Burnley, which we won 1-0 thanks to a Super Stevie Taylor penalty. Before this game, I didn't know anything about Rochdale FC and you could say I barely knew it existed. The moment I walked up the steps on to the terracing next to Sandy Lane, I looked around and instantly fell in love with the place. Immediately it became my club and my team and I hadn't even seen a ball kicked. It didn't matter. I felt a great sense of belonging. I just knew I would support this team for the rest of my life and I remember thinking why it had taken me so many years to discover the Dale. I couldn't wait for the next match, against Tranmere, so I could buy my Dale hat and scarf and wear my colours with pride. The lack of success has never made me think twice. It has just strengthened my bond to the club. I am immensely proud of my football club and we have risen in stature both on and off the field in the last 10 years. We are no longer poor little Rochdale. In fact, we are one of the most solvent clubs in the lower divisions. As for the Plymouth game, well, I stood with my hands on my head, trying desperately to hold back the tears and it felt like someone had just died. The disappointment was immense and I was so choked, I could hardly speak. Yet at the same time, I was extremely proud of making it so far. I am now looking forward to next season with great optimism and high expectations.

John Leonard, Glasgow: Well we didn't go up did we? I suppose we wouldn't though, it just wouldn't be like us. Anyway, it's still been my most memorable season watching Dale, and after 10 years I know there is no way back. I knew that from the first time I set foot in Spotland. Plymouth was disappointing but one overriding emotion was left. Not sadness, but pride. I love supporting Dale, and - sitting in the pub afterwards - me and my folks agreed. We love supporting the Dale. Not for one minute after the game did we think that the boys or Steve let us down. They tried bloody hard. There was definitely a lump in the throat at the final whistle as 1,000 Dale fans sang to their heroes. We'll be back next year. The Dale are goin' up. Thanks for advertising our amazing little club. It is amazing isn't it? I suppose that's why we love it. My 1,100 mile round trip was worth it. I wouldn't and couldn't have been anywhere else.

Nick Kingsley, Bury (formerly Rochdale): They wouldn't be Rochdale if they hadn't fallen gut-wrenchingly at the final hurdle; yet fans, management and players can hold their heads high knowing that we gave it our best shot, and this year it wasn't quite good enough - but there's always next year. We might be a million miles from the Champions League but I am proud to support our lads and will always be so.

Dave Coupe, Luton: "Do you think we will do it then?" "No," I replied. "Something is bound to go wrong. It always does." Two hours to go, and our season boiled down to one match - 90 minutes in Plymouth. I tucked into my mixed grill. The others watched enviously, waiting for the fate that was to befall them at 4.50pm that afternoon. A younger member of our group, still blessed with the optimism of youth, suddenly voiced his opinion: "I just have the feeling this is our lucky season." "Lucky?" I replied. "How many lucky teams lose 7-1 at home to Shrewsbury?" After my meal, it was time to walk the short distance to Home Park, Plymouth. It is a ground which time has forgot. It belongs to a bygone golden era of football with its sweeping terraces and vast spaces. As we walked up the steep hill to the ground, the sun disappeared, the clouds took control. It was almost as if the sun had withdrawn her blessing from the good ship Rochdale. The match started and, inevitably, news of Blackpool goals began to drift through. This was no surprise. In all honesty, we all knew we needed to win - things are never easy for Rochdale and today would be no different. At around 4.40pm the last rites of the season were about to be read. A last-minute goal, however, would save us. Last-minute goals belong to Liverpool, Manchester United and Arsenal, not Rochdale. I decided to watch the last five minutes away from the mass of Rochdale fans. I strolled to the far corner of the terrace which was empty of people. I wanted solace, time to think, to be alone, to reflect. I did not watch the last five minutes of the game. Instead, I watched the faces of the damned, the fans. The same faces I see week in, week out. I was not alone in my suffering. Most faces are even more seasoned than mine. They have suffered more than me. But time and failure have not diminished their enthusiasm. They have suffered so many failures over the season that they were damned if they where going to miss this, the coronation. I decided to share the final minute of this season with the person who introduced me to Rochdale AFC, my dad. He had decided to stay well clear of Plymouth, preferring his back garden and mobile phone. He waited for my call, waited to hear me breathless and exhilarated by a Rochdale goal, but it was not to be. I rang him up to share with him the final moments of the season, an exclusive live commentary of missed chances. Why should I be the only one to suffer? The players knew they needed a goal and in the dying embers of the season chances came and went. This made the suffering all the more hard to take. There was to be no glorious salvation to a season that had promised so much. The referee blew his whistle. I confirmed the worst to my dad. He took it very well, he had seen it all before. Despite my sceptical tones, I do genuinely believe that our time is coming. As we marched down the steps to the exit, a chorus broke out: *Always look on the bright side of life.* "It could be worse," said the chap next to me. Just ask Barnet.

Rory McNicholas, Charlotte, North Carolina, USA: Many times over the past 20 years or so I've been asked the same question, and I've thought about it long and hard, asking myself the same question - why do I love the Dale? There isn't a short, one word, comprehensive answer to that, apart from perhaps 'I just do', but that's not an explanation is it? It may be an answer, but it's not a reason. So why do I? Part of the reason is a huge amount of local pride. We'll never win the League or the Cup, we probably won't even come close, but that's okay, we know that, but we know we'll always be Dale. It's like being a part of something, something that you can't describe to others, something that no-one else can feel unless they're a part of it. You know familiar faces, but you never know the names - like the guy who always stands down in front of you to your left, or the one always behind the goal, third step up. Then there's the bloke who's match-day routine makes him take a pee just before kick-off then run like crazy to his usual place just in time to see the boys run onto the pitch. A nod, a wink, an 'alright' or a 'how-do' is the most interaction you get from one season to the next, but that's all you need, you know what it means, you know what it's worth. Even away from the footie, that special something is still there - you see that guy from behind the goal in the pub, or in Asda, and it's a nod, a wink, an 'alright' or a 'how-do'. I have been fortunate enough to watch the game at every professional level - as one of 961 fans crammed in at Spotland, 58,000 packed in at Old Trafford, and watching England in the World Cup in France 98. And, while you're always a supporter, a fan, or a spectator, you're never really 'a part of it' like you are at Rochdale, not really. When next season starts I'll be back in Rochdale, visiting from the States where I now live. And even though Spotland has changed, I know the people won't have, and by the time the ref blows for the start of the game, I know it'll feel like I never left - the nods, the winks, 'alrights' and 'how-do's' And it doesn't really matter what the result is - a record victory, a dull no-score draw, or an all too familiar, frustration filled 'could have, should have, if only'. The point is, I'll be there, and I'll always be there, wherever I am. Up The Dale!

Luke Bainbridge, Manchester (ex-Rochdale): Yes. Course I was gutted that the Dale missed out on the play-offs. Or that's what I told everybody. But if I was being totally honest with myself I knew it was never meant to be. Football clubs are not supposed to be reliable, but ever since we were first introduced I've always felt I could rely on the Dale. I could rely on them to lull me into thinking, each autumn, as they started the season with a flourish, that maybe this could be Dale's year after all. And then I could rely on them to make it abundantly clear, usually by Christmas, that it clearly wasn't, and why hadn't I learnt my lesson yet. And I could also rely on most friends and family to be incapable of grasping how you could support a club whose greatest player was a moustachioed, signet ring wearing, spiky gel-haired guy called Keith.* I'd imagine I'm not unusual amongst Dale fans, in that most of the memories - from the earliest ones like drinking a cup of gravy at half-time because it was freezing and we were too young to drink tea or coffee, to more recent ones like the linesman last season who turned round and engaged in a lengthy decision with the old fan who'd just 'questioned' his offside decision - don't actually involve football. The sloganed T-shirts that were printed for the big cup game away at Crystal Palace** - surely the wonderful Keith Welch's finest hour - that declared 'Last team to win at Anfield' (Marine had moved the tie to a Friday night at Anfield rather than give Rochdale home advantage). The slip by Dave Redfearn which presented Frank Stapleton with one of the easiest goals he's scored at Old Trafford. *** The penguins - the origin of which still remains a mystery - that were held aloft on Sandy Lane and the Willbutts, during football's flirtation with all things inflatable. Getting on the bus to Spotland, only for Dale stalwart Tony Brown to get on two stops later. The countless players I've seen turn round and confront members of the crowd individually after taking offence at a particular insult hurled. Those fans who turned up with Mickey Mouse ears against Whitley Bay.**** Dean Walling having to change a pair of ripped shorts, during the game, on the pitch. Or my favourite memory, from the first game after the Main Stand was rebuilt, boasting Rochdale's first ever executive boxes. A kid from the year above us at school came and stood next to us and half way through the first half he nodded towards said executive boxes and sneered: "Look at them lot all watching the match... go on, get back to work you lazy gits!" Towards the end of the second half, when those around us had stopped laughing, we managed to explain to him that they weren't actually offices. Yes, the ground is a different and much-improved beast to that of even 10 years ago and, yes, the chances of Rochdale one day achieving something are more realistic than even two years ago, when a fellow Rochdale supporter said to me "I don't aspire to promotion, I just aspire to the odd 3-0 win!" But, in many ways, that's irrelevant, because as Rochdalians Kalpihz rapped: 'If you don't know by now, you'll never know'. Up the Dale.

* Keith Welch, Rochdale's goalkeeper from 1986 to 1990, total appearances - 239.
** Rochdale reached the fifth round of the FA Cup in February 1990, losing 1-0 against Crystal Palace at Selhurst Park.
*** Rochdale lost 2-0 against Manchester United in the third round of the FA Cup in January 1986.
**** Rochdale beat Whitley Bay 1-0 in the third round of the FA Cup in January 1990. Before the game, their manager said he was disappointed his team hadn't drawn a well-known side, rather than a 'Mickey Mouse club.'

Peter Ward, Lancaster: As a 'Wartime baby' my life sentence has continued for longer than most Dale followers. One of my earliest memories? At the age of four, I suppose, running around on the Spion Kop at the Pearl Street End with blues and reds on the rich green pitch below and yes, it was brilliant sunshine and a blue sky! But there it ended - the brilliant sunshine and blue sky, I mean. It has been a long, dismal, dreary life sentence ever since, a life sentence with hard labour! By way of background: we left Rochdale for Manchester when I was five but kept up our strong links through family connections and then the visits to Spotland started, my father taking my brother and me while mother dealt with the relatives. Then my brother, older than me, turned to Manchester United and I was dropped off in Sandy Lane while both parents went on to ailing grandparents and others. I had a taste of United too, being brought up on the pre-Munich team, but I stuck doggedly to the Dale - a fact recognised by the *Rochdale Observer* in an article about the Dale Junior Supporters Club when it was recognised that even the great Manchester United took second place to Rochdale for one young supporter, yes - me. My name was mentioned in the paper, and it was also in the Rochdale programme when it was my birthday (a big thing in those days before mascots and half-time penalties). I wanted to be a professional footballer and - surprise, surprise - lead the Dale to and out at Wembley for the FA Cup Final for a 5-2 victory over United with me scoring a hat-trick. I did sign as a junior for the Dale and played on the hallowed turf, gained access to the inner sanctum (actually went in through the Main Entrance after years of peering in from the outside and up the tunnel from my spot in the Paddock, went into the home team dressing-room, ran down the tunnel and out onto the pitch - all a great thrill!). But almost at once I realised that, like thousands of others, I wasn't anywhere near good enough - and I wore glasses. My idea was that I would get contact lenses when I made it to the first-team. It took a long time to be 'fitted' for contact lenses and I didn't make the first-team anyway! I scored at the Sandy Lane End in a trial match; played in a couple of practice matches with the professionals; surprised Burgin (former England B international) with a classy shot from an acute angle that hit the post and stayed out (story of my life!); was clattered in the back by Martin (former Scotland B international) after a crafty feint; brought down by Aspden (after what was probably the finest body swerve ever seen on the ground); given advice and encouragement by Bodell; given a lift back to Manchester by Peter Phoenix. Of course, it has not been all gloom and doom. There has been highlights (not many though), but to make it worse I missed the one glorious, joyous occasion that would have made most of it bearable - May 10 1969 when our only promotion was gained by the 3-0 home victory over Southend United. A truly great day for the Dale - and I was in hospital - well, not really: I was released late on the Saturday morning and ruled myself out of the game on medical grounds, something I've bitterly regretted from that day, that minute, to this! The reason for not going probably sounds a tad wimpish now. At the time, I was at my parents' home (at Cheadle, in what is now called Greater Manchester) after a third (in a few months) operation for a troublesome nasal complaint. At this stage (1969) I'd already had many years of following the Dale and was well accustomed to having hopes dashed, enduring huge disappointments, being 'kicked in the teeth'. Looking back, I probably rationalised my decision thus: there was a medical risk in going out to the game and this had to be offset against the strong (we had a good team that season) likelihood the Dale would win and secure promotion, and I would be there to witness the event and share in the unforgettable glory of it all. On the other hand, there was the very, very slight chance a germ might get up my nose, infect the sore, gangrene would set in, and my nose would have to be chopped off. So even if the Dale won promotion, I should still suffer (following the Dale is a bit like this). So, I decided against going and reinforced my rationalisation by reflecting on the fact that I'd seen most of the home games in the run-in, including the penultimate home victory (against Halifax, won by Dennis Butler's glorious goal) that 'really set promotion up', and also the three times we scored six that season (and turned-up for the midweek game a few weeks earlier against Southend, which was postponed at the last minute - yes, you've guessed it, waterlogged pitch!). So I tried to come to terms with my loss. But I should have gone. I had to wait for the result via Grandstand and Frank Bough until 5pm or later. The match at Spotland was the only League game that day, in addition to the 'Home Internationals' (perhaps Wales v England), so the Rochdale result had low priority, and we did not have GMR and Mikes Brookes*, and score-flashes in those days so it was a long wait. And good for Frank, after he announced the score he warmly acknowledged the significance of the result - Rochdale's first-ever promotion. I should have gone, I should have gone. Last season? Well, having seen it all in a long, long sentence I knew, I really did, that it was just too good to be true. In fact, the fortunes of the Dale have become so relentlessly predictable I can forecast most of the scores. If I was a betting man I'd have won enough to redrain the whole of the Spotland pitch in a week, and buy a centre half with pace! Last game of the season? I thought fleetingly of a Dale victory and the pleasure this would bring (until the play-offs), but I knew we weren't really up to it. Yes, it was disappointing but at least the after-effects, the ever-so-familiar deadening sense of despair that engulfs even after so long a sentence, even knowing most times what the score will be, did not endure on this occasion. The strong sense of low expectation and realism, developed to the 'nth degree by years of disappointment and unfulfilled hopes, helped. And God help us, with the way 'the game' is now, if we ever do get promoted. Let us remember, though, those who risk not only their sanity but their money - the directors. Despite it all 'we' have survived while others have fallen by the wayside. As long as we keep on going there is hope. There is always hope, there is always a new season ahead. Thank you directors, current and past. Where would we be without you?

* Mike Brookes is *GMR*'s Rochdale correspondent. His dry, succinct and honest appraisals delivered in an authentic Rochdale accent have afforded him cult status among fans. He contributes articles about Rochdale to the *Manchester Evening News*, *Rochdale Observer*, the match programme and various websites. He has also been known to make the half-time announcements at Spotland, such is this one-man industry.

Trevor Hoyle, Rochdale: Nearly every home match, when I was a kid (we're talking the early-1950s) my dad would ask me if I wanted to go and watch Dale with him. More often than not I said no. I wasn't a sporting lad, no interest in football, always had my nose stuck in the *Rover* or the *Wizard,* and of course Biggles and *Just William* books. My dad had played amateur football and had a spell as a semi-pro boxer before the war, so he probably thought I was too much of a swot with a superior attitude problem. (Probably right - I passed for the Grammar School.) Suddenly, and for no reason, in my mid-twenties and married with two kids, I got the yen to make the trek to Spotland, I used to pick my dad up on the way - he lived in the town-centre flats - and we went together, rain or shine, for many years. Then after a lifetime of supporting Dale, right up to his sixties, he just stopped going, and I carried on, and carried on, up to today. Don't ask me why. It defies reason. A natural-born masochist I suppose. After years of staring from the Sandy at the rusting corrugated-iron shed and hill of cinders that was the Pearl Street End, I recall the shock of seeing a spanking brand-new stand there with row upon row of shiny seats rising to infinity. I thought: my God, it actually looks like a real soccer stadium, like what you see on the telly. Now, of course, with the new Willbutts Lane stand (can't remember its name) we have the best stadium in the third and possibly second division too. An early novel of mine, Rule of Night, was inspired by a visit to Dale. It was in the early-1970s when skinhead 'bovver boys' were starting to be a nuisance, and now and then a fight would break out behind the goals (I'm pretty sure this was before the fans were segregated). Anyway, the police grabbed this Rochdale yobbo and frog-marched him past the Main Stand and up the players' tunnel to the jeers, catcalls and flying spittle of the home fans. And the thought went through my head: they're treating him like an animal and yet this lad has a mum and a dad and mates and probably a girl-friend, and I was curious as to what made him tick. So my character Kenny Seddon was born, a tough-nut and a loser with a taste for violence who ended up in Buckley Hall detention centre. Several copies of the book found their way into Buckley Hall library - and all of them were nicked by the inmates. Which is the most flattering reaction I've ever had to a book of mine; what you might call literary criticism in action.

John McDonough, Idle, Bradford (formerly Deeplish, Rochdale): How many blokes, frozen to the bone and miserable after another dour performance, have left Spotland muttering, 'Bloody rubbish, that's the last time I'm going'. My dad was no exception, but unlike all the other moaners who went back on their word and trooped along to the next home game, he never did. And neither did I. Well, not for a decade or so. No, it was decided for me that resurgent Bolton Wanderers would offer a better football education for an impressionable young lad in the mid-1970s. And so began a series of relationships involving Lancashire clubs that were bigger, more successful and certainly better supported than Dale. They weren't difficult to find. My beloved team, that had won promotion from the fourth division, appeared on Match of the Day, beaten the Championship-winning full-strength Everton side in a pre-season friendly and, unforgettably, dumped Coventry and Noel Cantwell out of the FA Cup, were now an embarrassment. The ground was falling down around our ears. The team was plummeting almost as quick. I remember hoping that we wouldn't draw a non-league side in the FA Cup first round because there was a fair chance of having more embarrassment heaped on us. Bolton by comparison were a breath of fresh air (moving up the League), followed by Man City (coerced by drinking buddies, I'm afraid) and finally Oldham (I worked there and my best footballing mate - a Rochdalian - had followed them from when they were on a par with Dale). So why return to Spotland in the late-1980s, with the club clinging to its Football League life and no immediate prospect of salvation? Guilt, to be honest. What right did I have sharing in the promotion celebrations at clubs that would only ever rate as high as second in my personal pecking order? 'First love never dies' goes the song and while Dale were more often than not a poor side with little prospect of improvement, they were my first football team, and, as such, the catalyst for a sporting odyssey that is still running as strong as ever today. I now know what I wish I'd been told 25 years ago; that football clubs are not something to be discarded when a better one comes along - like girlfriends. They are with you for life, for better or worse - like wives. On returning to The Sandy it all made perfect sense. The Saturdays spent away from Spotland watching some other team and hoping Dale hadn't lost, were the right feelings to have. It was just a matter of time before me and my first love were reunited. Now look at them! It's like being transported back 30 years. There's a genuine interest in the town, kids are wearing Dale shirts and we've a stadium that would not look out of place in a higher division. Which is just as well, because that's where Dale are heading. To have gone up this season would have been too much too soon. We're not quite ready yet, just give it a year or two. As for the sceptics, let them go and watch City, or Bolton, or Oldham - and suffer like I did.

Alan Main, Salisbury North, South Australia: I started watching Dale round about 1960. I'd just left school, and started to go regularly with a group of mates from work. It was certainly then that I got the bug, or got into bad habits (which ever way you want to look at it). There then followed the years of semi-highs and trough-like lows, but, unlike my mates, I was not lured away by the more fashionable clubs. I still found it better to watch my hometown team, and to suffer or be elated by their performances. Believe it or not, many a Saturday night has been made or spoiled on the outcome of the match. There are many memories - the promotion season; of being called the Cavaliers of the fourth division; of Reg Jenkins, Tony Buck, Alf Arrowsmith, Dave Cross, Stan Milburn, and so many others. So I guess I support the Dale out of tradition, out of loyalty, and as a way of supporting my hometown. Even now, though I live in Australia, come Saturday night, my thoughts are with the Dale. The first job every Sunday morning is to log on the computer and get the result. The disappointment of us not making the play-offs this year was just as great out here as I'm sure it was for everyone in Rochdale.

Still, it's been a good season and my best wishes go to the board, the manager and the players for the future.

John McNicholas, Cottingham, East Yorkshire: It's nearly half a century since I was last at Spotland; I moved away from Rochdale in the early-1950s. But I've been to see them when they play Hull and my brother goes when they play at home. And I've two nephews that play for them - Liam's the one with the trumpet and Simon plays the trombone - you've perhaps heard them. I've followed Rochdale for all these years, so it's been a delight to read the articles this season. Much of the delight comes from the memories they bring back and the pleasure that comes from knowing that, despite the big changes - like the new stands - some things don't alter. Even little things. Mark wrote about the woman who stood at her gate on Sandy Lane and asked supporters going home how they'd gone on. She was there in the 1940s, you know (well, perhaps it was her grandma). What used to puzzle me was that she didn't go back in when someone told her the score. Perhaps she got more details from other supporters - "Was anybody sent off?" "Did they get any corners?" I used to go with my dad and his mate, Harry Shaw. We went to every home match and we always stood in the same place - half way up the slope to the left of the goal facing Sandy Lane. There was a sort of a stand at that end but we never went in there, even when it was raining, which it did a lot. I don't remember the names of many of the players. One that's stuck in my mind is Walter Birch, who must have been good or played for a long time.* Perhaps both, because he had a testimonial match. That was the game when Frank Swift, the ex-goalkeeper for Manchester City, played, saved a shot, then rolled it back to the forward to have another try. And there was a player who had a tremendous throw-in, who wore glasses. I think his name was Reid**. The manager was Ted Goodier, who bought and sold players a lot. The leather ball that got heavier when it was wet, and that had to come back into play when it was kicked into touch - none of the current speedy substitution of another (plastic) ball. Was that because they had to continue using a ball of the same weight, rather like using an equally-worn ball after a lost ball in cricket? Or just because they only had one ball? And if they kicked it into Sandy Lane, there was a man who had to go and fetch it: a good time-wasting tactic. Back passes were rare and always booed. I agreed with that. It seemed somehow unmanly to go backwards, like retreating. The players had proper numbers on their backs, so you could tell where they ought to be. I remember teams coming like Accrington Stanley and Bradford Park Avenue, which have almost dropped out of sight. Where's New Brighton? But Rochdale's still there, still doing better at the start of the season than at the end. I'll still look for their result before any other team's.

* Walter Birch played in 243 league and cup games for Rochdale between 1946 and 1952, scoring 10 goals. He was a centre half who joined Rochdale from Huddersfield Town, for whom he did not make a first-team appearance. He retired from football after leaving Rochdale. He died in 1991, aged 73.
** David Reid, a Scotsman, wore glasses while playing for Rochdale. He joined the club in January 1948 from the amateur club Glasgow Perthshire and played 36 matches, scoring two goals before moving to Bradford Park Avenue in September 1950. He later played for Workington and Crewe Alexandra.

Bob Hutchinson, Sheffield: A nostalgic visit to Spotland in 2000, plus the articles in The Times brought back memories of days on the Kop with my late dad and Uncles Gilbert and Clifford plus the faithful fanatics. My first memories are of FA cup games v Notts County with Tommy Lawton and v Charlton Athletic and Sam Bartram. Playing for the Dale were my heroes, Trevor Churchill in goal, Walter Birch at centre half, Jimmy Anders and Jackie Arthurs on the wing and Jack Connors at centre forward (such positions now extinct!) Another bright memory is of the introduction of the wooden floodlights and evening matches. How I longed to play on the hallowed turf under the lights. Harry Catterick was the manager and a former England International, Jackie Haines, the star signing. Following success at county level I was invited to sign-on and train under Tom Nichol (now in his eighties but still playing an active part at the club) on Tuesday and Thursday evenings. We lapped the hallowed turf and then did exercises under the Main Stand on the wooden sleepers and ashes. It was heaven! Even the primitive one-large-bath-for-all did not put us off. The first-team squad, which included Frank Lord, Brian Green, Stan Milburn, Ted Burgin, Stan Hepton, Jimmy McGuigan, Ray Aspden, and Norman Bodell trained using the same facilities by day under, first, Jack Marshall and then player manager, Tony Collins. It was very special to play matches at Spotland and to enjoy the privileges of the club, sitting in the stand at any club fixture, being known and signing autographs. Chairman Fred Ratcliffe gave me my first International tickets for Wembley. Joe Fagan was the groundsman prior to moving to Liverpool. A foot operation put paid to any hopes of a soccer career. I sat with Derek Dougan at a game versus Blackburn when he too was in pot! I became a PE teacher and moved to Sheffield and since 1964 all my school teams have been trained on refined Rochdale tactics! I have suffered and triumphed vicariously from afar. Other Rochdalians, Bob Harrison and Graham Taylor, have given moral support but it is difficult in a city with two first division teams to get the pupils to take me and my love of Rochdale seriously. Having spent too many years worrying about re-election, this season has shown a hope of play-off glory, only to be dashed on the last day. The present ground with such wonderful facilities is a far cry from the 1950s and 1960s. The players and supporters have never been so privileged. Rochdale is still the first result I look for on a Saturday and the result can still affect my mood (for a few minutes!) and I still think of my dad who is to blame (or takes the credit) for a lifetime of addiction to the game and especially to Rochdale.

Paul Fidler, Ipswich: Why do I do it? I mean, whenever I pluck up the courage to mention my team in football discussions down the pub, I'm faced with almost certain ridicule. There are those who know nothing about Rochdale. There are those who know little about Rochdale ('Aren't they in the Conference?'). Regardless of how well they are doing, no one seems to care anyway. But, I'll support them to the end. Being exiled 250 miles away in Ipswich doesn't help. Still, they are my home team. They will go up, and I will be there. I feel proud to support them, and support them I will. I can face whatever comes my way in the form of sarcasm. But, that all goes away when I'm in the Sandy, listening to the roar of, 'Daaaaaaaaalllllllllll.'

Evan Hollows, Stockport: My Grandpa used to take my dad to Spotland when he was a lad. After many seasons of lowly league positions, my dad finally cracked and gave up on them. After that, the closest he ever got to watching Dale was the BBC's vidiprinter. As I grew up, football became a bigger part of my life. I loved playing and I wanted to play for Dale just like my Grandpa had*. In the playground, all the other lads were City, United or County players. I'd never seen Dale so I didn't have a clue who I was. My dad couldn't really help me find my playground identity; he knew surnames from the results in the Sunday papers but that wasn't good enough to stop the taunts and jibes that I had to endure. It was hard being a young wanna-be Dale fan in Stockport. After plenty of pleading, dad finally took me to Spotland with a mate of mine. We stood right up by the boards while dad stood leaning against the old stand looking at the hills, daydreaming. We drew 0-0 against Torquay. I don't think he enjoyed it that much. I thought it was bloody fantastic, I was a real fan. I'd seen them play and was now suitably equipped to put across a decent argument should the need arise on Monday at school. When I was a bit older my dad used to just drop me off and spend the afternoon with my Grandma. He said it was better for him that way. Over the past few seasons, my dad has become the Dale fan he was as a lad. He's got a new-born enthusiasm and optimism. This season was made even more disappointing by the fact that I wanted the team to prove to him that he was right for finding his faith again. We just missed out and, at the moment, he's happy enough. There's always next year for some success but I don't know how long his patience will last, so 'Come on the Dale'.

* Evan's grandfather was William (Bill) Hollows. There is no record of him playing for the first-team, but Evan believes he may have appeared for the reserves or another of the club's affiliated sides.

Col Cavanagh, Rochdale: The final game of the season at Plymouth summed up the entire season for Dale. Almost every single emotion that we endured throughout the season came out again at Plymouth, only 10 times as strong. Has there ever been a moment to be as proud to be a Dale supporter, as it was down at Plymouth, knowing that we had taken over 1,000 supporters to Home Park? Was there a more nail-biting end to any match throughout the season than we had that day? And had a final whistle ever hurt as much as it did that day? It's easy now to look back and point fingers to where we went wrong. Vital penalties were missed, controversial team selections, dodgy referees, the pitch and its postponements, our egg-chasing lodgers; the list goes on. However, above everything, let's remember that this was still a great season for Dale. We may have missed out by a point, but there were so many great memories that we will never forget: the 1,600 singing their hearts out at Ewood Park, the 4-0 thumping of Shrewsbury, the win at Exeter, the signing of Paul Connor. This was a season to be proud of. Let's never forget that, and let's make sure next season is as good, if not even better.

Steve Hill, Woolmer Green, Hertfordshire: At the beginning of the 1978-79 season I decided to follow the club that had finished bottom of the Football League the previous season. No other reason really. Rochdale had picked up just 24 points all season - it couldn't get any worse. At the age of 14, I just assumed that we couldn't drop any further down the league. Twenty three seasons later and we are still in the bottom division. Our only promotion during this time was when they abolished the old fourth division. I've seen us lose in every corner of the country. I've been the butt of endless jokes and comments, many unprintable. I've also spent a small fortune following a club 200 miles from my home in Hertfordshire. I travelled to Plymouth in hope and expectation that we might finally make it to the play-offs and eventually to the promised land of the second division. But good old Dale were to disappoint again. It seemed that their failures of the last 20 years were summed up in those agonising 90 minutes - a few highs and near misses but ultimately nothing. And why do I still follow them? Because I am the proverbial football optimist and one day I want to say to all those people who have asked me 'Why Rochdale?' - it's because we are a successful, non-commercialised, well-run, friendly club that plays good football. Oh well, only another 20 years to sort the successful part out!

Steve Stott, Cork, Ireland: What is it about Rochdale? I lived there for six years; born in 1942, left in 1948 to go to Cork when my dad got a job in a textile mill in Blarney. Hardly old enough to remember very much of Rochdale. I lived in Cambridge Avenue. My parents watched the bombs drop on Manchester but I remained oblivious to the war. I went to school in Norden (I think). I never went to Spotland - I have never been to Spotland. I wouldn't know how to get there! But since I became old enough to understand Sports Report on the Light Programme, I've listened for and identified with the Dale. I've never been back to Rochdale even. But now my lads, both thirty-something and hardly ever north of Watford, are among the faithful as well as myself. We go to see them at Barnet on wet Saturday afternoons, slogging uphill at Underhill. We took a family pilgrimage to Anfield to see the 7-0 glorious 'Rochdale Cup Final'* We don't want them to continue improving because they might get promoted one day and think of the gloom next year if they were immediately relegated. We seek mid-table respectability or else the agony of just surviving. We feel emotional about a team we hardly know. We think it might be love.

* Rochdale lost at Anfield 7-0 in the third round of the FA Cup in January 1996.

Chris Fitzgerald, Norden, Rochdale: I've been a Dale supporter since I was eight-years-old and in the 13 years I have supported Rochdale one thing has enthralled me the most: the unpredictability of the team. From game to game Dale will make you laugh and Dale will make you cry. I know this could be said of most football teams but we always seem to carry this form from season to season. This is the exciting thing about supporting a local third division side.

Gary Grindrod, Milton Keynes: I am a Dale in exile, residing as I do in sunny Milton Keynes for some 20 years, and recently joining the Web, where, to my surprise, I found the Dale website. I still go to games if visiting family. When I left the forces in the mid-1970s, I joined the fire brigade in Rochdale and started going regularly to games. A colleague I worked with was on the fringes of professional football and ended up in Dale reserves, where, on Saturdays, I used to run around the empty stands getting the ball for them!

Farringdon Ibsley: The season just past has been one of learning and new horizons strange to many. Learning of that rare thing, success - yes, success, a new sphere for the Dale enthusiast. Its odour wafted rich beneath our noses, we were teased, enticed and left clutching for this temptress, as a proud yet cruel draw at Plymouth broke the dream with the painful wake-up call of reality. Do not despair! It is my 'thing' so to speak, to reflect such of life's delicacies into poetry and prose, but I admit to struggling over a review of this season more than any in a long history rooting for Rochdale Football Club. For the first year in many, I can honestly say I am enjoying a close season. The break from such unique (to us) emotional trauma is a relief. Form to savour and to scorn. Connor, arriving like the stereotypical super hero, Coleman, cast as Benny Hill's bald stooge. If we supported the likes of the congenial Manchester City, we would be hardened to it all. But, we are not, so we struggle to cope. From 0-4 away to 1-7 and 6-0 at home, a roller-coaster. Rare excitement after years of broken dreams and depravity. Lasting out with genuine hope until the final contest of 46 - precious indeed. Yet a minority seem to consider this level of achievement as yet 'another' failure. A sense of history and perspective suggests this is not so. For what we have coped with since our last relegation is our nonachievement, and that is a strength that I doubt any other league club in the country could have managed. We are still here. We have been entertained, good and bad in this time. Some may say as long as the entertainment is good and the social side of being a Dale fan is maintained, we can plod along quite safely. Is that our destiny? There can and will be more. We have failed to achieve promotion in all that time (or relegation either) but still, we fight on. Our numerically-challenged but devoted loyal band of supporters grows despite this. Still we survive in the age where sordid affluence has taken the 'big' club away from the fan into the stock market. The club is still ours - and I as a fan am more proud of that than any share issue or dividend would make a shareholder. That makes us real. We have a manager, who, though not faultless, is actually improving our prospects year on year. Enjoy it. What we have to learn now is how to deal with the prospect of success which is so near to us, and has been so rare in seasons past. Enjoy it. Transpose the survival skills into getting behind the prospect of achievement, not throwing the chance away with the hindrance of negativity, the 'we always lose out' despondency. We have more spirit and determination amongst us than we dare realise. Please use it.

* Farringdon Ibsley was a regular columnist on Rochdaleafc.com throughout the season and his florid, erudite prose won many admirers.

Chris Bocock: Towards the end of the Brighton home game, the hypothermia and nostalgia combined in a dangerously heady mix. I pointed to where the Spion Kop had been and described to my youngest daughter Ellie how the short-trousered kid stood on the grassy slope next to his dad and old Mr Riley with his pipe smoking. The season was 1968-69 and I remembered how the youngster's eyes often filled with tears of joy and elation as his heroes and warriors triumphed again and again towards promotion. Colin Parry and that head of hair; the swashbuckling Billy Rudd and the gorgeous Norman Whitehead on the wing. The echoes down the years tasted delicious and Ellie indulged me as only daughters can. Reverie over: free kick to Brighton - they score and I'm back to Mother Earth with a bang. I've been a long time in exile from the north. Over 25 years a veteran of games in London, the South East, East Anglia, the Midlands and now, Worcestershire. Those years have witnessed mixed fortunes for the Dale and me in roughly equal measure. Sometimes it's felt Siamese-like in our connection as we've experienced the good times and the bad, both together and apart. I still hold those 20 shares I bought when Dale's very existence was threatened by financial ruin. I still keep programmes from games in exotic places like Aldershot, Wimbledon, Maidstone, Cambridge, Walsall, Shrewsbury and Kidderminster. Why do I continue to suffer those severe mood swings on a Saturday evening when I'm through the menopause and into my grown-up years? And so to Plymouth on the final day. Enormous feelings of pride and passion while I'm driving South, mixed with apprehension from all those years of following Dale. Waves and gestures of fellow fans en route to Kismet only add to the occasion. Was there just a hint of those tears of joy and elation - that childlike fascination and enthusiasm? You bet there was! Thirty-two long years since the last time round with my heroes and warriors and I'm not sure I'll be here in another 32. This time it's my lover who is with me and I can't think of anyone I'd rather share this experience with. Not a football fan, her interest is aroused by the people, noise and passion, but she still finds time to read her book. The game's over, we all know the score and the barmy army troops disconsolately away. A few of us remain immobile on the terraces and the tears and emotion of a young lad nearby moves me: there can be no words at times like this. As the crowd descends the steps away from the terrace I hear the strains of Always Look on the Bright Side of Life. For the briefest of moments a thought flits across my mind and then it's gone. It's not until an hour or so later, sat on Plymouth Hoe drinking wine and watching the sun go down, that the thought emerges into full daylight. And then amid the ghosts of Francis Drake, the Tolpuddle Martyrs and seafarers on The Mayflower I know with absolute certainty I will be there in 2033 looking for my heroes and warriors in blue.

Steve Harrison, Sandbach (pop group manager and Paul Connor's representative): I'd love to take all the credit for bringing Paul Connor to Rochdale, but it wouldn't be strictly true. In fact, I have a business partner in Gary Mellor who is a lawyer. We operate within the sports industry as a firm of solicitors, as opposed to out-and-out agents. I first met Paul in a very 'Alan Partridge-seque' hotel on the outskirts of Cambridge when he was on-loan at the Abbey Stadium early in the 2000-2001 season. Paul scored five goals in eight games for them. I found him humble and unpretentious. My colleague and long-suffering Stoke City supporter was already a committed fan of the boy Connor. Moreover, our mutual friend and instigator of our sports management partnership, David Williams, another long-term Stoke fan, was clearly devastated at Paul's eventual move to Dale - the loss to Stoke was, in David's mind, unfathomable. It was clear that the boy Connor was a well-liked servant with the Britannia Stadium faithful. Paul wanted to play first-team football. He wanted to realise his potential; he needed to feel wanted and part of a team. He had no less than four managers at Stoke. Continuity was not the order of the day. Gary and I were instructed by Paul to represent him in his affairs. His picture went up on the office walls alongside his new musical associates including Tim Burgess of The Charlatans, Peter Hook of New Order, Mark Burgess of The Chameleons and Lee Gorton of Alfie, together with a scattering of Gold and Platinum discs. His sporting counterparts included Irish internationals Graham Kavanagh and Clive Clarke, and cricket internationals Dean Headley and Mushtaq Ahmed, and Dave Harold - the world-ranked number 10 snooker player. Steve Parkin at Rochdale was keen, very keen on the prospect of signing Paul Connor. An agreement was made between the clubs, which on the face of it, would totally contradict Stoke City's lack of commitment to the lad. Stoke City demanded a significant sell-on clause as 'clearly' Paul was going to go on to greater things. Sell-on clauses are essentially the domain of clubs such as Crewe Alexandra, a club of exceptional ability and coaching resources that regularly spots future potential prospects, get the best from them, yet accepts the inevitable scenario of the players moving on to greater plains. The club always insures that its short-term involvement and development pays dividends in the future. Obviously, someone at Stoke City rated Paul, beyond face-value impressions that emanated from the club - a brace of goals on his Stoke City debut, two goals in two starts in the current season and five goals in eight while on loan to Cambridge United in the second division. Now if that isn't Stoke City 'reserve form' then what is? Paul was not getting the opportunities. For our part, we needed to ensure that Paul was positioned in a club where he could realise his potential. I really wanted him to stand tall and make a difference. We needed background information on Dale. The season was going well, the attendances up, but it seemed to have peaked early doors. The goals had dried up and the pitch was suffering in the inclement reality that is the Pennine weather. Fixtures were beginning to stack up. As a Manchester City supporter since 1967, a season ticket holder since 1971 and my lifelong newspaper being the *Manchester Evening News*, Dale was familiar if not domestic meat and two veg in the Harrison household. I called Mark [Hodkinson], a Rochdale aficionado. I discussed the various issues with Mark and promised him that Paul would score 10 goals for Dale providing that we completed the deal without too much 'heavyweight' negotiations between the two clubs. For our part, we had all-but agreed the personal terms and package for Paul. The deal was done. On arrival at the club the relative enormity and excitement surrounding Paul's signing immediately struck us. The stadium was impressive; the personnel were simply charming. It was clear that this was a club steeped in passion and loyalty. It had a heart and soul. We all felt good. It felt like home. Paul was undoubtedly 'wanted'. On the following day, I met Paul to take him through his medical and then on to his press conference, alongside the Rochdale directors. I was keen to be introduced as Paul's 'representative' as both Gary and I squirm at the very idea and stigma associated with the expression 'agent'. The chairman extended the courtesy as he introduced me to the chief executive as Paul's 'representative'. "'Oh you're his agent. Let me check if I still have my ring and watch," he jokingly exclaimed after shaking my hand. I really did almost feel the need to justify my very being. "I'm one of the good guys", a sports consultant to a long-standing firm of solicitors; I love my wife and child - I'm kind to animals! I monitored the club websites. I loved the Dale fans' 'song for Connor' campaign. I felt for the Stoke fans' loss. The headline following Paul's start at Dale on the front cover of the Stoke City fanzine, The Oatcake - 'Potters on lookout for Goals? Prolific young striker uncovered at Rochdale'. It went on to elaborate: 'He just looked like a proper centre forward, always giving defences a hard time. Could we live to rue his departure?' I saw Paul on his debut for Dale. The reception he received was fabulous. I met his dad for the first time. What a lovely, dedicated and proud man. He never misses a match. Every week he travels from Durham City. Like father, like son. I have since watched Paul play a number of games at the club. The people I meet are always welcoming. The pies are great; the fans are true, loyal and as 'expert' as the next. The heart beats strong in the club. Paul scored 10 goals in 12 games and I kept my promise to my friend. I really believe that Paul Connor made a difference at the club. I 'almost' went to Plymouth and Paul 'almost' scored. On the day of the game, I left Paul a message wishing him all the best and felt the urge to say how proud we were of him. He brings that sense of loyalty out in you. The boy done good. He did us all proud. Nearest thing you've had to a 'pop star' in some time. Enjoy every moment while he's at the club. One thing for sure, it's Rochdale that has given him the chance to shine. I recently attended the England v Mexico match at Pride Park. As I took my seat, I noticed that the girl next-but-one had a Rochdale shirt on. I wanted to share my 'secret' with her and talk about Paul Connor - pride and all. I didn't. It's all that bloody insecurity about this agent business. Is T.W.A.T. really an anagram of agent? Paul Connor. Great bloke.

Scores goals for fun. Pop star looks, rates Tellin' Stories [a Charlatans' LP] as one of his favourite all-time albums. He also plays for the Dale. Now how cool is that?

Neil Watts, Stowmarket, Suffolk: 2000-2001, a Rochdale odyssey: Amazing highs, unspeakable lows - so near, yet, so far. A bright beginning, a cruel end, a season so typical of life as a Rochdale supporter. I've been there before you know - ever since my father started taking me in my childhood years. Initially spending the 90 minutes kicking the dirt on the Pearl Street terrace, then teenage freedom standing in the Sandy Lane End with my mates - returning to Rochdale town centre on the football specials with toes and fingers 'burning' as the blood returned to frozen extremities. A time of scrapbooks and, yes, success - promotion in the 1968-69 season - joy unknown, pitch invasions and that wonderful man Fred Radcliffe* speaking on a rickety public-address system in a tiered wooden stand. Then the 1970s - lean and barren years for the most part - life for me as apparently the only Rochdale supporter in the whole of Cambridge University, relegation, and early adult life away from the bosom of Spotland. Then the rites of passage and a new girlfriend - taking her on a pilgrimage from the soft South to the beloved homeland - in particular to the ground. She suffered the cold, frozen days with pigeons undisturbed in the goalmouth, and did not complain - even understood that an early date away at Southend was a clear sign of interest and affection! Then marriage and children - no time for really following the Dale, but a subscription to the Football Pink kept me in touch, and occasional away games at Peterborough, Cambridge and Colchester. We persevered, Rochdale persevered, and our family grew. Rochdale also grew - a new stand, financial stability. Buy a brick in a second new stand - in memory of Ken Watts - a great father still supporting from heaven, and children getting Rochdale scarves and hats for birthday and Christmas presents - stealthy indoctrination. Then family trips to see the Dale - the appointment of Steve Parkin - proper football being played - the signing of Clive Platt; real hope for the future, which brings us to the season just departed. The websites kept us close to the action all season - the usual roller-coaster ride. A family Christmas treat, away at Leyton Orient, a point earned on promotion rivals territory. Conning our way into a friend's household for a Sky game. Who else arrives for Sunday lunch bedecked in blue and white hats and scarves? Even that game was nearly lost to the bloomin' weather - fog - but a famous 3-1 victory, what a team! Then the rain kept on coming, the season stalled, a trip to a matinee performance of Aida at the Royal Albert Hall on Saturday 24 February followed by dinner in Covent Garden. Marvellous? You must be joking, telephone news of a 7-1 defeat ruined the day! Season's over, but no - a late equaliser in the Brighton game and we were off up the table again. A family pilgrimage at Easter, not to Jerusalem, but to Rochdale - people who know us just smile! Away at Macclesfield, a draw which should have been a win, and then on Easter Monday, my mother (who was on the pilgrimage with us) pays her first visit to a match at Spotland for many years and a glorious 3-1 victory ensues. Meet the players, and the Bayliss family. We're almost there aren't we? Sadly not. And despite an heroic last few games, dastardly Blackpool steal our play-off place. Oh, if only Gary Jones had scored that penalty at Macclesfield. If only, if only, if only - life as a Rochdale supporter. Still, there's always next season. Promotion? You bet!

* Fred Ratcliffe, a local engineering company owner and lifelong Rochdale fan, was club chairman from 1952 to1979. Almost single-handedly, he kept the club afloat for most of this period. He is generally recognised as the most important figure in the club's history.

Matt Smith, Spotland Bridge, Rochdale: When Dale went into the last two games of the season, both against Plymouth, we all knew that winning both would be a necessity. A win in the home game on the Tuesday night would give us all hope for the long trip on the Saturday; for some it would actually give them a reason to make the trek down to Devon. The thing was, even though winning the game at Spotland would not actually mean we had achieved something, it would give us that rare feeling of 'We have a real chance now!' We knew we had only won away once in six months, but winning the home match would give us the opportunity to celebrate. We would make the most of it and what follows is the piece I wrote the day afterwards: Last night was a strange moment for me. After following Dale for the last 20 years, I was able to celebrate in the way I have seen countless fans of countless clubs in the past. I was able to experience nail-biting tension without the all-too-often experienced (and expected) goal from the opposition minutes before the end. I was able to go onto the pitch running and punching the air with as much exuberance as the horde of kids who do it when we have finished 11th at the end of the season. As I did this, I knew I didn't look stupid, well maybe I did, but seeing as though everyone else was doing it nobody was going to say so. I would like to say it was just one of those nights where everyone present is just so happy to be there, but it wasn't 'one of those nights' because it was the night. I know we have not made it yet, but whatever happens on Saturday at Plymouth we have to all remember last night for a long time. We may not have won promotion, but for Dale fans last night it felt like we had. Trying to recreate that feeling will be difficult, but the most exciting thing is that we all know it is something we could all be feeling a few more times before the end of May, and that's why we want this great run to continue. We have had a taste of our first pint on a very hot day, and we want a few more before we retire to our beds for the night. I now know, at least, what celebrating something at the end of the season is like, even though we all knew that it wasn't really the end of the season. That night we went through all the feelings that fans of clubs who clinch promotion on the final day go through. It was something new, something different, and for that reason we will all remember the home game against Plymouth in May, just as much as we all do our best to forget Plymouth away four days later.

Chris Hynd, Larbert, Scotland: Having lived in Scotland all my days and never visited Spotland, many people will scoff at my claims to be a Dale fan. Having met friends from Rochdale on holiday one year, I made a promise to 'look out for their score' on a Saturday. My mate would do the same for my local team - Stenhousemuir. This name may ring a few bells with some Dale fans as Rochdale have visited Ochilview during the past two pre-seasons. It is a consequence of that first visit that the Dale bug well and truly bit me, so much so that I purchased a Dale top with 'Ellis 24' proudly emblazoned on the back. I have been watching the team's progress closely during the past two seasons through Teletext and Sky but, so caught up in play-off fever, I made the trip to Plymouth only to be disappointed. To round off a bizarre story, I have now met a fellow Dale fan at university and hopefully we'll be having a celebratory drink in the union next summer.

Patrick Groarke, Thailand: Home is where the heart is. Those rolling hills, mills, and a Town Hall to die for. And then the life sentence begins, a visit to Spotland somewhere back in time sat on a grassy knoll, mesmerised by the passion a football provokes. Elton John was in the crowd, I think; why else would my cousins Catherine and Angela take me to such a place?* A seed was sown. I am sorry to say I tried Leeds; it was a story of success at the time. The Gelder End was at its best, our children will never know. And then I came home, to my roots. I played footie with Dave Thompson ** at school. Moggy - known only from a distance - made it more than real.

* Elton John visited Spotland on Saturday, 18 September 1976, to watch Rochdale v Watford. He had just been made Watford chairman. Rochdale won 3-1.
** Dave Thompson, a winger, had two spells with Rochdale, 1981-1985 and 1994-1996. He played, in total, 266 league and cup games and scored 24 goals.

Phil Barton, Bishop's Stortford, Hertfordshire: You don't see many Rochdale replica shirts in Bishop's Stortford. Like the nearby

M11, football is acknowledged but leaves this Hertfordshire town relatively untouched. To wear the shirt in neighbouring Harlow, though, turns an act of eccentricity into one of suicidal courage - Space Mountain after a Big Mac. This is Holsten and Dreamcast territory and we don't much care for strangers in these parts. The native eyes weigh you up as you walk by, looking surreptitiously and trying to remember if Chelsea were ever sponsored by Carcraft. Then, behind you comes the muffled thud of body against lamppost and someone exclaims in Southern speak about 'four' and 'kennel'. I still sometimes have trouble with the local patois. But, down these mean streets a man must go, for I am one of those known as 'Dale in Exile'. I'm a bit unsure about the exile label. It has the ring of someone being punished for wrong-doing. Perhaps you could say we expats do feel some sense of betrayal and we wear the shirt as an act of penance for desertion. But I think it goes even deeper than that. The shirt is my football club and a statement of where I come from. I may be here, but these are my roots. And football is the link. You may be friendly with Spurs, on talking terms with Arsenal, but the Dale is family. For me Rochdale Football Club was born on September 21 1968 in the Sandy Lane. By the corner flag to be exact, almost directly under where the electronic scoreboard is now. 'Rochdale 6 Bradford City 0' it would have read. I still have the scarf, one of those in alternate blue and white segments; remember these and you remember Supercar, let alone Thunderbirds. If you hold it to your ear, it's like a seashell. Listen carefully and you hear echoes from the terraces of yesteryear, names shouted in joy, exasperation and supplication by men in flat caps and lads in big boots: Graham Smith, Norman Whitehead, Reg Jenkins, Stevie Melledew. Caught in the fabric is the faint smell of Woodbines and, in your mind, you see the ball sailing above the wooden floodlight that was graced with a half-time scoreboard like an optician's chart. I keep the scarf next to my replica shirt. Thirty years or more separate them. There are 200 miles separating Spotland and its image on my dining room wall. If you left Rochdale you'd understand; there's not even any hills here. Let me try to explain. I parked my car down here the other day.

When I came back , a note was tucked under my windscreen wiper: 'Lad from Rochdale parked next to you - how ya doing?' Here was an unknown person sharing the bond generated by a community far distant. A fellow exile, a kindred spirit drawn to the message implicit in my replica shirt but explicit on the scarf in the window of my car: 'Proud to be Rochdale AFC', whether home or away.

Nick Johnson, Castleton, Rochdale: From a pre-1990s perspective, I don't think you ever chose to become a Dale fan, you had to be born one. How did us 1970s-1980s schoolkids become Dale fans? The club wasn't promoted in schools, there were certainly no free tickets given out. For me, a born Rochdalian, there can be no other club. The club has changed immensely. The ground is unrecognisable from what was in place 10 years ago and huge sums of money have been put into team-building. For me, it's all down to one man - an honest, committed chairman, who - in the past - many fans (locals) and ex-managers have said 'has no ambition'. This man has always offered to step down if any came forward and proved that they could do a better job. We all know, however, that will never happen. We will always have our 'small team' tag but, one day, you never know! We will soldier on, and we can certainly dream. God bless the good ship Dale and all that sail in her.

Mike Brown, Manchester: Well, we're looking forward to yet another season in the third division. The season gone has, for me, summed up what it means to support Rochdale, with the team managing to lull you into the false sense by Christmas that promotion was at last a real possibility, with the televised 3-1 performance against Orient in January providing the icing on the cake. Obviously, being Dale, things had to go pear-shaped, culminating in the Shrewsbury result. This was made worse, if that is possible, by the fact that I must be one of the few Dale supporters whose girlfriend and girlfriend's family are all avid Shrews supporters. Luckily I was snowed in at a hotel in Aberdeen at the time the full calamity struck home, and the gloating messages could only arrive by mobile when we came back to civilisation on the Sunday evening. Some might say it was rough justice for the delight I took in the 4-0 drubbing we inflicted on them earlier in the season. After the run in February and March when even the teams at the bottom of the league seemed guaranteed three points against us, there remained, by Easter, miraculously the glimmer of hope that the games in hand could be turned into points against the likes of Carlisle, Lincoln and Plymouth. At the end of the day, however, it was probably the night in Blackpool that reality sunk in that another year in the third division lay ahead as we were totally out-muscled and outplayed by a typical McMahon team. Still, there's enough to take from this season, with the highest placing for 20-odd years, to remain optimistic about next year, provided the Plattini and Connor strike-force remain at the club and a few sensible additions are made in the summer to the defence and midfield. Maybe the promised land next season?

Andrew Greenwood, Norden, Rochdale: The repetitive tone of the older supporter still lingers on, harking back to the days when Spotland was a haphazard collection of old sheds and when players played for the love of the game rather than the pound. When the teams lined up with five attackers and when the pies were real ones from the local bakery. God, they don't half go on, but then surely the older we all get the more we all reminisce; there's more to remember I suppose. When the day comes to relate how Spotland used to be and how football used to be to the kids of 2050 what will we find ourselves saying? Leading a Dalestruck 12-year-old grandson across the genetically-modified playing surface, the conversation could go something like this: "Where that Main Stand is now, there used to be a small single-tier stand and it used to have a dozen little executive boxes. Inside the stand there used to be a boardroom, where a few local men would debate the issues of the day before deciding on the best policy. There was none of your being controlled by the London financiers like today, who send their decisions straight to the club's computer. When I used to come, the whole crowd could have fitted into that Main Stand and before that stand, well, it is impossible to describe what the original one looked like. Believe it or not, there used to be another sport played here called rugby where grown men would chase after an egg-shaped ball. But it never caught on and when attendances fell to below 200 they called it a day. Over there is where Dale (sponsored by www.everythingmustbesponsored.com) fans used to stand. Ah, those were the days, when you could actually move with the flow of the game, get swept away by the emotion of a goal and share the disappointment of a defeat and stand with your mates come what may. There was none of this, 'Shall I watch the game on the Internet or shall I go to Spotland sponsored by Worldcraft?' You used to have these things called turnstiles too, where you paid with cash; you know, those old coins that gran gave you last week, and when you'd given the turnstile chap your money, you would push through a metal grill that clicked to record your admission for the attendance figure. I couldn't believe it when this retinal scanning admission system was installed. At the other end, there used to be an all-seater stand, the WMG. Now it's just a corporate, multi-storey, glass-fronted executive area. They called that 'progress' when they knocked down the Family Stand to build it. It used to be quite a noisy end on match days and they had a bar underneath where supporters would go for a pint, sometimes during the game if it was crap! Finally, this old stand over here was the jewel in the crown when it opened in 2000. It was the envy of every club in the division and now it looks small and run-down in comparison to the rest of the stadium. That's why any visiting fans who happen to come are put there. When I was your age coming here, and in those days it was always on a Saturday at 15.00 hours, things were so different. You'll never experience the buzz I used to get and that's why you can take Dale or leave it. A bit of a shame really, but at least Rochdale still has a league club. You won't remember the likes of Grimsby, Shrewsbury and Tranmere Rovers." The 12- year-old looked up at his grandad and said, "But surely it's better now than it was 50 years ago?"

Terry Moore, Bristol: My dad introduced me to Spotland way back in 1949 or 1950; not immediately to the Dale, as I seem to remember it was a schoolboy match one winter's morning. He left us soon after, so he never did get to take me to a proper match. However, as I grew up and circulated around all the neighbouring grounds between Preston and Old Trafford, I inevitably ended up at Spotland more than anywhere else. In all those years what highlights we have had: one League Cup final, one promotion, one or two managers who have gone on to greater things, the big boot of Stan Milburn, and the occasional 4-0 win! But, once hooked, it's difficult to get away. Unfortunately, distance and family commitments prevent me from attending as often as I would wish, but at least the west country and London are within striking distance, and the odd trip up north is still feasible, Virgin Trains permitting. Living in Bristol and supporting the Dale is like starring in one of three films, dependent on the circumstance. First is *Zulu*. I am surrounded by hordes of natives wearing red or blue. Each and every one convinced that this city should be able to support a Premiership or First Division side, except they cannot agree on City or Rovers. What makes them think they have any more divine right than any other place with two teams? They tell me to support my local team, and I say that I do just that when opportunity arises. Next is *55 Days at Peking*. A motley collection of foreigners surrounded by hordes of natives as above. The difference being that on any given Saturday night in the pub there are any number of refugees like me, following their teams, Premiership down to the Doctor Marten league plus the obligatory 'never been to Old Trafford' MUFC lot. All of them going along with my right to support whoever I like, although they do doubt my sanity on occasion! The latter seems to go with the territory for exiles. Finally, we have *The Loneliness of the Long Distance Runner* - not wishing to drive far these days I usually settle for a train; travelling alone is not much fun. I am sure that Virgin, Great Western and the Underground do not deliberately set out to make passengers' lives a misery, but they usually manage it on the timekeeping and catering fronts. Getting to games is a work of art, but returning is frequently a nightmare, and depressing to boot if results have gone wrong. In fact, I often wonder whether I'll manage to meet my mates in Peking. So there you have it. The joys of supporting, no matter who. But may we Dale fans continue to cope with disappointments like Plymouth not for much longer. Live in hope and with pride. Maybe, just maybe, 28 is our lucky number.

Suzanne Geldard, Sports Editor, *Rochdale Observer*: I joined Rochdale's campaign relatively late in the season after taking over from Simon Crawford following his move to the *Hull Daily Mail*. I immediately adopted them as my second.team. There is so much passion at the club and I firmly believed that this would be their season. Having watched Blackburn Rovers through four play-offs - with their only success coming in the 1992-93 season - I wouldn't wish the nerve-racking experience on anyone. Except Rochdale. They deserved a place in the top seven and a chance to reach the second division. The second that Paul Connor clicked with Clive Platt, things looked promising. After Lee Todd's sensational free kick earned a late point at home to Brighton, Rochdale went on to destroy struggling Carlisle United and Exeter, earning a point at a rain-soaked Macclesfield in between. They were stung by the Bees, losing 3-0 at Barnet, but recovered to beat Lincoln City 3-1 to get themselves back on track. But the backlog of games they had to squeeze in at the end of the season because of earlier postponements took its toll as they went down 3-1 at Blackpool. Home wins over Mansfield Town and Plymouth, and it was down to the wire on the final day. For the last 20 minutes or so at Plymouth, I was shaking. A goalless draw was the last thing I expected, and I was praying Blackpool would slip up at Darlington to ensure Dale would stay seventh. But they couldn't break the deadlock at Home Park and news filtered through that the Seasiders had taken the lead at the Feethams. The bad news seemed to be transmitted to Steve Parkin's men on the pitch, but they carried on regardless, knowing their fate was in their hands. Hope sprung eternal when The Quakers equalised but Blackpool hit back straight away. Lee Todd was to the right of me in the press box, co-commentating for *GMR*, and he was visibly tense. The more time ticked on, the more animated he became, especially when Paul Ware, Gary Jones, Mark Monington and Clive Platt all went close in the dying minutes. Being ruled out through injury and having to watch from the sidelines, not being able to do anything about what's happening on the pitch, must be so frustrating. I normally keep quiet in the press box and just get on with my job, but it was hard to do that on that particular afternoon and there were a number of local press willing the ball to go in - much to the annoyance of the home supporters in front of us! It wasn't to be, and it's hard to know what to say in those situations for post-match interviews. But there's always next season to look forward to, and if Messrs Platt and Connor stay injury-free, who knows?

Bob Crowe, Sprotbrough, Yorkshire: Like most loyal Dale fans, it's where to start. I've lived in South Yorkshire for 17 years. Born and bred in Rochdale, missed a handful of games in the last 30 years and have two sons who live and breathe for the Sandy (can't get used to calling it 'the Thwaites' - it always gave me a headache). I do a 120-mile round trip when we're at home, more if I'm dropping the youngest off at university in Salford, or even more if the eldest lad forgets to put petrol in his car (he's in Stoke). Started watching football when we used to get in Giggle Lane [Gigg Lane, Bury] for nowt at half-time, but changed when they gave me the afternoon off to watch "Noel, Noel" get his cum-uppance in 1970-71*. I've watched 'em disappoint me now for nigh on 30 years. The wife has it sorted: 'Why do you get so upset, when you know they'll not win when they have to?' or 'Go on then, what was wrong with the referee this time?' Even the classic, 'They might be third now, but give 'em a couple of months and they'll be back in the bottom half'. Little does she know that this is a ploy by the lads just to make all the away games easier and quicker for me to travel to (not impressed with the short hops to Luton, Oxford, Swansea and Bristol). Anyway the point of all this dribble (remember when they could) is that about 17 years ago when I crossed the Pennines to the choir of 'Hey up duck tha don't half tok funny tha mus be from Manchester' (bloody thickies). I felt so proud that I didn't watch Leeds or Sheffield Wednesday or the Blades (oh and Donkey Rovers), but that I went to watch Rochdale (no, I haven't met Lisa bloody Stansfield and Reg Jenkins wasn't an MP). I'm so proud of all the stick I have had to endure at work over the years, like the classic brew-time comments: 'It's my turn to wash the pots, where's the Rochdale Mug?' - 'I think he's still in his office.' Ha Bloody Ha. But we showed 'em, losing to a Golden Goal in the 'old transit van trophy' or missing a wide open goal against Cheaterfield (sic) or even missing a penalty against the Parkin old boys [Mansfield Town]. Better still losing to York, then Halifax and failing to get the other against Hull - God I hate being over here sometimes. Never mind, we'll go up next year. I can feel it! I'm so confident I might even get within 400 numbers of that elusive Golden Gamble ticket. I might not have been able to shout for the lads as they stood forlorn in the sunshine at Plymouth, only because I was trying to stop my eyes from filling up, but I joined in with the, 'Always look on the bright side of life - de dum de dum de dum etc,' as we walked through the park. Why? because I'm Rochdale till I die, I know I am, I'm sure I am, I'm Rochdale till I die.

* Rochdale beat Coventry City, 2-1, on Monday, 11 January 1971, in the third round of the FA Cup. Before the match, Coventry's manager, Noel Cantwell, on hearing his team had drawn Rochdale, commented: 'Where's Rochdale?' He should really have known because he spent six years at Manchester United as a player in the early 1960s - just 12 miles away. Coventry refused to play under Spotland's floodlights, claiming they were not bright enough. The game was held on a Monday and thousands of children were allowed to take the afternoon off to cheer on Rochdale. David Cross scored the first goal. Coventry equalised before Dennis Butler scored the winner with 11 minutes remaining to record Rochdale's most celebrated FA Cup giant-killing act. Noel Cantwell remained a figure of ridicule in the town for many years afterwards. One of the more popular songs was based on the carol, Noel, with the lyric changed appropriately: 'Noel,

Noel, Noel, Noel…that is the name of that bastard Cantwell!'

David Garside, Rochdale: The first year in which the new league format of third and fourth divisions operated (1958/59 season) was, coincidentally, that which saw my attendance at Spotland commence on a regular basis, although my interest had been fermenting for some years. Why the considerable hassle of a journey to the next town? A 10-minute walk through Rochdale Cemetery and along Sandy Lane to watch my own local team seemed to be a much better proposition. The standard of play was not always of the highest order, but there were ample compensations. The general ambience of a match day, the banter of opposing fans, and the smell of newly mown grass, liniment and Woodbine cigarettes. Standing, as always, against the front wall near the Willbutts Lane/ Pearl Street corner of the ground, it was possible, for a time, to be treated to the delights of the intricate wing play of Tony Collins in one half of a match, to be followed in the next by the considerable defensive talents of Stan Milburn, now the senior member of a footballing dynasty and, without doubt, a most wonderful gentleman. Season 1961/62 was one of the most memorable in the history of the club. Whilst form in the League was patchy throughout, it was the team's exploits in the League Cup that caught the eye. Defeating Southampton and Charlton Athletic (both of the second division), then Blackburn Rovers of the first division who boasted England internationals Douglas and Clayton in their line up, Rochdale eventually succumbed to Norwich City, yet another second division side, in the final. The side was replete with characters and, amazingly, the season was completed with the assistance, principally, of only 14 players. In the close season of 1968, Bob Stokoe established a most remarkable number of free transfer signings to supplement the remnants retained from the previous season. Each was an inspired acquisition, and together they formed a unique blend of youth and experience, brain and brawn, skilful flair and unyielding efficiency. It was Christmas before they gelled but from Boxing Day until the season's end 24 matches later, only two matches were lost. Abiding memories are of Norman Whitehead evading the tackles of despairing defenders in a mazey run, the flaxen hair of Tony Buck soaring skywards to head the ball towards the goal, the perceptive passes of Vinnie Leech, and the awesome shooting power of Reg Jenkins. The finale, the last game of the season when Southend United were defeated 3-0, brought scenes of unbridled joy to Spotland. Promotion to the third division was confirmed! The momentum continued into the following season. It was then possible to go home after a match feeling a warm glow of contentment. There were many further outstanding matches, most notably the cup triumph over Coventry City played in front of 13,011 on a Monday afternoon in January 1971. Ultimately, however, all good things come to an end and by 1974/5 season Rochdale were back in the fourth division but what treasured memories!

George Brigham, Sudden, Rochdale: I have always followed the Dale because I was born in Rochdale. I have watched and cheered for other teams, but none could ever take precedence over Rochdale. Having now quit amateur sport on Saturday afternoons, I have had the pleasure of almost 100 per cent attendance home and away coinciding with Mr Parkin's tenure and what a pleasure many of those away games have been. I remember away hammerings of the magnitude of 5-1 at Exeter and 5-0 at Fulham, but some of the away performances of the last two seasons should have seen the Dale demolish the opposition similarly. Where I work, on the Lancashire coast, I am one of two Dale season ticket holders. Apart from the fans of the local Conference side, Southport (where former Dale players are put out to grass), the Liverpool, Everton and the ubiquitous Stretford couch potatoes look at us in obvious shock that our 'shitty' team gets a column every week in The Times (well, so they are told by me, because they would not know otherwise.) And then they hear about our away performances and our young manager and our octogenarian winger (MBE) and I think they would like to think of us as mad, but they cannot. Because we go to watch - home and away. The Premiership version of home and away is the front room or down the pub. Then there is the day itself. Everything is geared around meeting in the Green Room (home games) or which decent boozer that allows kids and does good grub (away games). The characters that this club attracts are remarkable and I am proud to be associated with most of them. The Blackpool triumvirate. The Senior Driver. The teachers. The local government officials. People with proper jobs. The man from London who likes Quo. And the retired. All of them characters, many with their offspring in tow. The away games attract many BURKS* and are always a good day out. *Radio 2FM* in Ireland adopted the Dale for a couple of seasons for their morning sports reports instead of that team from Stretford. I was so proud, particularly spending 10 weeks a year over there working. By the way, Dale won this right in a poll! I wonder if they still follow us. The abiding, indelible memory of last season for all the wrong (and typically Dale) reasons was the Shrewsbury home game. I took my nephew for his first taste of Spotland for six years and even he could not drag me away from watching the humiliation. It was like a morbid fascination - an out of body experience. At work on Monday I had never been so popular. Everyone sympathised and no one took the piss (to my face). Consoling words and concerned looks were the order of the day - and I was the fan! I think it had won them over and they had started to care about this nation's greatest-ever nonachievers, which is some achievement.

* BURKS is the acronym for the Bath University Rochdale Keen Supporters, an idiosyncratic collection of Rochdale supporters that formed in November 1978 at Bath University. They attend occasional matches and members are awarded 'caps'. It has a roll of honour, boasting Madeliene Bell as the youngest BURK at 29 days, while Bob Champion holds both the pre-match drinking record with seven pints and the pie and peas eating record, with a tally of four trayfulls.

John Ridehaugh, Belgium: I woke with a funny feeling in my stomach. Silly really, as I was hundreds of miles away and unable to get to the match. But then I always felt that way on match days when I lived in England. Why should things be any different now I lived in Belgium? "God, I wish I was at Home Park," I said out-loud. As kick-off drew nearer I became more and more restless. 'It's natural to feel this way,' I said to myself. After all, it's not every day Rochdale have their destiny firmly held in their own hands. But this was something special. My father (an avid supporter for over 60 years) had only ever experienced the extraordinary feeling of success once. He was going down to Plymouth to (hopefully) experience something similar again. 'I envy him,' I thought. My girlfriend knew how I felt, which was a comfort. We had flown over to see the last two home games, both of which we won. Spirits were high, but then I remembered: we are Rochdale and nothing good ever happens to us. 'Forever the optimist,' she said jokingly. Well what do you expect? I have endured over 30 years of this and you have only known the last six months. The game got underway and the first piece of news appeared on my monitor over the Internet. "Bloody Blackpool are winning 1-0," I shouted downstairs. "Don't worry love, Connor will score in a minute," came the reply. I waited and waited but Connor was to have a rare off-day. My spirits were briefly lifted as Darlington equalised against Blackpool. I hung onto my scarf and adjusted my Dale hat as the tension began to show. I must have looked a right idiot sat in front of my computer wearing my Dale shirt, hat and scarf and everything else blue I had, including my undies. I wondered if my Dad was wearing his lucky undies too. It had been a standing joke between us for years. By the time Blackpool had scored twice in quick succession, I was just left with a thin thread of hope that we might just sneak one in the last couple of minutes. But it was all to no avail as my plans to show my girlfriend the delights of the Welsh capital at the end of May went flying out of the window. The phone rang shortly afterwards. It was my dad. He was gutted, but as truthful as ever: "We never really looked like winning," he said. Still, at least he had got to see it. My reply to his remarks about the game had a ring of familiarity to it: "Well I guess there's always next season!"

John Vincent, New Zealand: As the bus wound its way over the Haast Pass, towards New Zealand's west coast, I spotted someone further up the bus with a copy of the Otago Times. Having spent the previous weekend hiking in the Mount Aspiring National Park, far from humanity, newspapers and the Internet, I was, by now (Monday lunchtime), desperate to find out the result from Saturday's match at Spotland. During Saturday night I had woken up at the precise time that the final whistle was due to go, on the other side of the world, and had naturally taken this as a good omen; victory was guaranteed. I borrowed the newspaper, and started looking for the important result. Tucked away in the sports pages, after the rugby, cricket and netball were the English football results. Quickly I found the third division, then scanned down to the last result that day - Rochdale 1 Shrewsbury 7! Naturally, my first reaction was that this couldn't be true, and obviously this provincial Kiwi newspaper had got something terribly wrong. My next thought - we must have had someone sent off, or more likely at least four players sent off. It took another four days for me to pluck up courage to read the match report on the Internet. I'm glad that I wasn't there, but in a sense I began to wish that I had been. After 15 years of following the Dale through thin and thin, I should have been there to provide my support in such a dark hour. Maybe the trauma would have been too much, maybe my love affair with my hometown club would have been irreparably damaged by such an event. I had left home, to travel around the world, straight after the creditable 0-0 draw with Cardiff, and immediately the team went into free-fall. I did feel some responsibility for that slump during February and March. The minute that I was out of the country, Dale just couldn't win. When they did eventually win, it was fitting that it was against Carlisle United. I had lived for five years in Cumbria, travelling down to Rochdale every other week for home matches, so Carlisle were the team that I had to endure saturation media coverage of. At half-time in the match against Carlisle, with the score at 4-0, I had to get on a train to travel from Wellington to Auckland. I spent the journey fantasising about what the final score would be, 8-0, 10-0, 4-5? As a footnote, while hundreds of fellow Dale supporters were down at Plymouth, willing the team on for that final play-off place, I was sat in an Internet café in Sydney, following the match through the early hours of the morning. At the end of the match, I emerged into a tropical rainstorm, which seemed fitting at the end of another heart-breaking season. Anyway, next season I will, like all the others, be back, sat in my usual seat in the WMG stand, convinced that this, finally, will be our year.

Colin Smith-Markl: My grandad took me to my first match in 1960 and I still remember how bitterly disappointed I was as I stepped into the ground for the first time. It didn't look anything like Wembley - the only stadium I had seen, on TV. I was five-years-old and that was going to be the first disappointment of my life sentence. Our dismal record has been well documented but let's not forget that there have been highlights - we won promotion in 1969 and there was the night we won at Crewe to avoid the drop and partied into the night as if we had won the League. There were also the (losing) trips to Manchester United, Crystal Palace and Liverpool. Not really very much for 40 years. I spent 10 years as chairman of the Supporters' Club from 1978. We used to spend Sunday mornings cleaning the changing-rooms, doing odd jobs from painting the crowd barriers to nailing tarpaulin back onto the rear of the rotting main stand. We organised car boot sales to raise money and I regularly rang everybody on the membership list (about 30) to try and swell the numbers on the coach to the next away game into double figures. And what have I got out of it all? A life focus and a well-rounded personal philosophy that allows me to take every disappointment and every problem in my stride. Watching Rochdale is the ideal preparation for life - at least that is how I justify it to my children. I know how to value success - no matter how minimal - and the fact that we nearly did it last season gives me an inner glow of contentment that no Man Utd fan could ever comprehend or appreciate. The times they are a changin'. My grandad watched Rochdale for 50 years and did not savour either the pride of a super stadium or the success of promotion. My children and I have experienced the former - as for the latter, we just might.

Bob Harrison, Sheffield: I ran on to a football pitch last night, nothing special about that you might think, but at 50-years- old maybe I should know better. Mind you, I have done it before, in 1969 to be precise. My mind was full of the promise of better things that a teacher-training course in Sheffield might provide. A big city, with two big football clubs, night clubs, theatres and a thriving industry. The anticipation of Rochdale being promoted thus playing in a higher division and a whole new city and the life it had to offer was a powerful and never-to-be-repeated feeling for an 18-year-old away from home for the first time. I can't remember my first Dale game although I have vivid recollections of Blackburn v Bury, sitting on my dad's shoulders as he stood next to my Uncle Bill. The colour, noise and smell are carefully stored on my hard drive. To be honest, the players and managers are a bit of a blur in the intervening 30 years or so, although some have resonance - George Morton, Joe Richardson (the reason he sticks in my mind was that he was a right winger and used to take corners and you could stand really close as he stepped back to take it and I could smell the liniment on his legs! Is that sad or what?), Laurie Calloway, Stan Millburn, and, of course, Reg. If you need to ask Reg who? you can stop reading now! In fact, I have seen more away games in recent years, luckily coinciding visits to mum and dads with a home game. From Sheffield it's easy to get to Scunthorpe, Lincoln, Chesterfield Hull, Doncaster (remember them?). Even Exeter, where I found myself embracing my pal, Steve, an avid Dale fan and cricket writer for The Guardian and The Observer and leaping in the air only to be asked by my teenage son to calm down. Oh yes, my sons are both Rochdale fans and my daughter, too. You would think a decent university education would teach them some sense. My telephone bill is enormous, phoning my dad as I do from most countries to find out how the Dale have gone on. It's the first thing he tells me on trans-Atlantic lines, regardless of the time in the USA; family news comes way down the call. He doesn't go now, being 83, but the last game I took him to when Rochdale scored my heart was in my mouth as the excitement got to him. What a way to go though! So I am on the pitch last night, we've just beaten Plymouth 2-1. I am still in my work suit and I catch myself and wonder why am I here? Then I remember the feeling the Dale have given me and it has stayed with me all my life in all situations and for which I am eternally grateful. Even if you are down at the bottom for long periods of time you are always standing on the threshold of possibility! Up the Dale!

Richard Brooks, Rochdale: Firstly, I must stress that I was living and had always lived in Norwich and my family had no connections with the north of England. My earliest memories as a follower of Rochdale originate from when I was maybe seven-years-old. I would go downstairs on a Sunday morning and look at the sports pages of my parents' Sunday Telegraph. Norwich City were usually in the bottom half of the first division. They were doing okay in the wider scheme of things - not like the teams at the bottom, right at the bottom: Workington, Stockport, Halifax, Aldershot, Tranmere and Rochdale. Rochdale were always there. I just noticed them. They stood out from their inability to climb out of the bottom four of the league. Week after week after week. The years passed and I continued to watch out for my team up north. Ten years later, and I had an office job in Norwich. I was working with Norwich City supporters who gleefully pinned '8-0' to the back of my chair when we lost at Orient. There were a few Ipswich supporters who usually kept their heads down, and the usual Manchester United supporters who had never set foot in Manchester. I had to go to Spotland. One of my first matches was a derby against Halifax. We won 5-3, and Rob Wakenshaw scored the best goal I have ever witnessed. I stayed in the Flying Horse Hotel and a few days later I watched as we secured our league survival for another year with a 2-1 win over Stockport. Now this was the stuff that dreams are made of, and I was hooked. For one season in the early-1990s, I took the train, and followed the

Dale on most of their away games. I was chatting to a guy at half-time at York. We exchanged predictions for the second half. I told him that I was from Norwich, and he was amazed, amused and probably thought I was a little crazy. I told him that I'd see him at Torquay next week, and now I was most definitely certifiable! So, to close, and to bring this story up to date, I am now 32-years-old. I live near Wardle, Rochdale, and I have just renewed my season ticket for my third season of 'Up the Dale - Down the Ale!'. The friends who I sit with in the WMG stand include the guy that I met all those years ago on the terraces at York City. As is the case every year, I'm hoping that we might finally make the play-offs next season, but supporting Rochdale, although sometimes very entertaining, does nothing if not instil a sense of realism.

Mike Johnson: It probably sounds a bit strange, but when I stood in the WMG on 12th August 2000 for the first game of the 2000-2001 season, as the players ran out onto the pitch, the hair stood up on the back of my neck. I was really proud, proud of my club. For the first time in my life, we had what looked like the makings of a proper football ground; new covered stands - the full length of the pitch, and when the new 'Willbutts Lane' stand is completed, a 10,000 capacity. Fantastic. And, for the first time as well, I actually thought we had a chance of promotion. The club's merchandise had the strap-line 'This Time!' - it seemed authoritative and believable. I believed it. I am 34-years-old. My dad started taking me when I was six or seven. During all that time, Rochdale have either been rubbish or really rubbish. I'm a hardened pessimist. It serves me well. I have got used to the pattern of mediocrity followed by brief hope, spectacularly brought down to earth, losing at home to...Shrewsbury or someone. This season felt different. We had resilience, fight, and a will to win. We brushed Orient aside live on Sky TV and held Cardiff in front of 12,000 at Ninian Park. I was one of the 208 that Friday night. Pessimism was unfounded. We weren't going to get turned over by anyone. I have lived away from Rochdale now for 16 years, nearly as long as I lived there. I now live in London. My Dale mug and wall-chart don't get a mention at work. Spurs fans know, but they don't understand but I reckon an extra couple of hundred people secretly check to see how the Dale got on every Saturday though! I got to 20 games last season, plus the Sky game. My record was Won 5; Lost 6; Drew 10. Rubbish, rather than really rubbish. Why? It's easy to support Man. U, Spurs or Chelsea. It always makes me laugh when you see gutted Gooners or Geordies after their latest 'failure'. They haven't got a clue. It's in my blood, I can't do anything about it. My brother has a season ticket. He missed three games home and away all season in all competitions. My dad was an ever-present at home. My aunt, uncle and cousin all turn up at home and sometimes away. I have irrational thoughts about Burnley and Bury. What else is there to do on a Saturday afternoon? It's an excuse for a trip out, escapism; and it's a bit mad. Scunthorpe is only round the corner from North London, especially on a Tuesday night in February! I love it! Even now, after being gutted in Plymouth, I'm fidgeting around waiting for news from Spotland. If we could just buy a couple of nippy, goal-scoring midfielders in the summer; next time it really should be 'This Time!'. It's the hope that kills you.

Simon McNicholas, Rochdale: I have followed Dale from afar for years. My job took me from Kuwait and Dubai, to the USA and beyond. I had to rely on dodgy BBC World Service reports and local press who seemed more concerned with camel racing and rounders. When I eventually made my way back to the hallowed turf of Spotland, the WMG stand had been erected where the hill used to be. I couldn't believe how far the club had come. What saddened me, however, was the 'seated fan' who wouldn't sing, or cheer, or clap, or egg the team on - but was concerned only with booing. I had to put a stop to this. I recruited my brother Liam (who was on leave from the RFA (Royal Fleet Auxiliary) and, as we were both trumpeters, decided that we would inject a bit of life into the WMG. Our debut was at York away. There was the petrol blockade, so we went on the coach. We kept our trumpets hidden as we went in. The York fans took the piss for 20 minutes - 'Can you hear the Rochdale sing' etc.

Liam and I were debating when we should make our debut. Then, as luck would have it, a York player dived to the ground, looking for a free kick. He was acting like something out of *Saving Private Ryan*. This was our moment. We played the Last Post. The Dale end pissed themselves laughing and joined in with the lament. Neil Edwards turned and clapped in appreciation. The referee was seen to smile, and even the York fans agreed with the irony of the moment. The fatally-wounded York player leapt to his feet as if the Virgin Mary had cured him of his broken leg. Me and Liam were the heroes that night. As we strutted into the WMG for the next home match, we were greeted by chants of, 'You can stick yer fucking trumpets up yer arse' - not from the away fans, but from the regulars in the WMG. Me and Liam have taken our 'fucking' trumpets to many games. Sometimes we are not allowed to take them in, and have trudged back to the car to secure them. Some grounds welcome us with open arms, and hope that our playing improves the atmosphere. The fans we have met along the way have treated us as a bit of a joke and harmless enough. We get abuse regularly for our efforts. What saddens me is that the worst abuse we get is from our own fans who want to know, 'Why you are bothering with that shit?', and 'Why don't you shut the fuck up?' Why are we doing it? To get these miserable sods in the WMG to cheer the boys in blue. Somebody has to.

Mark Rothwell, London: L'hotel Kunst near the Gare de l'Est in Paris and Plymouth, the English seaside town, may not seem locations to mention in one sentence but for this Rochdale supporter the two were entwined on the last day of the football season when a win for Rochdale against Paul Mariner's former club, Plymouth Argyle, would mean a play-off against Hull, Leyton Orient, or whoever. So the phone call to my Rochdale-based spy suddenly took on the importance and expectation of something like finding out your degree result, finding out whether you had bagged the winner at a Grand National or won a photo-finish at an international sporting event. 'Rochdale drew,' said my spy, on reflection sniffling and morose but I still had Blackpool's result to come. Chance was they had drawn or lost but, being a Rochdale cagoule (sick of the anorak label), you could only expect the worst. And, you know what, the worst came like a ten-tonne truck about to run over me. 'Blackpool are through to the play-offs,' raced along the intercontinental land-line. End of season, end of boasting about Rochdale's dizzy top-of-the-table heights. Next season we'll do better I repeated to myself as I cast a glance behind my shoulder and summoned the question, 'why Rochdale? Why support a team who, if they were in the food trade, would be Kwik-Save to Manchester United's Harrods'? Well, the honest truth, a hurtful, embarrassing kinda truth but also a truth bursting with pride, is that Rochdale is my hometown. It is my neck of the woods, where my family have lived since 1850, well before Rochdale Football Club kicked their first ball. Why is the truth hurtful? Any flick through Rochdale's 91-year form guide will tell you, sadly, that Rochdale equals got-out-of-the-relegation-zone-by-the-skin-of-a-Spotland-blade-of-grass-ad-infinitum. The guide will also tell you about such 'magical, playboy characters' like Jason Peake who have made some dreary afternoon at Underhill - no longer - or Cambridge a tad more exciting, enlivened. So, the club sit firmly in the basement, along with cut-price Alvin Stardust CDs, bootleg Pokèmon posters and, wait for it, a special offer on a canine nibble known as Winalot, (something Rochdale need to do in bucket loads if mega-progress is to be made). Jokes aside, Rochdale is a small club with stacks of enthusiasm, energy and inventiveness - am I right in saying a night match many moons ago was lit by candle? If true, it's that kind of making-do against the odds which pulls at the heart strings and commands - certainly from me - (blind?) loyalty, respect and a yearning feeling for a taste, just a small taste of Harrods' finest foods. I ambled towards Barbes Rochechouart, surveyed the street, changed direction to Anvers and popped into a cafe where some chanteur from Lyon was folding an accordion to let out the refreshing Ciel Bleu. Tres bien, je pensais, tres bien.

John Kirby, Belgium: How many passions or interests could there be that would endure years of underachievement and disappointment; cold; wet; abuse from supporters of more successful clubs; and a series of tongue-in-cheek articles that devoted more newsprint in one series of Saturday articles than 25 years worth of reporting Rochdale's matches? Strangely it begins with the thrill of the unknown. The £8 paid last season to enter the Sandy Lane End in no way entitled you to a predictable outcome. Some luck, some skill, that bloody idiot of a referee - they all combined to stimulate the unpredictability of 90 minutes football. The senses are massaged in the knowledge that at home, most of the crowd feels the same as you, and without any effort you tap into the mass of feeling around you. You become part of a conspiracy that contrives by some attempt at the paranormal, to influence the result, a player, the referee. Willpower is poured onto the pitch, resulting in emotional reactions to a great shot, a good save, a foul by the opposition, a goal against us. Of course, the use of sound is the most obvious extension of this experience. But the mind exerts the greater feeling, blocking out normal life, concentrating emotion, yet all in the knowledge that this power cannot be gathered and used by the players. Ordinary people with a range of intellect join together in this collective experience. Our backgrounds and our culture are harmonised by the need to win and the £8 entrance fee. Why Rochdale? Well, like many first experiences when young, the initial impact is high and was capable of being developed, channelled and enhanced with maturity. For me, aged seven-years-old, taking the train from Heywood with my dad, then a short walk down the back of the Town Hall to jump on one of the many waiting blue and white corporation buses which wound their way up to Spotland. The adrenaline began when my dad gave me sixpence and left me in the queue for the children and pensioners' gate with a promise that he would meet me inside. In those days Dale regularly attracted 5,000. To my eyes it looked like 500,000. You can guess how I felt when he was not on the other side. So my senses were already heightened and receptive for this new experience. That first game was against Chesterfield. I think Dale won. In the emotional bonding made that day, they did win. At school in Heywood I was totally alone in my support for Rochdale.

United, City, Bury and Bolton all figured highly in my schools respectable-clubs-to-support stakes. As I travelled through the town decked-out in a (in those days black and white) scarf and bob-hat and clutching an enormous wooden rattle, no one recognised my team's trademarks. But this didn't matter; my support was then - as now - born out of a pure affinity to my club. Pure in the sense that without glamour or glitz (who could find glamour in the old Spotland or in my long-time hero and centre-half Ray 'thou shalt not pass' Aspden?). You are a part of the crowd. The unpretentious, unbridled passion, coming from plain people, some with grey lives with only this experience to spice up their week, others with pressure jobs, giving a massive channel to let go of the current problems, or me, a small boy who could join this unofficial club with no credentials needed or questions asked; it was then and is now addictive to us all. Some 46 years later, the addiction continues to be unsatisfied. On a lovely autumn afternoon standing on the terrace at Shrewsbury, witnessing Dale outplay, out-think and silence the home crowd as they won 4-0; like fine wine, it was to be savoured. Later that year, stood on the Sandy Lane, the other side of the coin, as the same Shrewsbury side demolished Dale, who showed the tactical naiveté of a Sunday league side, to the tune of 7-1. The aforementioned unpredictabilty kept us all in check as the season proved to be good but not good enough for promotion. But Dale fans are conditioned to this sort of outcome, so the hurt is nullified. Even at 7-1 down people were still urging their team on. That could - in the Premiership - be construed as foolish. But it's wrong to think that. It is a result of the pure, genuine and uncomplicated association with the players, management, but above all with a collective meeting of east Lancashire minds which has only one desire, to see the Dale do well.

Nationwide Football League
Third Division Final Table

	P	W	D	L	F	A	Pts
Brighton	46	28	8	10	73	35	92
Cardiff	46	23	13	10	95	58	82
Chesterfield	46	25	14	7	79	42	80
Hartlepool	46	21	14	11	71	54	77
Leyton Orient	46	20	15	11	59	51	75
Hull	46	19	17	10	47	39	74
Blackpool	46	22	6	18	74	58	72
Rochdale	**46**	**18**	**17**	**11**	**59**	**48**	**71**
Cheltenham	46	18	14	14	59	52	68
Scunthorpe	46	18.	11	17	62	52	65
Southend	46	15	18	13	55	53	63
Mansfield	46	15	13	18	64	72	58
Plymouth	46	15	13	18	54	61	58
Macclesfield	46	14	14	18	51	62	56
Shrewsbury	46	15	10	21	49	65	55
Kidderminster	46	13	14	19	47	61	53
York	46	13	13	20	42	63	52
Lincoln City	46	12	15	19	58	66	51
Exeter	46	12	14	20	40	58	50
Darlington	46	12	13	21	44	56	49
Torquay	46	12	13	21	52	77	49
Carlisle	46	11	15	20	42	65	48
Halifax	46	12	11	23	54	68	47
Barnet	46	12	9	25	67	81	45

Dale/Pomona Player of the Month

August - Clive Platt
September - Gary Jones
October - Mark Monington
November - Paul Ware
December - Gary Jones
January - Dave Flitcroft
February - Dave Bayliss
March - Paul Connor
April/May - Wayne Evans

Bibliography and suggested further reading:

Kicking in the Wind by Derick Allsop (Headline, 1996)

The Definitive Rochdale AFC by Steven Phillipps (Association of Football Statisticians, 1996).

The Survivors by Steven Phillipps (Sporting and Leisure Press, 1990)

A to Z of Rochdale AFC by Darren Phillips (Breedon Books, 2000)

Rule of Night by Trevor Hoyle (Futura, 1975)

Rothmans Football Yearbook 2000-2001 by Jack and Glenda Rollin (Headline, 2000)

The PFA Premier and Football League Players' Records 1946-2000 by Barry J Hugman (Queen Anne Press, 2000)

Rochdale FC on the internet:

www.Rochdaleafc.com: Excellent website, with match reviews, comprehensive statistics, lively message board and unrivalled news service.

www.rochdale-football-club.co.uk: The club's official website. Plenty of information and sassier than most official sites.

www.geocities.com/rafc99/: Dale Bullet's. A new website with laudable ambitions, even if short on content. The sound of random bullet shots and cheesy music accompanies the text.

http://members.aol.com/rochdale21/: The Rochdale FC Picture Gallery. Photographs taken by Dave Coupe of all things Rochdale - fans, action shots, the ground; just as the site's title suggests, actually. Worth a visit.

www.fortunecity.co.uk/shangrila/acapulco/191/: Up the Dale. A website built in Belguim, no less. Neat and authoritative site, but not fully completed.

http://homepage.ntlworld.com/alan.wilson3/: The official BURKs website. Strictly for fellow BURKs and anyone intrigued by this bizarre cult.

Supporters soon rallied after the disappointing end to the season. A visitor to Rochdaleafc.com by the name of Chaff contributed an hilarious spoof of Queen's 'We Will Rock You' and suggested the club adopt it as a new anthem. Flicker is Dave Flitcroft and Taffy is Neil Edwards - the other players should be easily identified.

We are, we are Rochdale
We are, we are Rochdale

Platty you're a boy making big noise,
banging in the goals, gonna be a big man someday.
You got mud on your face, you got good pace,
scoring us goals all over the place.

We are, we are Rochdale
We are, we are Rochdale

Flicker you're a young man, hard man,
shouting at the ref, gonna take on the world someday.
You got blood on your face, try and keep up with the pace,
starting on players all over the place.

We are, we are Rochdale
We are, we are Rochdale

Fordy you're an old man, small man,
running down the wing, gonna make you something someday.
You got mud on your face, your oldish face,
glad to see you keeping up with the pace.

Taffy you're a Welsh man, short man,
saving loads of shots, gonna get us promoted some day.
You're always in the right place, your keeping's ace,
we love it when you dive all over the place.

LIFE SENTENCE

Bayliss you're a scouse man, rob yer house man,
gonna tackle every forward all day.
You leave 'em for dead,
you're great with your head,
we can hear you saying 'calm down,' 'come 'ed'

Coleman, you're a bald man, old man, slow man,
might win a tackle some day.
Away or at home, you aimlessly roam,
with a head looking like the Millennium Dome.

Connor you're a big man, strong man,
and by scoring all the time, you'll take us up by May.
You always make space, you finish with grace -
no need to panic as you pick your place.

Toddy you're a small man, hard man,
and you never give up is what they say.
Stick a man on the deck, destroy their threat,
then you'll curl a free-kick right into the net.

We are, we are Rochdale
We are, we are Rochdale
We are, we are Rochdale
We are, we are Rochdale

Twelve

Afterthought

Two months after the end of the season, I received a telephone call from Francis Collins, Rochdale's chief executive:

"I know this is a bit unusual, but I wondered if you minded coming in and having a word with Steve Parkin."

Naturally, I was surprised by this request.

"What does he want to talk about?"

Now, Collins is an astute operator. I knew the response would be guarded.

"I'm not right sure to be honest. It must be about some of the things in your columns."

"How come it's taken him so long to get round to this?"

"I don't know. He's just got back from holiday. Maybe he took them with him and read them there."

I agreed to meet Parkin. I re-read the columns and tried to imagine the impact they might have had on him. In places, especially during the drastic slump in form, I had been critical, though I felt it justified and written without vindictiveness. I was willing to defend anything I had written about him on a one-to-one basis, even if I didn't expect to enjoy the experience.

I did wonder whether I had been economical with praise. While it was true he had a larger budget than any other Rochdale manager, this in itself did not guarantee improvement. Managers at other clubs had been similarly trusted with funds down the years but had not made the same quantifiable progress as Parkin.

On the day we were due to meet, an overnight storm had left debris in the streets around Spotland - broken branches, clusters of toffee wrappers and cans. Although July, it had been strong enough to dredge up last autumn's leaves and scatter them over the road and pavement. The air was cool and the sky overcast, as if someone had abruptly turned off the summer.

I was nervous. I had been here before, of course; it was a basic principle of journalism that you had to stand by your words. It came with the territory. I had faced irate footballers and football managers before too. All the same, as I walked across the club car park, I had the feeling that this was different. It was my club, so the professional and the personal were indistinguishable.

"Hope you've got your armour-plating on," joked Collins.

He phoned through to Parkin and was asked to take me to the boardroom.

"The boardroom, hey? Must be serious!" he said as he put down the phone. Ho ho. Oh dear.

I followed him out of his office, up some stairs and into the boardroom. He couldn't stop smiling, his joy shining bright on this pallid day: at last, a journalist flushed out from the shadows and made to account for himself with a proper, crunching tackle of a football bloke. I'd smile too, if it were happening to someone else.

My mouth was dry. I wanted a drink, but did not want to show a transparent sign of anxiety. After a few minutes, Parkin entered. Quick on his feet, nimble. We shook hands. It was a firm grip, but not one of those wretched measure-of-the-man clenches. I made a pre-emptive strike, a stab at humour:

"Francis tells me you'd like a fist-fight."

"Not at all, not at all."

He had several of my articles in his hand and laid them on the table as he drew up a seat. Some of the paragraphs had been highlighted in thick green pen. He folded the cuttings flat with the side of his hand. He was wearing football boots, shorts and a training top. He leaned forward over the table and read a section, and then leaned back in his chair. He had the thighs of an ex-footballer - wide, fleshy.

At first, he didn't meet my eye and seemed shy and awkward. It was clear that he'd given some thought to how he'd make his case:

"You're entitled to your opinion and I've no problem with that, but you've said here that you don't trust me…" He was referring to the column of Saturday, 31 March 2001 (*Rochdale Talisman Manages to Strain the Bond of Trust*), written in the midst of our poor run. I had hinted in it that I no longer trusted his judgement. Words, of course, are open to various interpretations and people find some more offensive than others. 'Trust', in the context I had used it, was objectionable to Parkin, though I had limited it solely to his football acumen and not used it in the conventional sense as a criticism of his integrity.

When he looked up from the article, his gaze met mine. His eyes narrowed, his lips pursed. He did this without affectation and seemingly unaware that he had done it; it didn't seem showy or forced. I was conscious that his expression changed constantly between hard and soft, smile and frown. I felt immediately that he would listen to what I had to say, and, indeed, respect honesty and robustness. I wasn't intimidated. I even swore.

"Steve, we'd not won a game for weeks when I wrote that piece and we were playing crap. I think if any fan said at that point they trusted you implicitly, they would be a lying." He didn't say he agreed, or that he accepted my point, but I could see he was at least reconsidering his feelings now I had put mine into context.

We didn't get round to the other green bits. Instead, we spoke at length and in detail about the season just gone. I felt fantastically privileged to be in a locked room with the manager of my football club. In two hours, I asked him question after question, all the points we raised in the car driving home from games: the niggles and worries, the right-footers played on the left, the rumours, the retained list, the salaries, the players with heart, the players without heart. He was remarkably candid. He did not airbrush the truth or issue platitudes.

He seemed most concerned about the lack of a training pitch and painstakingly talked me through the rigmarole of the squad's itinerant existence. He had grumbled all season about this, but only when he outlined the daily hassle did I realise how difficult it was to improve players and work on team-play when a good deal of the time was spent travelling to various venues (most of which were barely suitable for a professional club), unloading, putting out the equipment etc. He also described his working week. It was long and fraught and much of it took place below the water level of a fan's perception.

He bristled with determination and ambition and seemed aware that although we were few in number, Rochdale's supporters had a deep affinity for the club. It was, of course, difficult to assess a personality in such a short time, but I noted in Parkin traits I had seldom seen in football people. He was self-critical. He did not evade questions. He listened, in a way that was neither patronising or inauthentic.

I asked him about a life in football. He was happy to move away from a discussion on the machinery of the game to a broader perspective. He agreed it was 'intense' and spoke about his life outside - his family, thoughts that drifted through his head during his journey to work, his Friday night ritual of a drink with his old pals. He smiled a different kind of smile at this point, relaxed and open, reminded of his off-duty self.

Despite my much-stated cynicism about football people, I warmed to Parkin. He spoke good sense. He was passionate. As I shook his hand once more, standing at Spotland's main entrance, I thought that he was someone heading to a better place; immediately I mused: I hope it's with Rochdale.

Rochdale AFC
2000/2001

President: Lillian Stoney.
Chairman: David Kilpatrick.
Directors: Chris Dunphy, Jim Marsh, Graham Morris,
Rod Brierley, Richard Bott.
Manager: Steve Parkin.
Assistant Manager/Player: Tony Ford.
Club Captain: Neil Edwards
Physiotherapist: Andy Thorpe.
Football in the Community Officer/Centre of Excellence:
Keith Hicks.
Youth Team Manager: David Hamilton.
Assistant Youth Team Manager: Jamie Hoyland.
Youth Team Coach: Trevor Jones.
Chief Executive: Francis Collins.
Club Secretary: Hilary Molyneux Dearden.
Lotteries and Merchandising Manager: Richard Wild.
Marketing and Sponsorship Manager: Les Duckworth.
Administration: Tom Nichol
Internet Officer: Stuart Ashworth.
Assistant Secretary: Bev Mansfield.
Lotteries Assistants: Peter Woodhouse, David Lord,
Paul Fishburn.
Groundsman: Craig Wooding.
Medical Advisors: Stephen Derbyshire, John Slack.